THICK SKIN

Field Notes from a Sister in the Brotherhood

Also by Hilary Peach

BOLT (poetry)

THICK SKIN

FIELD NOTES FROM A SISTER IN THE BROTHERHOOD

HILARY PEACH

ANVIL PRESS // VANCOUVER

Third printing: March 2023

Library and Archives Canada Cataloguing in Publication

Title: Thick skin : field notes from a sister in the Brotherhood / Hilary Peach.
Names: Peach, Hilary. author.
Description: 1st edition.
Identifiers: Canadiana 20220274487 | ISBN 9781772141955 (softcover)
Subjects: LCSH: Peach, Hilary. | LCSH: Women welders—Canada—Biography. | LCSH: Welders (Persons)—Canada—Biography. | LCGFT: Autobiographies.
Classification: LCC HD6073.W42 C27 2022 | DDC 671.5/2092—dc23

Cover design: S. Grand Black
Interior layout: HeimatHouse
Represented in Canada by Publishers Group Canada
Distributed by Raincoast Books

The publisher gratefully acknowledges the financial assistance of the Canada Council for the Arts, the Government of Canada, and the Province of British Columbia through the B.C. Arts Council and the Book Publishing Tax Credit.

Anvil Press Publishers Inc.
P.O. Box 3008, Station Terminal
Vancouver, B.C. V6B 3X5
www.anvilpress.com

PRINTED AND BOUND IN CANADA

CONTENTS

FOREWORD || KATE BRAID

I met Hilary Peach many years ago, as a younger sister in the trades. At the time I was active as a carpenter in Vancouver but I didn't see much of her, partly because she was always on the road, and partly because she lived on one of the Gulf Islands. Our main connection has been through her other work — her other life — as a writer and arts producer, organizing literary festivals and events on her home turf in between work assignments. By that time we had this in common too — that we were both writing poetry. I loved her poetry. Some of it was about being a boilermaker — of course. And it was both very funny, and profoundly true to anyone who knew the trades culture. Much like this memoir.

Thick Skin is a wonderful book, a gift not just to any person who might be curious about what it's like to be a boilermaker on the move, but also to anyone who wonders what really goes on behind all those sparks in the industrial towers and boilers around us. I not only learned a lot about welding, and travelling construction, but also about where determination and grit and hard work can take you — all in the company of a smart, funny, wise, tough woman. Here we learn the importance of small things, not just of the delicate motions of a good weld, but of choosing the right swear word, or picking the right moment to speak up. Along the way, we are introduced to some difficult characters, but we also see the kindness and care, the friendships and loyalties that are forged in steel.

Peach says this is a book about working in the trade, not about being a woman working in the trade. But women who work in construction know the statistics: they generally make up less than five percent of the crew, which is about double the number who have entered the trades since I started in construction in the 1970s. A gain of two percent over fifty years! This astonishing imbalance can't help but inform the stories in this book, and is underlined as mainly male crews figure out how to adjust to having a woman on board. Or don't.

For anyone who hasn't been there, *Thick Skin* begins to break down the mystery of the construction trades. Traditionally, boilermaking is a closed shop, and keeps its secrets. This book takes us up those scaffolds, into the confined spaces, and gives us an insider's look at what these tradespeople actually do, dirt, filthy language, and all.

Every man or woman who takes up a trade — any trade — has to get used to its particular "culture." When I was on the tools, my fellow carpenters prided themselves on being the "gentlemen" of the trades (though I must say, not every single one of them actually qualified in that regard). Electricians were known as the "smart-asses," mostly, I suspect, because they must deal with far more math than the rest of us. *Thick Skin* allows us to watch one of the few women boilermakers at work, introducing us to both the skill set and the famously "badass" culture of this little-known trade. It wasn't always easy, as you'll see. But boilermaking teaches endurance, forthrightness, patience, and strength, as well as those survival skills that many women are specifically discouraged from learning: how to let things roll off your back. How to gain confidence and skills you can be proud of as you take on more and more complex work. How to make excellent money.

Thick Skin reveals the challenges of the job, both physical and emotional, but it's also a love story. It's about choosing your battles, fitting in, getting along, and it's a study in sensitivity and toughness. How can a boilermaker's story be loving? This one is.

This is a wonderful book — not just funny but a rare, insider's look at the life of a travelling welder — the good, the bad, the ugly, and always, the fascinating. A collection of hilarious stories by a master (mistress?) of repartee, it is also an homage to the trade she loved.

I was sorry to see this story end, but as the boilermakers say, "See you on the next one." I hope it is soon.

PART 1:

Booming Out

THE SHIPYARD

In the middle of the industrial hustle of the Esquimalt waterfront, two enormous, blue gantry cranes tower into an even bluer sky. They travel slowly back and forth on railway tracks, picking up heavy objects and moving them from one place to another along the side of the dry dock. Everything is huge, and the busy forklifts weaving in and out of the roadways seem tiny. Two workers stand under one of these cranes, shouting into the industrial noise. To one side is a cluster of old single-storey buildings that house various shop activities — the carpentry shop, the paint shop, the electrical shop, storage buildings, and sea cans full of tools. Next to the cranes is one of the welding shops, with large steel tables outside, their tops made of slats of flat bar, set up for cutting steel with the oxyacetylene outfits. On the other side of the crane is the dry dock, then the walkway, a few more buildings and some stacked up ATCO trailers, and beyond that is the ocean, stretching to the horizon, dazzling in the afternoon sun. One of the cranes groans, kicks into gear and begins travelling, a steel dinosaur with big blue legs. It is empty, its hooks pulled up to its belly, on its way to pick up a shipping container.

Running parallel to the crane tracks, between the buildings and the sea, is a huge, rectangular excavation in the side of the bay, surrounded by a steel railing. It is a hole in the ground, lined with concrete, as long as two and a half Canadian regulation-sized football fields, end to end, and as deep as a three-storey building. They call it "the ditch."

The Esquimalt Graving Dock is the largest hard-bottomed dry dock on the west coast of the Americas. It is where enormous ships — freighters, tankers, ferries, cruise ships, cable-laying ships, and barges — are taken out of the water for refits and repairs. There is a giant, movable wall at one end, called the caisson. It opens to the ocean, and when it is open, the dry dock floods and fills up to sea level. As long as the caisson is open, the water level goes up and down with the tides. Ships are floated in through this opening, and positioned over dozens of large blocks that are under the water. Then the caisson is closed, the water is pumped out, and the ships are landed on the blocks, fifteen metres below sea level. The caisson is as watertight as it can be, and keeps the ditch from flooding while work is being done.

The whole thing is built of concrete. Manlifts, welding machines, and other equipment are strapped, lifted, and flown down into the bottom by cranes. Workers go down through hidden stairwells built into the walls, on either side. To get to the bottom, you descend through a concrete entryway on the sidewalk, sixty-six steps down a secret passage, where there is a door. It is an eerie feeling to step out on to that concrete expanse, three storeys below the sea, with the ocean on the other side of the wall, while people are busily racing around in forklifts, moving equipment. It is an even eerier feeling to put on a harness, clip into a man-basket, and ascend beneath the hull of a 200,000-ton cruise ship, where bright pink barnacles the size of dinner plates cling to the hull.

FOR A FEW years in the early 2000s, I worked there, dispatched out of the Boilermakers, Iron Ship Builders, Blacksmiths, Forgers and Helpers, Local 191, in Victoria. I'd moved to the island to take a job welding aluminum ferries at a fabricating and machine shop in Sidney, near the airport. It was a big project that lasted a couple of years, and when it ended, I was in the union and put on the dispatch list for the shipyards.

The work was mostly plate welding, running a wire-feed machine. There were not many women working in the yard. There was Judy, an excellent welder who was a few years older than me, but she was often on the opposite shift. And there was Sue, one of the crane operators. Every day was a little bit terrifying, and I was inexperienced, which meant I was not always assigned the best jobs. But many of the jobs in the shipyard were lousy. It rains a lot in Esquimalt, sometimes for days or weeks at a time. We were issued the cheapest yellow rain gear, which tore easily, and I spent a lot of time standing or kneeling in four inches of water on the decks of rotting barges, with 450 amps of electricity running through an electric air arc gouger. My work day often consisted of ten hours of self-inflicted shock-treatment.

Eventually I figured out that if I put plastic bags over my socks before they got wet, and surgical gloves under my leather work gloves, and stabbed the electrified carbon straight down through the water at the lowest point where I had to cut out the deck plate, I could make a drain hole. If it was draining at the lowest point, and I started gouging at the high points where the deck plate was bubbled up, I wasn't actually standing in the water, and got shocked less often. I didn't know that the shipyard should be building me a hoarding so I wasn't welding in a downpour, and that they should be providing rubber boots that weren't a size 12.

THE SUMMERS WERE all big blue skies and shining water. Sometimes I was sent to the bottom of the dry dock and told to climb into the basket of a man lift. My partner would operate it, flying us up the outside hull of a ship to weld on some lugs, or to cut them off. But the winters were rain and wind, then snow and ice. If you were excellent at your job, which I was not, or good friends with supervision, which I definitely was not, then you could score a job inside the ship in winter, warm and dry. They occasionally did put me inside, balanced on a plank tacked to the side of a cargo hold, or sliding along in the double-bottom of an oil tanker. Usually that happened when the rain stopped, when the sky was a brilliant blue and the sun flashed off the water, when the guys on deck wore dark glasses and worked with their sleeves rolled up.

The caisson at the end of the dry dock was not completely watertight, and there was always a big puddle, called the moon pool, at that end. One afternoon I arrived for night shift and a crowd of guys were standing at the railing looking down into the enclosure. At the bottom was a young sea lion, a big male, roaming around the inside of the dry dock, trying to find a way out. He had been caught in the enclosure, swimming around when the caisson closed, and when the water was pumped out he was stuck there, at the bottom. You could see a track circling the perimeter of the chamber, from his body dragging over the concrete. He had been in there for hours, desperately trying to find a way back to the ocean. The nightshift workers would have to cross the gangway to board the ship, or work on shore. No one would be down in the bottom that night.

"But what about the sea lion?" I asked, over and over.

WHEN IT WAS dark, I crossed the caisson to the far side and started down the stairs. I popped out at the bottom just as the sea lion was turning a corner, coming toward me. He stopped abruptly, about ten meters away, and we looked at each other. He was panting, and I was hypnotized by his huge brown eyes. Then I started talking to him.

"Hey," I said. "I just came down to tell you what's going to happen. Because I asked around, and I thought you might want to know. Here's the thing." He moved a little ways away, then stopped, facing me. I explained that the next day they were going to drop a basket down into the bottom, with a crane, and people with long poles were going to herd him into it. He was not going to get hurt, just directed into the cage, then lifted out, set down on the other side, and released.

"I know it seems unbelievable," I said, "and it's going to be scary, but that's what's going to happen. And you'll be fine. You won't get hurt. They can't do it at night because the animal people aren't here, so you have to wait until tomorrow." He bobbed his big head and moved a little closer. I stepped back toward the stairwell. "So tonight," I told him, "you just need to relax. Nothing's going to happen tonight. It was a hot day and you've been doing laps for hours. You need to take it easy." The sea lion huffed. I told him to go to the moon pool and cool off, rest up. Everything was going to be OK. Then I retreated to the stairwell and climbed back up the sixty-six stairs to ground level.

When I got back to my workstation my foreman asked where I had been.

"I was talking to the sea lion," I said.

He looked around, then said, "What are you doing here? Why don't you go home? Get married, have some babies. This is no place for women."

The sea lion finished his lap, then went to the moon pool and lay down in about two feet of water. I'm sure it had nothing to do with our talk, that he just went there because it was starting to get dark. When I left at dawn, he was almost invisible, lying in the moon pool in the shadow of the caisson. The next day they moved him out.

They used to say at the shipyard that you would never advance if you didn't have the ring, by which they meant the masonic ring, the one my grandfather and uncles had. The one where there weren't any women in the cabal. I don't know if that was true, but I do know that you needed thirty days on the same job to get seniority, and that I was consistently laid off on my twenty-eighth or twenty-ninth day. Like the sea lion, I was destined to go around and around, doing laps at the bottom, until someone flew me out in a basket.

SINCE I DIDN'T have seniority, I only got called to work when they were busy. Like any boom-or-bust industry, the shipyards would swing from all the overtime you could handle to completely empty. One Christmas, the administrator at our union hall was handing out scratch-and-win lottery tickets, and an apology, when guys went in to ask about upcoming work. Jobs were scarce and getting scarcer. But a few of our members had won a different kind of lottery; they'd been called out to work in the United States.

When a boilermaker local is short-handed they will put a call out to the locals in other regions looking for union people to fill the positions. If you go, it's called pulling a travel card. You're out as a guest, working under the other local's contract. The foremen shake your hand and thank you for coming to help out. They don't give you anything too tricky, using their own superstars for the pressure work. I had gone out four times as a travel card in BC, with the field local, 359. They had put me on demolition, tacking with a fitter, welding skin casing, or other non-critical work. When the job ends, the travel cards are laid off first. Last ones hired, first ones gone. They were fun trips with good money and better stories.

Union locals that were looking for travel cards wanted pressure welders, meaning people who could weld piping and tanks as well as plate. The stresses on a joint made in a pipe that has high pressure liquid or steam running through it are different than the stresses on a section of deck or hull plating. The materials are strictly controlled, and rated for the kinds of pressures and temperatures they'll be subjected to. There is a narrow margin of error and the joints are X-rayed. The film might reveal inclusions or porosity, lack of fusion, or a failure to fully penetrate the joint and get enough weld re-enforcement at the root. If any of these issues show up in a measurable way, the joint will fail, and have to be repaired. If the joint fails a second time, more of that welder's joints are X-rayed and checked, possibly leading to more failures. And if the second repair fails, it's a cut-out. The section of tube or pipe is removed, a new piece is fit in, and then there are two joints to weld, both of which have to pass X-ray. By this point the welder is usually out of chances, and is sent somewhere else.

When I started travel carding at pulp mills, it was clear that the pressure welding was a high stakes game, a tricky business. There was a level of technical difficulty, and a welder who could quickly and consistently make the joint and pass the shot was a star. You got the best jobs, all the overtime, better hotel rooms, overcooked steak dinners with the boss at Moxy's, served by underaged girls in short skirts. And if you couldn't make the shot, stardom quickly faded. As my colleague, Elvis, used to say, one day you're the dog, and the next day you're the fire hydrant.

IN THE UNITED STATES, travel carding is called "booming out," and getting a job there when you are Canadian is extra complicated. Still, boom times in the rust belt meant they, too, needed pressure welders, and various wheels were being greased. BC members were going to work in Philadelphia, New York, Wyoming, and California, and making enough money in three months to buy a new truck. My friend Judy left for a job in Boston, and when she came home, she renovated her old house, and added on a painting studio. She said the crew would set up barbecues on the roof of the recovery boiler and have lobster boils on Fridays. The Canadian dollar was worth seventy cents US, which meant if you were getting paid in American money you were rolling in dough. Guys were booking long vacations in Hawaii and winter houses in Mexico.

When an American local had a big job, they were obliged to fill as many positions as they could with American members. If there was still a shortfall, they would send a request to Canada. By fax. Each local, notably Toronto, Sarnia, Alberta, Winnipeg, and BC, would canvas their membership to see who was interested, then send back a list of the qualified workers they could supply. It was a hassle for the Americans to process foreign workers on temporary visas, and expensive for the companies, around ten thousand per worker. But it cut down on the administration if they could send out a bulk order with all the paperwork to just one place. So it was to the advantage of the Canadian locals to supply as many people on the list as they could. If BC could offer twenty welders as required by a dispatcher in New York, and Toronto could only offer ten, BC would get the contract. To that end, the boilermakers in Vancouver and Victoria collaborated to offer as many qualified bodies as they could for the American orders. That's how shipyard welders from BC ended up getting sent to work in the middle of the desert.

Lots of guys said they wanted to go, but there were hurdles. The Americans didn't need many fitters, and would only take pressure welders who had passed something called the Common Arc test, a qualification that wasn't offered in Canada. You also had to pass a drug test and have a clean criminal record, which narrowed the field considerably.

For me it was unrealistic, a pipe dream reserved for the most experienced and talented in my trade. I was still struggling to set the heat on my machine, setting up the wrong polarity, making all the rookie mistakes. But it was an attractive daydream, the prospect of working away, making money and having adventures. Traveling to huge sites in places I'd never been, working with the Americans. Eating their strange, chemical-laced snack foods and drinking cheap beer, staying in hotels with swimming pools and stumbling upon poorly maintained roadside attractions. But I had zero experience welding tubes, and in the boilermakers all the pressure work went to the superstars, or to keen young guys with great eyesight who would do anything to prove themselves. They weren't handing out pressure joints to green-as-grass thirty-something lady welders from the shipyard. There was no chance to weld without experience, and no experience without a chance.

All I could think of, was to keep practicing so that I would get better. And if I was going to get any good jobs at all, I would have to learn to TIG weld.

LIGHTNING

Stick welding, also known as shielded metal arc welding (SMAW), is the most common process in the industry. It uses a flux-covered electrode that you tap or scratch on the work surface to strike an electric arc. Once the arc is established, you maintain the correct rod angle, speed of travel, and distance from the material, and the electrode burns slowly down to the nub, depositing molten steel into the weld puddle as you go. You throw the rod stub in a metal bucket, insert a new one into the holder, or stinger, and start again, picking up where you left off. You can weld stick in any position and only need two cables, the stinger, and the ground clamp. The chemical flux baked on to each rod melts and forms a protective coating over the weld puddle, so you can weld in cold weather, and when it's windy. It's good for any work outdoors: structural steel, towers, bridges, tanks. It has a high deposition rate, is fast, versatile, cheap, and easy to learn. For many welders it is their whole career.

Tungsten inert gas, or TIG welding, is more complex. The electrode is a piece of tungsten about the size of a large nail, that has been sharpened on a grinding stone to a fine point. It's inserted into a ceramic cup that has an electric current and a gas line running to it. The shielding gas, usually argon, is released through a diffuser lens into the torch head, and protects the weld from the atmosphere. Without a shielding gas, the molten puddle becomes contaminated, resulting in a dirty weld, that is prone to porosity and cracking.

The welder controls the torch with one hand, and adds the filler metal with the other, feeding long pieces of stiff wire into the molten puddle. The result is a finely controlled heat source and a weld puddle that can be manipulated to create small, clean, high strength welds with minimal distortion. It can be used to weld almost any alloy, including stainless steels, aluminum, and exotic metals. It's quiet, except for the hiss of the gas and the hum from the current, and there is no smoke and no sparks. All the parts of the torch head, and the wire, are strictly controlled and kept in a clean, dry place, to prevent contamination. It's a specialist's tool, a scalpel. The small percentage of welders who become proficient with TIG are considered highly skilled and very employable, anywhere in the world.

I had completed most of my welding training, and could get by in stick and wire-feed, but TIG was the money shot. I decided that between work contracts I would go back to school, pass all the provincial procedure qualifications, and my destiny would be my own. I was living on one of the Gulf Islands, and early one crisp October morning I packed my welding helmet on to the motorcycle and boarded the small ferry to Nanaimo.

Outside the welding shop a couple of young guys were goofing around and eating drive-through breakfast sandwiches. Around the side of the building, a small, scruffy-looking older guy leaned against a railing and smoked a hand-rolled cigarette. He wore a welding hat and a blue lab coat.

"First day?" he asked, looking at my helmet. I nodded. "TIG welder?" I nodded again. "TIG welding is easy," he said. "That's why they invented it."

INSIDE I COMPLETED some paperwork and the scruffy guy came out of the office with two meter-long pieces of thin, stiff, copper-coated wire.

"Watch," he said. He held the wire in between the first two fingers of his right hand, stabilizing it with his thumb, and quickly fed it through his fingers, spinning it at the same time, until he had worked from one end of the wire to the other. "The first thing you learn, is how to feed wire. Fast. Because once you're welding, you're going to need it to be there." Then he told me to take the wire to the cafeteria.

"Come back when you can feed it, like this," he said, "with both hands," and demonstrated again, using his left hand. I did as I was told, and after a couple of hours came back to show him.

"Not fast enough," he said. "Go back." This was Denby. His students and colleagues knew him as Glen, but Denby was his artist's name, his real name. Back I went to the cafeteria, and practiced for the rest of that day, and all of the next day. Then it was the weekend, and I took the wire home and practiced some more. By Monday I could feed the wire through my fingers with both hands. For the rest of my career I would see welders struggle and get hung up because they couldn't control the wire, or could only weld right-handed. I never had that problem, because of those first days.

Denby was my on-again, off-again teacher for years. After I stopped going back to school for good, I would still drop in to see him at the college, as did many of his students. He was of small stature but a powerful force. He had a wiry beard and shaggy hair sticking out from under his black welding hat, and sported antique aviator glasses with leather side-shields, steam punk before there was steam punk. When it rained he wore a battered Australian bush hat and carried a long black umbrella, with a handle made of forged steel in the shape of a goat's head. He had made it in his blacksmith shop, as he had made so many remarkable things.

On one of my returns to school, the workbenches in the main area of the fabricating shop had been pulled back, out of the way. In the middle of the floor, standing a metre high and at least two across, was an octopus. It was realistic in every detail: the mournful eye, the confusion of thick legs wrapping around invisible objects, the beak.

Denby had sculpted it from mild steel, each individual sucker carefully forged and shaped, and it appeared to be in motion, traveling across the ocean floor. He was trying out different welding rods and overlay techniques to make the perfect texture for the skin. When it was finished, he used a pickling mixture that accelerated oxidation and turned the surface a rich, burnished orange.

Denby is one of those people who, when he takes an interest in a subject, will focus a fearsome energy on it. He is driven by his curiosity about a thing, by the what ifs, as in, *what if I made a Garry oak tree out of steel*...which was his next project. He forged every leaf and acorn, and a little hidden nest, tucked away in the upper branches, with a perfect little steel songbird, standing over three perfect eggs. His interests ranged wildly, from art deco design to building whisky stills, from Tolkien to the Grateful Dead.

"They pay me for my weld," he'd say. "They don't pay me for my thinking time." One of the most common complaints about welding is that it can be boring. But Denby had a mind that was on fire behind the welding hood: a cacophony of ideas, visions, music, calculations, science, and poetry. He taught me to weld without thinking about it.

"I don't want to be thinking about welding while I'm welding," he told me. "I want to be thinking about... rococo architecture or... how to build that steam hammer."

HE WAS ALSO a diver, and the octopus was his friend. Denby had been diving in the pass outside his home when the octopus popped out of its den, surprising them both.

"He acted like a dog," he said, "he'd charge if I got too close, but then settle back down when I backed away." He became fascinated with the octopus that summer, putting on his tank and slipping into the frigid ocean early in the morning. The octopus got used to him, became curious, and the two of them spent a lot of time together, just hanging out. When winter set in and it was too cold and rough to dive, Denby made the sculpture.

He also helped me build a box out of aluminum that bolted on to the back of my motorcycle, so my border collie could ride with me. I stopped by the school one afternoon with Flash happily sitting in his box with his doggles on, to show Denby how well it had turned out. He was delighted. A couple of days later his old Harley Davidson pulled up outside my house with his Jack Russell, Niles, balanced on the tank bag. Not to be left behind, my neighbour's Russell, Louie, took to riding on the front of my bike, while Flash relaxed on the back. Many weekends we would go for a slow turn around the island, two motorcycles with the three dogs, an odd little gang.

As talented and eccentric as he was, his gift was for teaching. He had an encyclopedic knowledge of welding, blacksmithing, blueprints, construction code, and metallurgy. He was consistently calm and good natured, never raised his voice, never lost his cool. The day he laid his motorcycle down on the highway and needed emergency surgery to put a couple of titanium pins in his leg, his wife arrived at the hospital just as he was being wheeled toward the operating room. Heavily drugged, he was lecturing the nurses.

"Do you even know how reactive and non-reactive metals interact in a saline environment?" He was hectoring them. "I don't need a surgeon, I need a metallurgist!"

AFTER I LEARNED to feed wire, we quickly reached an agreement. I would practice welding pipe in the mornings, and we'd spend the afternoons blacksmithing.

"Look at you," he said, one afternoon while we were building Victorian candelabras. "You're like lightning with that hammer."

"Really?" I said, dubiously, "Lightning?"

"Yeah," he said, his eyes twinkling. "You never hit the same place twice." It was an old blacksmith joke, but I hadn't heard it. His teacher had told it to him twenty years earlier. And twenty years later I was running little blacksmithing workshops in my own shop, and heard myself saying to a student, "Look at you. You're like lightning with that hammer."

THE COLLEGE NEVER fully appreciated Denby, how inspirational he was to generations of students, the depth and breadth of his knowledge and imagination. The administrators couldn't see past his misdemeanours, like building an unsanctioned smithy at the back of the school, and creating a nine-foot long, rather voluptuous, reclining mermaid. He was a consummate gentleman, the students loved him, and he trained many excellent welders during his thirty years in the department. On Vancouver Island, if you showed up on a job and the foreman knew that Denby had trained you, you were expected to know what you were doing.

Welding is not easy to teach. You can explain it, but like blacksmithing, it needs to be demonstrated. Demos are tricky because it's hard to watch the tiny, fluid puddle and high-amperage electric arc when you're both looking through darkened lenses. Denby was precise in his teaching and gave excellent demos. But as I progressed in my training, he answered fewer and fewer questions.

Sometimes he would say nothing, but often he would respond with a line from a Bob Dylan song.

"I don't think I want to turn the heat up any more," I'd say, studying my latest attempt on a piece of pipe. Denby would shrug.

"You know what you want," he'd say, "but I know what you need." It was his way of telling me to figure it out, that I already knew the solution. Eventually, we only communicated in the shop with Bob Dylan lyrics.

"I've never engaged in this kind of thing before," I'd say.

"First among equals," he'd answer. "Second to none." Or when I'd stop welding for a minute he would pop his head into my booth and ask "How does it feel . . . to be on your own?"

"When you've got nothing," I'd answer, "you've got nothing to lose."

MISS LONELY

In the United States, the Boilermakers International had collaborated with a company called Common Arc in an initiative designed to eliminate the high costs of arranging a job test for every welder before every job. Welders were testing constantly, sometimes ten or twelve times a year, often doing the same test for the same contractor in a different location. Each test coupon had to be X-rayed, or bent in front of a welding inspector, and it could take days to get results back. The annual expense of all those tests was costing contractors millions of dollars. The Common Arc program promised to eliminate redundancies by creating a single qualifying test. If the welder passed, they could legally weld almost anything, for the next six months, anywhere in the country.

The test had to have wide parameters, so the program took elements from all the existing procedures and distilled them into one. They called it the gun barrel test, because of the super-heavy-wall tube and narrow inside diameter. The two pieces of pipe were tacked together on the bench, then lifted on to the stand and welded in the 6G position, which meant at a forty-five-degree angle. The welder would start welding at the bottom of the joint in the overhead position, climb up the side into the vertical position, change angle and move into horizontal, and finish in the flat. Then go back to the bottom of the joint, and repeat the procedure on the other side, left-handed. There are multiple passes, so the sequence repeats over and over, until the joint is filled.

The heavy wall meant the tube acted as a heat sink, so you had to either turn the heat up and risk blowing a hole in the root, or preheat the bevel face. The narrow inside diameter left very little room to maneuver the torch, and the thickness meant it took an insane number of passes to fill; the cap was more than an inch wide by the time it was finished. It was an endurance test, to be completed within a four-hour time limit.

The advantage to such a difficult test is that if the welder passes, they are qualified to weld material from paper thin, to three quarters of an inch thick, on plate, pipe, or tubing in any diameter, in any position. But contractors wanted the welders to be able to use either process — stick or TIG, so they decided to use both, changing the process halfway through the joint. The welder had to put in a TIG root and hot pass, then break down the equipment, shut off the gas line, disconnect the torch, change the polarity, and switch to stick for the fill and cap. If they passed, it was more or less an unlimited qualification.

I had read about Common Arc in the union newsletter and was curious; we didn't have anything like it in Canada. Boilermaker locals in the US held testing clinics at their halls, and in the spring, contractor representatives were invited to the event to assess the results. Canadians were allowed to participate, so when a clinic in Spokane, Washington, was announced, I decided to give it a try. It seemed unlikely I'd pass, given my lack of experience and extreme test anxiety, but it would be good practice. So I dawdled on down on my motorcycle, stopping at the taco stand just south of Bellingham, and staying at a roadside motel I couldn't afford.

AT THE HALL in Spokane, there were a dozen contractors milling around, talking with the welders, networking. Everyone seemed to know each other. There was handshaking and backslapping, a young guy congratulated for just becoming a father. Others pressing the contractor reps about rumours of upcoming jobs. I realized these guys weren't just here to qualify, they were going to be competing.

We were each assigned a welding booth and two test coupons. We were instructed to go into our booths and tack the coupons together, whereupon the inspector would come around to approve the fit-up. He would wait while we welded the test piece into position, and once it was on the stand, we weren't allowed to move it. Then we would work through the steps printed out on the welding procedure, waiting for the inspector at each hold point. When the test was completed, we would cut down the piece and the inspector would stamp it and put it on a table with a clipboard. The contractors would walk around the table, and if they liked the welding, and thought it conformed to the code and their requirements, they would sign your clipboard. That meant you had qualified, and could work for that company when a job came up. If you had a good test, you could get a dozen signatures, and qualify to work for everyone.

I took a preheat, running the torch around the face of the bevel with no filler metal until the inside of the joint turned a deep purplish blue. I was anxious and my hands shook. I dropped my helmet and started moving the torch in little backwards circles with my left hand, adding filler metal with my right, teasing it up the inside of the joint. When I was finished, the root was flush at the bottom, but you could get away with that as long as it wasn't low. There were no fisheyes, the little pinholes that appear when you break the arc and pull out too fast. I put in a healthy hot pass, feeding wire like crazy so it didn't overheat and suck back. Then I stood outside the booth as instructed, until the inspector came over. He peered into the tube with a flashlight, lowered in a tiny mirror to see the bottom side of the root, and put a little check mark on my procedure sheet. I switched over to stick and started filling it up, putting in pass after pass. I'd occasionally go off the rails a bit, my welding crooked, and have to correct it. It was hot. The clock ticked. I was about two thirds done when I heard the first welder power down his machine and put his piece on the table. It became quieter and quieter as they finished, one by one, and went out into the parking lot to talk and wait for their pieces to cool. I was the last to finish, coming in just under the time limit, and the inspector was already stamping ID numbers into the other pieces. Instead of being neatly stacked and uniform, the stringers on my cap narrowed and widened, sometimes crossing over each other. The inspector peered at it with his flashlight from one side, then the other, looking for undercut. He found a couple of spots and told me to take them down with a file. The contractors were already coming in when I put my piece out on the table.

The reps went around the room, signing off on different welders. A lot of them were very good, had done the test often, and were only there because their six-month qualification period was up. The contractors that knew these guys signed off on them right away. Two welders didn't finish — one left at the beginning when he couldn't get his root in, and the other gave up about halfway through.

Some of the contractors glanced at me and walked by without looking at my coupon; they weren't interested in having a woman on their job. Others came up to my station to look at my weld, picking it up and putting it down again without signing the clipboard. Near the end a contractor rep introduced himself. He asked where I was from.

"Canadian, eh?" he asked, smiling. "What brings you down here?" I told him I came down because I wanted to try the test. He nodded.

"It's a tough one," he said. He picked up my coupon and held it up to the light, looking down the inside at the root. Then he put it down and signed my clipboard. "Don't give up." he said. That day I got one signature out of fourteen contractors.

A COUPLE OF months later I signed up for another testing event in Portland, Oregon. It was a five-hour drive, and I was still three hours out when the rain came. It was one of those horrendous storms where the sky opens up and the roads are awash. The feeble headlight of my twenty-year-old bike only lit up the rain, making it worse. I slowed down as much as I dared, but couldn't get off the freeway. Cars were pulling off the road because the drivers couldn't see. I couldn't pull off because it would be too dangerous to try to get back on. Eventually I tucked in behind a red pickup truck that was rolling at a steady sixty kilometres per hour, and followed his tail lights, desperate for an exit. It was nightmarish, kind of like the welding test I was headed toward. Eventually the truck signalled and I followed it off an exit ramp. Half an hour later I came across a Super 8 motel and checked in, feeling like a shipwreck. Everything I had with me was wet. I made a clothesline out of bungie cords and strung it across my motel room.

IN THE MORNING there were clear blue skies. I got up early and rolled into the union hall in Portland, damp but on time. My nerves were not as jangled this time. Compared to the harrowing ride down, the test didn't look too bad, and it was my second time. I finished in three and half hours, ending the day with four signatures on my sheet.

If your coupon passed the visual, it was sent out for an X-ray. A few days after Portland, a little laminated card arrived in the mail, saying my test had passed. So when our dispatcher called to tell me Local 11 was looking for tube welders to go on a maintenance turnaround at the largest coal-fired electric power plant in Montana, I accepted. Jim, the dispatcher, had to call me because I was on the list, and he had to run the list in order, but it was clear he didn't expect me to say yes. He became very quiet.

"Do you even weld tubes?" he asked.

"I'm qualified," I said. "You can look at my tickets." I could hear him shuffling papers over the phone.

"Do you even know what you're doing?" he asked, finally, in his nearly impenetrable Scottish accent.

"No," I said. "But I'm qualified." More papers.

"I'll fax you the information," he said. "If you change your mind, call me back."

It was true that I was qualified, and also true that I didn't know what I was doing.

I had three years of welding school, journeyman's papers, a provincial Red Seal, and all the right tickets, but I had never welded a pressure joint on a job. I had a logbook full of qualifications, but the only one they cared about in the US was the Common Arc. Oddly enough, I had done that too. The paperwork arrived like it was supposed to, the criminal record check came through, and I passed my drug test. The only thing left was to tune up my skills.

Denby was leaning against the handrail by the fire door, smoking a hand-rolled cigarette.

"What are you doing here?" he asked.

"I need the booth," I said. "I'm going to a job in Montana." His lips peeled back in a reptilian grin.

"Ah," he said. "So you're finally going down south to learn how to wear your hat."

"Maybe," I said. "If I can make the job test."

"Well," he said. "You've been to the very finest school, alright... Miss Lonely."

FOR THE NEXT three days he helped me prepare for the weld test. The contractor in Montana wasn't one of the ones that had signed my clipboard, so I would have to test again when I got there. It was make or break, which meant that if I failed it there would be no job, and I would be going home. My anxiety was off the scale.

For three days I practiced in the booth, trying to put a root in that wasn't too shallow, making tie-ins that didn't fisheye. Denby showed me some tricks: how to move the molten metal on to the upper bevel and avoid undercutting the bottom, how to tie-in without leaving a lump on the cap.

On the third day he said, "Nobody ever taught you how to live out on the street so now you're just going to have to get used to it."

"I just know what I know," I answered. "I go where only the lonely can go."

ON THE MORNING of the fourth day, the day before I left for Montana, Denby intercepted me as I was getting a handful of TIG wire.

"What are you doing here?" he asked.

"How can, how can you ask me again? Well it only brings me sorrow," I said, thinking we were playing the game.

"No," he said, shaking his head. "No more sport welding."

"It's hard," I said. "It's a hard rain's a-gonna fall."

"You only work for money now," he said, and gently took the wire out of my hand. I started to get choked up, convinced I wasn't ready, and swallowed hard. I retrieved my work bag and helmet from the booth and secured the gear on to the motorcycle. We shook hands.

"The same thing I would want today I would want again tomorrow," I said.

"You're invisible now," he said. "You've got no secrets."

MONTANA

It was unsurprising that there is no direct flight from Vancouver, BC, to Colstrip, Montana. But it was a little surprising to learn that it would take twenty-four hours, four flights, and a hundred and fifty miles by taxi. At the time I had the old motorcycle, which was finicky, and in the winter I switched to a little S-10 pickup of similar vintage. I didn't think either of them would make the 1,800-kilometre trip, even if I had the time and courage to attempt it, which I did not. The company wasn't offering travel money or a living out allowance, which was another reason not many welders from BC took these jobs. *Lot of trouble for nothing*, they said. But I needed to work, so I started booking plane tickets on my credit card. The flights would cost more than $1500 Canadian, one way, which was a lot for an unemployed welder in 2001. I had a $2000 limit on my Visa, which didn't leave a lot for setting up house.

For out-of-town jobs, I don't usually bring tools, but I take my own welding helmet, steel-toed boots, a respirator, and work clothes. I assembled a pile of gear everything I would need to live for a month, and jettisoned most of it, including my lunch-kit and a stack of books. They don't supply coveralls in the US so I kept a few shirts and one pair of Carhartt overalls. In the end I left with a suitcase and a backpack, the old oilskin rain jacket that my mum had bought me tied on to the pack, welding helmet, and gloves crammed on top. I wore my boots so I didn't have to carry them.

I was up at five and my boyfriend drove me to the 7:00 a.m. float plane, worried and wishing me luck, conflicted but unsure of what to say. He wanted to be supportive, but clearly was not convinced it was a great idea. The float plane was a luxury, and I had debated the expense, but my flight for the US left from Vancouver at 10:00 a.m. and I wouldn't make it on time if I took the ferries. The de Haviland Beaver was the same age that I was and skimmed over the waves at three hundred feet. I could see seals swimming just under the surface as we took off into on overcast sky, and twenty minutes later the plane slid into the river mouth, flying low over lines of Brandt's cormorants, standing together on deadheads, drying their wings.

My mum lived near the airport, picked me up at the float plane terminal on the south river, and drove me to the international departures gate at the main terminal. She had brought me a cup of coffee. She told me my grandmother had been born in Butte, so I had roots in Montana. Then she pulled over to the curb, cutting off a taxi, and gave me a plastic bag with a cheese sandwich, a granola bar, and an orange inside. Also, two one-hundred-dollar bills.

"It's all I had in American money," she said. "Save it for an emergency. Or buy yourself something nice." The emergency scenario seemed so much more likely.

VANCOUVER AIRPORT IS a pre-clearance centre for people entering the US, so I had to clear customs before getting on the first plane. In security they searched my luggage, taking everything out: my clothes, shoes, washbag, a deck of cards. At immigration there were long lineups, and I had my passport, a blue piece of paper from the US government, and a letter from the union. Eventually I stood in front of a hefty lout with a military haircut who read my paperwork, slowly moving his lips. There was a problem because it was made out for a different port of entry; the Americans had assumed I would be travelling by car, and would therefore be crossing over from Grasmere, BC, to

Eureka, in northern Montana. Grasmere. Eureka. I repeated the words back to the immigration agent. I had never heard of these places.

"It doesn't matter anyhow," he said, closing my passport and sliding it with the papers back across the counter, "because you can't travel on your husband's papers."

"What?" I asked.

"Ma'am, you can't travel on your husband's papers," he said, more slowly. "If he's going down there to work you can't travel on his papers. You need your own papers." He was looking behind me, as though this husband would suddenly step up and translate what he was saying so I'd understand.

"I'm not married," I said.

"Ok, well your boyfriend then," he allowed.

"I don't know what you're talking about," I said. He sighed.

"These papers say he's traveling to the United States to work as a welder on a temporary work permit for a turnaround in Colstrip, Montana," he explained. "You can't travel on his..."

"Whoa, whoa, whoa..." I interrupted. "Those are my papers. I am the welder. I am going to work in Montana. See the name? See the name here, on my passport? How they are the same...?" The lineup behind me was getting longer. He studied the papers again, frowning.

"It says the International Boilermakers," he said, finally.

"Yes it does," I replied. "Would you like to see my membership card?" I would not move from my place in front of the desk, and gripped the edge with my fingers. The officer left his station with my papers and returned with a supervisor.

"You're trying to travel on your husband's papers?" the supervisor asked, puzzled. He was chewing a sandwich.

"No," I told him, "your colleague is confused. I don't have a husband, but I do have a job, and I have a flight to catch ..."

When I had finished my explanation, he said, "You know you're at the wrong port of entry. This says you're crossing at Eureka."

I explained that I was not at the wrong port of entry, they had put the wrong place on the paperwork.

He said, "I'm from Montana. Livingstone."

"Ah," I said. "Let's see where that is." I pulled out my paper map and he showed me his hometown. He finished his sandwich, took off his glasses, and gave me a long look.

"You're a welder?" he asked, again.

"Yes," I said. He looked at me for a while longer.

"My daughter wants to be a welder."

"Tell her to join a union," I said. "She'll make twice the rate." The supervisor nodded and flicked his hand over the paperwork, which the loutish officer stamped and handed back to me.

"Welcome to the United States," he said.

We were still in Vancouver. I was the last one on the plane.

THE PLANE HAD two seats on one side of the aisle and one on the other, only eight of us flying. I sat in a single seat, anxious. We took off into a fierce West Coast storm, the morning sky a dark grey, and bounced and rattled toward Seattle.

Just enough time for a coffee in Seattle, where they searched my luggage again, this time finding and opening a box of crackers and confiscating a pocketknife. I boarded the flight to Great Falls. This was a small-town outpost, a single, low-lying building with a coffee shop and a newspaper vendor, both closed. "Tequila" was playing in the ladies' room. The airport was deserted, except for a large, coffin-shaped glass case in one corner of the departure lounge. Inside the case, standing upright, was a moth-eaten black bear. There was only one flight to Billings each day and it left at 4:00 pm. I ate half of my mother's cheese sandwich, alone with the bear in the glass coffin. It raked the air with its front feet, snarling. I had four hours to kill and sat in a moulded plastic chair across from the bear, staring it down.

The plane from Great Falls to Billings was bigger, four seats across, and I was served a cup of hot coffee and a bag of peanuts. The anxiety was becoming excitement. People looked different, and two passengers wore large belt buckles and cowboy hats. Billings was hot and dry, which was a good thing as I'd forgotten my oilskin coat on the flight from Seattle to Great Falls. In Billings, the cook in the cafeteria had an eagle and an American flag on his ball cap. He was eating a bowl of soup and watching a rerun of *Buffy the Vampire Slayer.* The security agent opened my knapsack and pawed through it.

"Go ahead," I said. "Take whatever you want." I boarded the final flight, another small plane, that dipped and dove through turbulent desert skies, the flight attendant clutching the backs of the seats as she passed by with her basket of snacks.

MILES CITY WAS about where my planning had ended. It was around 6:00 p.m., and I didn't know how to get to Colstrip. The only bus going east had left for the day. I summoned a cab and made a deal with the driver to take me the 123 miles. I was on nightshift and was supposed to start at 6:00 p.m., finishing at five in the morning. There was going to be a welding test, and I would be up all night. I told the driver to wake me up when we got there. I had to show him the money up front and held up the two one-hundred-dollar bills for him to see in the mirror. Then I made a nest in the back of the cab, pulled a sweater over my head, and slept.

I'd had a solid hour's sleep by the time the cab pulled into the Super 8 hotel in Colstrip.

When I checked in, the desk clerk beamed and said, "Your shift started at six. You're late."

"I know ... but how do you know that?"

"Oh, I heard. Lady welder from Canada." She beamed again. I asked if she could call me another cab while I changed my clothes.

She laughed, "No, there's no taxi here." No taxi? "Don't worry, I'll give y'all a ride."

HER NAME WAS Kathy and she handed me a styrofoam cup of coffee when I came down from the room. Kathy drove me to the power plant, a couple of miles outside of town, even stopping at the gas station on the way so I could pick up two Snickers bars and some chips. She drove an old Nova, swinging it out on to the highway like a yacht. About halfway there she swerved, and a huge round shape bounced on to the hood and rolled up the windshield and over the back of the car.

"What the hell?" I ducked down under the dashboard. She laughed and said "Tumbleweed. Don't you have those?"

Kathy swung the Nova into the parking lot and pulled up to the security gate. A little window in the gatehouse swung open and a man in a brown uniform shirt peered out.

"Hi Bill," Kathy said. "We got a new hire here on the night shift. From Canada." She beamed again. The man cleared his throat.

"Do you have any drugs, alcohol, or firearms in the vehicle?" he asked sternly.

"Well you know I do, all of the above. What d'ya need?"

"Will you stop that Kathy?" he said. "I got a job here, ya know. This is serious."

"Just open the gate, Bill. The girl's had a long day and she's late for work." The man slammed the window shut and the gate went up. "That's my brother-in-law," she said. "He just got this job for the turnaround and he thinks he's somebody now 'cause they gave him a nametag. OK girl, you have a good shift. Just ask one of the boys to drop you off, OK? Everyone drives by the hotel." Then she was gone, and I was standing in a dusty parking lot on the edge of the desert, in front of a massive power plant facility.

SORRY FOR YOUR LUCK

The Montana power plant at Colstrip is the tallest man-made structure in the state. The brain and heart — if it had a heart — of a sprawling, fifty square mile industrial wasteland in south-eastern Montana, the power plant is a blinking, cacophonous monster. It crouches on the edge of the townsite, its chaos of blue and red and orange lights, sirens and alarms, all within range of the town's 2300 residents.

I STOOD IN a parking lot swirling with dust. It's everywhere in the town, a thick grey-brown coating that covers the buildings and washes across the roads, obscuring the lines. Incomprehensible announcements blared through a radio system. I headed for the administration building. A security guard checked me in and assigned a temporary visitor's pass and eventually I was sent to the contractor's trailer. The crew was just going back on the unit after their coffee break. A foreman called Dan introduced himself and shook my hand. He looked at his watch.

"You're a little late," he said.

"Yup," I answered. "I came from Canada."

"Canada," he said. "That's far."

"Yup." So far, so good. Dan had me wait in the lunchroom while he went to find out what to do with me. Since the job in Montana,

I've been left in the lunchroom a number of times. Usually they do it because they don't have a place for you yet. Sometimes they just don't want to deal with a woman on the site and claim you don't fit in anywhere. Sometimes they want to make you nervous, and sometimes it's just mean, and they will sit you in the lunchroom for a whole shift, drawing attention from the rest of the crew, underscoring your difference, and that they have no need for you at all. Over the years, I learned to love these down times, and would read, do my nails, play Scrabble on my phone, and read The New York Times. But in Montana I had no newspaper, and no phone, and just sat in the lunchroom, which was a temporary structure made of plywood and plastic hoarding, and waited. It feels like being the last, and least desirable kid to be picked for the softball team.

DAN RETURNED WITH a young safety office, Tyler. Taylor? Travis?

"The new hires are just finishing their safety orientation," he drawled. "You were supposed to do a welding test, but there probably won't be time now. You might as well go home and come back and start tomorrow with the new guys if you want." I didn't answer. Home was a long way away, and it was a Saturday. Saturday meant ten hours of double-time was on the table, I wasn't going anywhere. "Or you can go with Tyler here and get your safety orientation out of the way."

"I can't do the weld test tonight?" I asked.

"The new hires are already testing," he said. "There might not be time." I did the two-hour safety orientation and we haggled again, and at midnight they let me go in for the welding test. The shift ended at 4:30 and the test had a four-hour limit.

"It's a heavy-wall test," he said. "You might use up all of the time, and everyone is out of here at 4:20 sharp."

DAN TOOK ME to the welding shop in the maintenance building where they had a couple of booths. Two welders had already tested and were puttering around the yard. They wouldn't get their results until the next night. The guy in the tool crib had a lean face, a droopy moustache, and a mullet. His name was Weasel. I was told he would "look after me" while I tested. There was no inspector, and no quality control guy. I asked Weasel if there was a weld procedure.

"Oh yeah," he said, dropping two pieces of pipe on the counter, "weld 'em up." The coupons he gave me were rusty and one of them was out of round. I had a bad feeling. I didn't pick them up.

"I don't have time for a practice piece," I said, slowly, "so I'll just take the test coupons now." Weasel smirked and nodded at the pieces on the counter.

"There ya go," he said.

"Naw ... I think I need a couple that are round," I said, "or they won't line up. I'll take two of those clean ones, if that's OK with you." I nodded at the box of coupons behind him and gave him my biggest, friendliest smile. Grudgingly he passed over two new pieces. I took them to my booth and set it up, adjusting the light, making sure the grinder worked. You were allowed to use the grinder, judiciously, but not on the cap. I had a little make-up case with me with a few tools in it: a flashlight, a little mirror on a handle, a dental pick. I went back to Weasel and asked him for some wire and a small, half-round file.

"You bring your own tools," he said, unhelpfully.

"Yeah," I said, "Well when you're crossing the border they aren't too big on you bringing in a file in your handbag, so if you don't mind ... and I'll take some 3/32 70S and one stick of one-eighth." He passed me the file, and reached under the counter and pulled some stubs of wire out, each about a foot long, and held them out to me. The ends were melted, they had obviously been used by somebody else first.

"That would be new wire I'm looking for," I said, "out of the box." With a heavy sigh he took two long, thin cardboard boxes down off the shelf and pulled a single wire out of each one. I checked the marking stamped on the end, verifying it was the right alloy. He was not making it easy.

BACK IN THE booth I was suddenly exhausted. All the airplanes, the immigration guys, the drug test, the days of practice, the conversations with family about whether or not I should take the job. Losing my coat. Not knowing where I'd be staying after the weekend. And the test. I considered lying down on the shop floor and closing my eyes, just for a few minutes, but didn't.

TEST ANXIETY IS like hostess anxiety – you either have it or you don't, and I have always suffered from both. Whenever I threw a party, I was convinced beforehand that no one would come (they always did), it wouldn't be fun (it usually was), and that I would be left with a case of Prosecco and an embarrassment of smoked salmon canapes. This was not the worst imaginable outcome — who doesn't like Prosecco? Unlike an under-attended party, a failed exam had more serious consequences. I suffered through it during university, even changing majors from linguistics to theatre because there were fewer exams. It was beyond nerves, I could get wound up into a state — sweating, dizzy, short of breath. Welding tests were as bad as university exams, only longer, with more people watching, and usually my livelihood depending on it. This time I was hyperaware that I only had about two hundred dollars left on my credit card. If I blew this test and didn't get the job, I wouldn't be able to get home. I simply had to pass.

Shaking slightly, I put the root in like Denby had taught me, preheating the bevel and adding to the front of the puddle, pushing the heat up the joint. It didn't take long, and when I looked inside with my flashlight it looked OK. There were a couple of flush spots, but I thought it would make the X-ray. I put in a hot pass and changed my machine over to stick. I had two bottles of water with me, drank one, and stepped outside to cool off for a couple minutes, then went back in to ask Weasel for some rod. He produced a handful that was dirty and cold, from under the counter.

"I'd like some new rod, please, out of the box. Three-thirty-two 7018. And an oven." I couldn't tell if he didn't know what he was doing or was trying to mess with me.

"You want me to open a brand-new box?" he asked. I nodded.

"Three thirty-two. This is a test. I'm not using dirty rod."

I WAS USING one of the most common and versatile welding rods there is, which goes by the number 7018. The number breaks down to indicate tensile strength, which elements are in the flux, and which positions it can be used in. 7018 is a low hydrogen electrode. The flux that keeps the weld puddle uncontaminated is made with minimal hydrogen content, because hydrogen in the completed weld will cause it to crack. But the flux is also prone to sucking up moisture from the air, particularly in a humid environment. Moisture reintroduces hydrogen. So once a box of rod is opened, it is immediately transferred to a portable rod can or oven, which is plugged into an outlet and keeps the rod hot and dry. Montana was so arid, I learned, the welders hardly concerned themselves with ovens. But coming from the West Coast, and working in a marine environment, I was pretty picky. That said, it was never unreasonable to request clean rod for a test piece. If the rod is damp or contaminated, it will cause porosity in the first inch or two of every pass, and the weld will fail.

"I don't have any," he finally said. "We only have one-eighth."

"Oh, I think you do," I said, glancing at the clock. I was falling behind. He was deliberately slow. "Maybe take another look. Or maybe they have a box in the office." I smiled. He narrowed his eyes. He didn't want me going to the office, telling his boss he couldn't find welding rod. Eventually Weasel found a box, but swore he didn't have an oven.

"I'll leave it in the oven here," he said, emptying the rod into the big oven in the tool crib. "You can just come and get it." He offered me a small handful.

"More," I said. "I'm going to need more."

THAT'S HOW WE spent the last two hours of the early morning, him dozing behind the counter and me struggling, sweating, cursing softly, grinding weld metal out and putting it back in. It was a fight all the way. I've had that fight several times since, and watched others do the same. You set traps for yourself, second-guess technique, start seeing flaws that aren't there and missing the ones that are. You're pitting inexperience against training, lack of confidence against faith. Eventually all you can do is put everything you know, and your steadiest hand, into it, and hope that it passes the shot.

Some welders are naturals, and master their technique pretty fast. Others struggle their entire careers. I kind of ran in the middle of the pack; I was never a natural, and had to learn and practice every step. Eventually I became reasonably good at my trade, could reliably produce a decent weld and make the shot with confidence. But that came a long time after that night in Montana.

I WAS FINALLY reaching the end, had welded my way all the way out to the cap. I had about four more rods to burn and could see the finish line. It would soon be over! And it didn't look half bad. I went to the tool crib and asked for a final handful of rod, which Weasel taciturnly handed over. Dan was back, leaning against the counter.

"How's she goin'?" he asked, glancing at the clock. It was five after four.

"It's going," I said. "Ten more minutes."

I put the rod into the cardboard box on the bench where I'd been keeping it so it stayed clean, pulled one out and started welding. But this one looked different. The arc wasn't the usually orange-white colour, it was more blue. And it sounded different. And through my respirator I caught a whiff of something — it smelled different. All this happened in seconds. I pulled out, and lifted my helmet. There was a hard, black flux over what I had just welded, about an inch long. I touched it with the file and it popped off, showing a shiny surface, much brighter and more yellow than the rest. I let out a shriek, and a barrage of filthy language. The curtain of my booth was pulled back.

"Something wrong?" Dan asked.

"That ... that rodent face ..." I said, pointing toward the tool crib, "... slipped some stainless in with my rod." Dan came in and examined my weld.

"Yup," he said, "Looks like stainless." He went out of the booth to talk to Weasel.

WHEN I CAME out, Weasel said, "Well, I guess that's that. Make or break. It's a one-shot deal." He smiled, "Sorry for your luck." Dan tried to calm me down.

"It is make or break," he said. "But this was ... uh ... unforeseen." I knew that the welder is responsible for having the right rod. You're supposed to check it before you put it in your stinger. I was on autopilot, exhausted, two rods away from victory, and I hadn't checked. So technically, it was my fault.

"I don't know what we can do about it now." Dan said.

"Well we're gonna have to do something," I said. "Because I don't accept this."

"You don't *accept* it?" he repeated. I shook my head. He looked at the clock again. "Come in tomorrow," he said finally. "Come in tomorrow and we'll see what we can do. Maybe they'll let you take the test again."

DAN DROVE ME back to the hotel. I was in shock. Take the test AGAIN? It was unthinkable. There was a beer machine in the lobby and I bought a couple of Coronas and a bag of Doritos. It was 6:00 a.m. and I'd been up for twenty-four hours, but wouldn't be sleeping for a while. I had to strategize.

I drank a Corona in the shower and thought things through. The rules were clear: if you didn't complete your test under the four-hour limit, or if it failed a visual, or if it failed the bend test, the job evaporated and you went home. *Sorry for your luck.* I was going to have to confront someone and plead my case. I didn't think I should have to go through the test a second time, and they wouldn't want to do that anyway. And I didn't want to go home. The only option left was to try to fix the test I had done. It was unlikely they would go for that, but I got out a notebook and started sketching out a script.

When I'd written my speech, I managed about three hours sleep, picked up some fried chicken and a couple of apples at the gas station, and rehearsed in my room. The trip had cost me a couple of thousand dollars, but it had cost the company at least ten to do my paperwork. More to the point, they needed welders. Maybe I could get them to see it my way. At 5:15 p.m., the company bus stopped outside the hotel to take workers to the plant. It was mostly full, and quite raucous when I got on, but quickly became quiet. These guys had never seen a woman boilermaker before, it seemed. I barely noticed.

I HEADED STRAIGHT for the office, an ATCO trailer, where there were four cowboys inside. I pushed the door open without knocking and asked, "Who's in charge?" The four guys in swivel chairs looked at each other in some confusion, unsure who exactly should be in charge of an obviously agitated female welder. They eventually all looked at one guy, an older fellow in a plaid shirt with pearlized snap buttons, who swivelled his chair to face me, sighed and said, "I guess I am."

"I came here from Canada yesterday to weld tubes in your power plant," I started my script, trying to breath steadily. "I took four different airplanes and a taxi from Miles City. I spent over fifteen hundred dollars because I wanted to come here and do this job. I did my welding test last night and that … *fool* … in the tool crib slipped some stainless rod into my sleeve. I don't know if it was an accident, which makes him incompetent, or on purpose, which makes it sabotage, but because of him I laid an inch of stainless on the last pass of the cap of my test coupon." I paused to catch my breath. The four guys looked at each other. "As you know it's a make-or-break test, which means your man out there thinks I'm going home and it's…" I took a dramatic breath, "it's HORSESHIT." Like the word fool, I'd chosen my cuss word carefully when writing out the speech. It had to be a word that cowboys understood, serious enough that they wouldn't use it at home or in front of a lady, but not so fierce that I would offend my male bosses completely. Bullshit was too mundane and had been co-opted by the middle class. Horseshit was perfect. Serious enough, with a whiff of Western vernacular.

When I was done, the guy in charge, Charlie, turned to another guy, and said, "Bill?" They were all still looking at me like I was an alien creature. I may have been over-reacting a little bit, but the stakes were high. Bill turned completely around in his chair to face me.

"Bill here is in charge of quality control," Charlie said, passing the buck. He was nodding his head, and leaning back in his chair, a funny smile forming under his droopy moustache. "What do you want to do about this?" he asked.

"I guess," Bill said slowly, "I guess, if what you're saying is true..."

"It's true," I said.

"I guess ... you can do the test again ..." He was clearly not big on second chances.

"I'm not doing the test again." I told them. I had settled down. They seemed like nice enough fellas, and I really did appreciate their dress sense. "I've been up for thirty-six hours, I'm cranky, I did the damn test and I'm not doing it again." I paused, and went back to my script. "I came here to work, not to hang around in the test booth for two days." This was a risk, this bravado I didn't feel.

Charlie turned back to me, and said very slowly, "What exactly is it that you want?" I took a deep breath.

"I want to fix the test I already did," I said.

"And just how would you do that?" he asked.

"I would take that slug of stainless out with a five-inch grinder, reweld it and finish the cap. The way I would on the job," I added, stabbing the air with my index finger. No need for them to know I'd never welded a tube on a job. Charlie nodded slowly.

"I think we might be able to do that," he said. "Bill?"

"The test is ruined," Bill said. "you won't be able to fix it."

"I can fix it," I said. "I know how to fix it." Bill stood up and walked toward me.

"Ok," he said, finally. "Have it your way. But I'm going to mark where that stainless was, and when we cut it for the bend test, I want one of the coupons to come right out of that spot." I nodded.

"Fair enough."

"And if it doesn't bend clean, we'll see it."

"Sure," I said. "No problem." As I was leaving, thanking them as I backed away, Charlie was saying, "Someone has to talk to Weasel."

FIXING THE WELD was not as difficult as getting the supervision to see things my way. Dan had saved the coupon, understanding that the issue would need to be resolved. I carefully carved out the slug of stainless, then welded up the groove with 7018 and finished the cap. I was pretty sure I got it all because the sparks are different when you grind stainless, fine and dark red, instead of orange and yellow. I wasn't too concerned about the test piece bending — stainless is full of nickel and is more ductile than carbon steel. If anything, a little stainless would give a better result.

I SPENT THE night working in the yard with a tall, gangly, and very laid-back Montanan called Gavin Reed. Like many of them, he had a squared-off handlebar moustache that crept down either side of his mouth. Gav was from Helena, about six-hundred miles away. He kept asking, "What did you say to them? They let you fix that test … what did you say?" I just shook my head and didn't answer. We moved welding machines around and unloaded a truck, preparing for the next stage of the turnaround. Around 2:00 a.m., Dan came loping toward us across the yard.

"You passed," he said. "Welcome aboard." I was dizzy with relief and shook his hand.

"Please tell Weasel…" I said. "I'm sorry for his luck."

SACRIFICE ZONE

Colstrip is a company town, invented for the workers who were needed to run the power plant and work at the mines. The housing consisted of bungalows and mobile homes clustered together in small developments and trailer parks, nestled right up to the edge of the plant. You could see the power plant from every house, or at least the giant haze of light that emanated from it at night. You could hear the machinery, the steam turbines, and of course the coal trains, coming and going, all day and night. You could feel the earth shudder under the dragline, and rumble from explosions at the mine sites, deep underground.

The American art photographer David Hanson spent several years in Colstrip, taking devastatingly beautiful photos of the landscape. In an essay that accompanies his collection, *Colstrip*, he describes the "eight-million-pound walking dragline" that was built at the coal mine at a cost of nearly twenty million dollars in the early 1980s:

> *The size of a large office building, complete with control rooms and power decks, the Marion 8200 is emblazoned with the image of a buffalo, the logo of the mining company. It has a boom that reaches more than three hundred feet out over the earth, and it has a shovel that can carry a hundred tons of rock in a single bite. The dragline works its way up and down the strips, systematically removing the earth and rock from one strip*

> *and dropping it into an adjacent strip from which the coal has already been excavated.*
>
> — David T. Hanson, *Colstrip, Montana*

The scale of the operation that Hanson describes is difficult to fathom. Together the mines, power plant, and related industrial sites make up more than fifty square miles, an area sometimes referred to as one of Montana's environmental sacrifice zones. In the last century, Hanson explains, enough dirt has been dug up and moved "... to fill both the Erie and Panama canals five times over." The boilers that feed the steam turbines at the Colstrip power plant "...consume 1,200 tons of coal each hour, or roughly one acre of land every day and a half." When I was there, the area had been in a drought for five years, yet dry as it was, the power plant continued to "consume nearly 22,000 gallons of water every minute," piped in from the Yellowstone River, thirty miles away.

Having the dubious honour of being deemed number nine in the 2009 report by Environment America called *America's Biggest Polluters*, the plant is one of the dirtiest in the nation. A vast system of wastewater settling ponds and dump sites encircle the power plant, leeching huge amounts of toxic chemicals and heavy metals into the groundwater and contaminating the aquifers. The town's drinking water was contaminated long ago, and almost all of the wells have been permanently closed.

In his essay, Hansen explains how toxic wastewater is channeled through evaporative sprinkler systems, leaving a crust of chemicals on the ground. In addition, the power plant belches smoke, steam, and a cocktail of chemicals including nitrous oxide, methane, and carbon dioxide into the atmosphere. It emits four hundred pounds of sulphur dioxide every hour.

None of this is immediately apparent when you first roll into town. In fact, the townsite is surprisingly picturesque, in a classic

Americana kind of way. There's a core of little wooden houses, a charming post office, and an irrigated park with some of the only shade trees, struggling to leaf out under the desert sun. At the core is a gas station that is also a laundromat, and is fitted out with a couple of slot machines so you can gamble while waiting for your clothes to dry. There is the grocery store, Rosebud Foods, that also had a one-armed bandit in the foyer; the Everything Beautiful Thrift Store; and, a mechanic's shop that doubles as a miniature Harley Davidson dealership and sells t-shirts and caps. Down the block is the Moose Lodge, a private club where members could gather to drink, talk, and gamble. The largest building in town is the Coal Bowl, an eight-lane, ten-pin bowling alley that includes a lounge, a small casino, and a restaurant that offers the only fine dining experience in town. I could hardly wait. In total there were four places to gamble and five places to worship in a town of two thousand people.

The motel was a few blocks outside of the centre, toward the highway, and was relatively new. A two-storey walk-up with a run of balconies looking out on to a dusty parking lot, it was the typical accommodation for travelling workers. It was also the only place in town, and therefore the motel of choice for travelling bowlers. I'd reserved my room for three nights, because that was all that was available. There was a bowling tournament coming to town, and all the rooms were booked for the following week. Not only was the Colstrip Super 8 packed, there was not a room to be had from Forsyth to Miles City.

I got in from work around 5:00 a.m., slept a few hours, then got up and packed. I headed to Rosebud Foods, convinced I could find someone in town who would rent me a room. I explained my situation to the checkout clerk and asked if she could think of anyone (grocery checkout clerks know everything in a town like this). She called a colleague over from the next till, and the two of them talked it over, discussing different possible candidates. When I left the store I had a phone number pencilled on my grocery bill.

I checked out of the hotel and met Loraine outside of the Coal Bowl. She talked non-stop, mostly about her kids and God. I could have her daughter's room, she said, her daughter was away in California pursuing her dream of going into show business. I didn't know if it was nervous chatter or just her way of being, and it didn't really matter. She had a room, and it was a hundred and fifty a week. This sounded just fine.

The house was a little yellow and white rancher with a large pile of dirt in the front yard, an American flag made of paper taped to the inside of the window, and a yellow dog tied up to the porch. The yard was grassless, cracked dirt, dust swirling around a couple of sheets that flapped on a clothesline in the hot wind. Loraine unclipped the dog.

"That's Lucy," she said. "She's fine if you're home. I only tie her up when I'm out. Everybody knows her." The dog bounded down the porch steps and ran off toward the neighbour's house.

THERE ARE THINGS your life doesn't prepare you for. Like packing your suitcase and your little backpack into the new house and realizing all the walls are covered in dead animal heads. There were large ones, mostly antlered, but also females, and small animals, like racoons and weasels. No bodies, no action poses or little varnished logs to suggest a natural environment. Just their heads, on wooden plaques, as close together as they would fit, encircling the living room. These were trophies only. It was not a display that cried *Behold! The noble muskrat!* It said only one thing: *I killed these*. Loraine ignored the animals and quickly showed me around the house. Down the hallway there were more dead animal heads, and more through the kitchen, their glass eyes following us from room to room. Loraine went into her bedroom to drop her handbag on the bed and I followed her as far as the doorway. There were more animal heads, and instead of a headboard there was a gun rack, holding several expensive looking rifles and shotguns. I stared.

"Yeah," Loraine said, in her spaced-out sing-song voice. "Yeah, he's a hunter, my husband." She stepped past me in the hall, pulling the door closed behind her, cutting off my view. "Come on, I'll show you your room." She said cheerfully.

Twenty years after that event, in retrospect, I can't believe I didn't run screaming from the house. But I was a young woman, and Canadian, and polite. I knew how to move over, to get out of the way. It was how you got through things.

"My" room was Loraine's daughter's room, and according to the décor she was a Black Sabbath fan. Loraine continued prattling away, nervously. "You just settle in," she was saying. "Make yourself right at home." I tossed my suitcase and backpack on the bed. There was a framed photo of the teenager on the dresser. Dyed black hair and heavy eye liner, a black leather vest, diamond stud on her lip, and a small tattoo of a cartoon devil peeking out of her cleavage. She was in a nightclub, her head resting against the back of a purple velvet booth, taking a drag from a cigarette and glancing to the left. Behind her, out of focus, were two figures on a stage. It was a strip joint.

The window faced away from the power plant, on to the desert. At one time, some grass seed had been thrown down in an attempt at a back yard, but the grass had dried up and it was mostly sand. There was part of a fence, and beyond that more sand, and sagebrush, sedge, fescue, and strange spiky plants I didn't know the names of. The desert stretched out away from the house, a slight hill off to one side, tumbleweeds caught up in the grasses on the other. The dog was out there, ears up, pawing at some creature in the sand.

In the living room, Loraine was rummaging through a small desk. She pulled out a sheaf of papers, took a couple of pictures off the mantle, and went back to the bedroom. A few minutes later she dragged two huge vinyl suitcases out to the car.

"Is that your son?" I asked when she came in, nodding at a picture on the wall. She jumped.

"Oh! You scared me." She laughed, nervous. "Yeah, that's my boy. He's in jail." She shrugged and kept talking, telling me Wednesday was garbage day, there was a bicycle I could use in the garage. I watched from the doorway while she took clothes out of the dresser and threw them into a duffel bag.

"What happened to the door?" I asked. I'd noticed my bedroom door had been damaged, a number of holes splintering the cheap wood.

"What?" she said. "Oh ... my daughter ... she ... she had a tantrum. You know, teenagers, she just decided one day she was going to destroy her room." She shrugged. I nodded.

"You're packing," I said. "Where are you going?"

"What? Oh ... I'm just going to my mother's for a few days," she said, zipping up the bag. "Just a few days, then I'll be back. He's coming out Friday, then I'll be back, oh, maybe Saturday, maybe next week." Her eyes danced around the room.

"Loraine ... who's coming out on Friday?" I asked. She finally looked at me, her eyes wide and blue. Her mouth twitched.

"Oh didn't I tell you?" she asked. "My husband's coming home Friday. He's been in the dry-out. He was going to be in for another month but then guess what, he's coming home early ..." she faked a smile. "I won't be here, not right away. I'm going to help out my mom for a few days ..." her voice faded out on the lie. Then she dragged the bag past me out to the car and heaved it into the back seat.

"There's cereal in the cupboard, just help yourself to anything you can find. Make yourself at home." She slammed the car into reverse and backed down the driveway. "Have fun!" she called, shifting into drive. She gave me a little wave, and was gone. I opened the doors and let the hot, sweet Montana wind blow through. I walked through the house, looking at things. I made a lunch for night shift and put my groceries away, unpacked my work clothes and lay down on the teenage stripper's narrow bed. I could squeeze in a couple more hours sleep before Gavin picked me up.

GAVIN AND I spent the night cutting away skin casing. It's the outside of the firebox, the thin sheet steel that covers the wall tubes. The insulators worked ahead of us, pulling down the outer cladding and the old insulation, exposing the steel. A couple of fitters came after them, drawing long straight lines on the outside of the boiler with sharpened soapstone, according to the drawings. We came next, with five and six-inch grinders fitted with thin, lethal zip-cut blades, cutting through the casing along the lines and removing it. When the soapstone wasn't sharp the line became wide and less accurate. Gavin shrugged.

"The thicker the line, the righter it is," he said. Once the tubes were exposed, some sections would be replaced and others would be thickness tested, their corrosion level measured, to see if they needed to be taken out. Gavin was an amiable guy, easy going and soft-spoken. At 6' 3", he didn't fit into the smaller areas, but had a long reach. We soon agreed that I would crawl on to the buckstay, where at 5' 4" I could actually stand up and reach the upper cut line. I'd make the cut, leaving pieces attached intermittently, and when a section was ready to take out, he would reach in and grab it and pull it down on to the walkway. You had to make the cut without going too deep and scarfing the tubes on the other side, which I knew how to do from back home. Small pieces we could wrestle out by hand, but for larger sections we welded on lugs, hooked come-alongs up to the grating or buckstay on the next level up, and swung the pieces of steel out on the chains, lowering them to the walkway.

"So how are things?" Gavin asked. "Things good? Looks like a nice house."

"Yeah," I told him, "things are good. I've got a place to live, there's a dog, and a bicycle." Gavin nodded. He drove right past the yellow rancher on his way to the apartment he'd rented, and had offered to pick me up and drop me off. Since I didn't have any other plan, I'd accepted.

"You let me know if you need anything," he said after the shift, at five in the morning, when he dropped me off. "You've got my number."

LUCY THE DOG was on the porch, and happy to be let inside. I walked through the house, checking that I was alone, showered, and headed for my heavy-metal goth bedroom. When I pulled the door closed, there was something odd. Something odd about the holes. I went out and looked from the outside, closed the door. Two things became clear. First, the holes had been made by an axe, they had the exact shape of an axe head. And second, they had been made from the outside of the room. From the outside, by someone trying to get in. I lay down on the bed. Typically, a teenager having a temper tantrum and destroying her room would do so from the inside. I got up. Turned the light on. I opened the bedroom window and popped out the screen. It was an easy drop to the cracked, sun-cooked ground. A bale of hay had been dragged underneath the window. The stripper-goth daughter had already staged an escape route, and from the shape of the hay bale, had been using it regularly. I swung one leg through the window, then the other, and dropped on to the hay bale. I walked around the house and in the front door. Locked it. Lay back down on the bed. Got up and retrieved my shoes from the front hall and put them in front of the dresser. Stuffed all my essentials into the backpack. I couldn't put anything across the door because it opened outwards, but I made a note to get a cord of some kind so I could tie it shut. I lay back on the bed, and fell asleep.

I spent three days and nights in the axe murderer's house. That's how I thought of him, the shadowy figure who killed things for sport and slept with weapons. The man whose wife didn't want to be there when he got home, whose daughter preferred the LA strip to the Man with the Axe. Throw in a cocaine or alcohol addiction, and it didn't seem like the ideal roommate situation. It was fine when he wasn't there. I rode the rusty bike into town for supplies, and before work would walk with Lucy into the desert, or hang laundry on the line. The problem was trying to get to sleep in the morning, after night shift. What if he came home a day or two early?

HOME. FIVE DAYS, eighteen hundred miles, three luggage searches, two hotels, and a $150 taxi ride away. Homesickness is wretched when it hits. I was on hold waiting to talk to the IRS, a tinny symphony playing a loop. A fat, blue-headed bird puffed up on the clothesline and fanned his tail.

Twice I had explained that I was a Canadian national working under a temporary work visa at the Rosebud Power Plant, and had been put back on hold. I didn't have a cell phone, but could stretch the landline on to the front porch. I was transferred to a department in Philadelphia, where the estimated wait time was more than ten minutes, and the symphony played on. I lay down the receiver and pulled my work clothes out of the washing machine. I took them out back, shook them out in the desert wind, and pinned them on the clothesline. Overalls upside down, brightly covered long-sleeved t-shirts, socks, black sports bras and panties mixed in with welding caps and bandanas. This is the way they do it here. Clothes come in stiff and dusty in Colstrip, Montana.

I found my camera. The recording of the IRS thanked me for continuing to hold, and the symphony began again. I snapped a couple of pictures of Lucy, the plump yellow dog who secretly wanted to bugger off into the badlands, shake rattlesnakes, and squint like a coyote into the setting sun. I took a couple shots of the laundry.

THE DAY BEFORE the axe murderer was officially due to arrive, Gavin pulled up at the end of the driveway, his big red Ford shiny, he had just washed it.

"Well," he said, "how's things? You get any sleep?" I didn't answer right away.

"I'll tell you how things are, Gav, and why don't you tell me what you think?" I hadn't spoken to anyone, confided in anyone, or really said how I felt about anything, since the welding test. "I'm living in the house by myself. The dog lives next door most of the time and my landlady has gone away for the weekend, but she's taken her passport, her clothes, the pictures of the kids off the mantle, and my money. Her sixteen-year-old daughter has run off to be a stripper, or possibly some kind of devil-worshipping porn star, in Los Angeles; her son is in jail, and her husband has been in a detox centre for the last two months. He gets out of the dry-out the day after tomorrow, so I'll be living here alone with him, just the two of us, the house is full of guns and dead animals, and there are axe holes the size of my head in my bedroom door. What do you think?"

He paused for a long time, turning over what I'd said. Then finally, carefully, he said, "I think it's time to get the hell out of Dodge."

I nodded. "Find somewhere else."

"Cut and run," he said. "Vamoose."

"Vamoose," I echoed. "Yeah, I think maybe it is."

THE GUN

Gavin ambled away after our toolbox talk, leaving me to set up our workstation by myself. Eventually he wandered back and sat down on a job box, stretching his long legs out on the grating. I was tired, worried, and afraid, and he was irritating me. Then he said, "You got an apartment. If you want it." He had been in the office, calling the woman who managed the only apartment block in town. It's where the guys who lived in Montana always stayed. She did short-term rentals for the shutdowns. There was one apartment that wasn't rented out, it was waiting for new paint, and Gav had charmed her into renting it to me for the month. "If you want it," he said again, shrugging boyishly and handing over a piece of paper with a phone number on it. "You can have it today."

After the shift, Gavin drove me back to the axe-murderer's house, I packed, then fell asleep in the punk porn star's room for a solid five hours, the most I'd had since leaving home. Gavin picked me up at noon, and took me to the apartment block where I signed on for a month. The manager waved me off when I explained I didn't have the damage deposit, and said she was fine to wait until payday for the rent. It was huge, a two bedroom, unfurnished.

"There's a Walmart in Miles City," Gavin said. "Take the truck if you want. I don't need it." He was going to the park to play basketball. Miles City was more than a hundred miles away. If I hurried, I could make it back for my shift. I did a quick calculation of how much credit was left on my card. A couple hundred and fifty dollars cash left from my mom was all the money I had. I had an apartment, but needed a bed. Gavin tossed me the keys.

THE TRUCK WAS a long-box, extended cab, and I had to grab the seat belt, then the steering wheel to climb up inside. With the seat all the way forward I could manage it, and big trucks weren't new to me, though the size and fire-engine red hue did seem ridiculous. I pulled over to the side of the dusty main street in Forsyth to stretch my legs and walked the two blocks of sidewalk. Someone had a sign up in the laundromat that they were selling puppies. Inside, a Prince video played on MTV. And next to that was the Barbed Wire Museum. A storefront in a low wooden building, the wide front window displayed a white painted plywood board. Nailed to the board in tidy rows were several lengths of some of the more coveted pieces in the collection. They had names like "Battered Leaf," "Two Strand Star," "Double Z," and "Sharp Point Ring Lock." I did not know that barbed wire is a thing, but apparently it is a revered American relic in some places, with more than eight hundred uniquely patented designs dating back to the 1800s. Barbed wire, apparently, eventually put an end to the open rangelands of the West, after nearly a century of violent fence-cutting wars between the farmers and ranchers who protected their grazing and water rights with fencing, and those who worked the open range. The museum, sadly, was closed, or I undoubtedly would have become too engaged to continue my trip. Hanging in the window next to the strands of razor and barbed wire was an election poster. In large letters it said "Elect Elliot Smuck for Coroner," above a picture of a plump, serious looking guy in a suit. This is Montana, a place where the official who investigates violent, sudden deaths is elected by the populous. Not only are his services recognized and needed, he is a well-known local personality, and there is competition for the job.

I GOT BACK in the truck and drove along the Tongue River, listening to a local country station on the radio, until I finally wheeled into the Walmart parking lot. There wasn't much time. I found a twin-sized blow-up mattress, a set of sheets, two pillows, and a light cotton duvet. I bought a four-inch pocketknife for work, because they'd taken mine at the airport, a towel, and a couple of dish clothes. I calculated what everything cost as I went, and still had enough money left for something nice — a small luxury. It was going to be a Discman — evolution of the Walkman — and a couple of CDs. Pickings were slim, but I found a two-disc collection of *The Essential Bob Dylan*, and Aretha's *Spirit in the Dark*.

Across the parking lot was Murdoch's Hardware, where I was told I could pick up a pair of Dickies. I piled my new bed into the back of the king cab and slid the CDs out of sight under the driver's seat. But there was something already under there. I reached under and pulled out a Glock 9mm semiautomatic pistol. I had learned to shoot a .22 rifle when I was in my twenties, but had never held a handgun before. It was hot. That is, it was a hot August day and the gun was hot. I was pretty sure it was loaded. I was sitting with it in my lap when a car pulled into the space next to the truck and a woman around my age got out with her four young kids.

"Stay close," she was shouting at them. "Junior! Watch your sister!" Junior? People here call their kids Junior? "Godammit, Junior, go git yer sister." They named their kids the same name as the dad? I gingerly put the gun back under the seat, a little further than it had been, and slid the CDs on top of it.

SHOPPING COMPLETED, I wheeled the big red truck back out on to the highway. The plan was starting to come together. I had the job. I had an apartment that was my own, and now an air mattress and a pillow. And Gavin, a friend. About ten miles outside of Forsyth the state trooper pulled me over. He didn't say anything for a long time, just looked at me through the open window, then asked to see my licence and registration.

"This is a licence?" he asked, turning my BC card over. I smiled and nodded. "You're Canadian?" I nodded. "This isn't your truck."

"No," I said. "It belongs to a colleague." The trooper asked where I worked. I explained I was a Canadian national working at the PPL power plant in Colstrip, and had come down as a travel card pressure welder for the Boilermakers union.

"So," he said, "Your boyfriend is a welder and you're out shopping in his truck."

"He's not my..."

"Are you married?"

"What? No..."

"Are there any drugs, alcohol, or firearms in the vehicle?" he asked.

"Yes..." I stammered, "I bought a bottle of rosé in Miles City..."

"No drugs?" he asked, "no firearms?" I shook my head.

"Not that I know of," I lied. The trooper's radio crackled.

"Tell your boyfriend that he has a tail light that's out," the trooper said, handing back my licence. "Tell him to get it fixed, OK?" I nodded.

"You'd think, nice new truck like this, they'd last a little longer," the trooper said, sadly. "He probably doesn't even know. Remember to tell him, OK? He'll want to get that looked after." I nodded again. "Have a nice day, ma'am."

IN THE LUNCHROOM, I slid on to the wooden bench across from Gavin Reed.

"You're tail light's out," I told him. "Highway patrol pulled me over. And there's a handgun under the seat."

"Yeah," he said, "I wondered about that. But you were already gone." Also at the table were two Navajo guys, Charlie Parker and his friend Tank, and Frank Bender from Spokane. There were about thirty-five men in the lunchroom. They were rough looking, lots of scars and prison tattoos, handlebar moustaches. Most of the locals knew each other from working at the Anaconda copper smelter before it shut down.

"Do all of you guys... carry guns in your truck?" I asked. Frank concurred that he didn't go anywhere without a handgun. Charlie gave a sly smile and said, "Why? Are you gonna rob me?" Tank didn't say anything. Then he offered something out of a plastic bag.

"It's animal jerky," Charlie Parker said, "you want some?"

"I don't know," I said, "what kind of animal is it?"

"Prairie dog..." Tank said. "Coyote..." and the two of them laughed.

WE WORKED THE rest of the night pulling skin casing and taking apart the buckstay at the corners of the boiler on the fifth floor. It was summer, and unbelievably hot. Night shift was a little better, but it was still sweltering inside. The boiler next to the one we were working on had just been shut down and was still hot, the boiler house was filled with steam. Everyone was soaked in sweat. At dawn, Gavin and I took the freight elevator to the penthouse floor, then up two flights of stairs to the roof of the largest unit. Up on the roof, the wind was warm but dry. The sun was a fireball rising in the eastern sky. As it lightened, something indistinct but moving became visible on the horizon. It was coming closer, a cloud of dust. I wanted to know if it was some kind of weather anomaly, a mini desert tornado or very localized fast-moving dust storm. But it was not.

"It's the buffalo," Gavin said, "coming in to drink." There were, apparently, a couple of herds of buffalo that roamed the area. One herd was part of a ranch, and the other was mostly wild. The came in at dawn to drink from the reservoir ponds at the outskirts of the power plant, because there was no other water.

THE FOLLOWING DAY, Saturday, marked a week in Montana. Back at the new apartment the sun was fully up when I pumped up the air mattress and ran a bath. I locked the door and put the chain across, no axe murderers here. I had glass of rosé out of my travel cup in the tub, then put the batteries in the Discman and lay down, Bob Dylan's eerie voice in the cheap headphones.

...so take heed, take heed of the western winds, take heed of the stormy weather and yes, there is something you can send back to me, Spanish boots of Spanish leather.

WOMEN AND CHILDREN

Night shift does strange things to your perception, metabolism, endurance. You just don't sleep properly when your night becomes the day. One of the welders, Pinky Lee, had given me tinfoil to cover over the window in the bedroom. I was getting four or five hours sleep, and usually had time to take care of chores, explore the town, then grab another hour's nap before the shift. I went to the laundromat, to Rosebud Foods, and picked up two lawn chairs and a few dishes at the Everything Beautiful Thrift Store. I bought postcards at the gas station and lined them up on the windowsill in the apartment. I didn't seem to have much appetite, but took an apple and a bottle of water and walked to the edge of town, away from the power plant, then headed off the road across the sandy expanse of sedge grass and low dry brush. I was wearing cut-offs, a sleeveless shirt and a ball cap, blinking in the sun, but enjoying its warmth. I followed a little trail around the base of a small hill, and in the distance could see the yellow and white rancher, the back door open, a beat-up grey truck in the driveway. About halfway around the low rise I called the hill, a ball of yellow fur hurtled toward me. Lucy! We started walking out on the plains together every day, me with my cheap headphones, her bounding into the bushes after the fast-moving lizards or flushing out a meadowlark.

At the time I was walking around the desert with the bouncing ball of fluff, I didn't realize that Montana is home to an impressive number of reptiles and amphibians, including alligator lizards, salamanders, skinks, and ten species of snakes. I was watching for gophers, and had heard there was a badger den not too far from the turnoff to the main highway. I've always wanted to see a badger.

The tumbleweeds were fascinating, and ranged in size from a small melon to a yoga ball. They were either in motion, travelling in surprisingly straight lines across the plains, powered by the relentless wind, or they were stuck, caught up against a chokeberry bush or a clump of sagebrush. I liked to pull them loose, then take them to an open area and let them go, spinning across the sand at the speed of the wind. I wanted to send them to the Arctic, in a big square cardboard box, with a simple tag attached, that said: Instructions: 1) *Take to open plain*. 2) *Release*. I started taking them home, arranging them in the living room, putting a few in the spare bedroom, so it didn't seem so empty. When I got back to the apartment that Sunday, Pinky Lee was tinkering with his truck in the parking lot. I waved, my arms full of tumbleweeds.

"Don't leave your tumbleweeds on the porch," Pinky called back, "they're liable to blow away."

MONDAY AFTERNOON A new foreman called Pete came into the lunchroom and pointed to Charlie Parker, Tank, me, and a local kid called Jaime.

"You, you, you and you," he said, "come with me. It's game time." Tank winked from across the table.

"Send me in, Coach," he said. "I'm ready to play."

PETE TOOK US over to the next boiler and up the elevator to the tenth floor. Following the guys, I checked in with the hole watch and gave him my brass tag, which he hung on a nail on a wooden board. We crawled through the manway. The superheater is the top end of the boiler, and is used to convert saturated or wet steam into superheated or dry steam. The superheated steam is used to run the turbines that generate electricity. There are primary superheaters, and secondaries, at different stages in the process. The superheater elements are huge panels, composed of a number of three-inch tubes, wound together. The tubes in a panel are bent at the top and bottom so they lie tight together, side by side, and snake way down into the boiler, all the way back up, then down again, and up, in elaborate coils that hang into the main boiler space. The tube panels are often more than thirty feet long. There are different types and shapes of elements, just as there are different kinds of boilers. But their main function is to absorb heat from the inside of the boiler and transfer it to the contents of the tubes, creating superheated steam.

When a power plant is having its top end rebuilt, the new panels have to be welded into the infrastructure above that feeds them. Each element is lifted with a crane and dropped in place, either through the roof or through a cut-out in the boiler wall. They are rigged and moved until they hang vertically, suspended, and positioned under the matching tube ends coming down from above. Once the elements are in place in an area, the scaffold planks are laid between the panels and the area is set up so the welders and fitters can access them. There is a system, a sequence of events, so that the elements hang straight and even inside the boiler. By the time we went in, the panels were hung and the scaffold planks set up. Portable halogen lights hung from the tops of the panels with tie wire or were wired on to the sides, so the welders could see. There were eight welders already working, four teams of two. Two more teams were being added into the mix, Charlie and Tank, and Jaime and me.

When you weld tubes like this you work with a partner. One person sets up on each side of the tube panel so that together you can get at both sides. Most tube welders in the States, and some in Canada, work with the same partner all the time and travel from job to job together. It's an efficient and effective way to work; partners learn each other's styles and work out a system. Tube welders who have been partners for many years seldom talk about their welding while they're doing it, they know what their partner is going to do before it happens. It's a kind of telepathy. It's like dancing.

My partner, Jaime, had just turned nineteen. He was skinny and pale with red hair and freckles, a farm boy from central Montana. Usually, if there were welders who didn't have partners, supervision would try to match an experienced person with a new, green one. But there weren't any more experienced welders, so in our case they matched green with green. Needless to say Jaime was teased for working with a woman, and an older woman at that, from Canada. But Jaime was unphased. He had brothers in the trade and understood the culture.

"Don't you mind me," he'd say, "you just mind your own self."

JAIME AND I set up next to Javier Gonzalez and his partner, Buddy. "The Canadian is here," Javier said, beaming. "Seems like we got you boys in a sandwich — Canada on one side and Mexico on the other. Be careful, or we might put on the squeeze. Right Canada?" He smiled broadly, flashing a gold front tooth. I liked him immediately. He was from Texas, and spoke with a movie star drawl I'd never heard in real life. He later taught me to make scorpions by twisting lengths of tie wire together. His welding partner, Buddy, was from Louisiana, and barely spoke at all.

Javier and I sat on plastic buckets on the scaffold planks between the elements and the boiler wall. There wasn't much room, but enough to move around, to work. Buddy and Jaime, both thin, skinnied between the panels and set up on the other side, pressed up against the next row of tubes. With less room to move, Jaime would be relying on me to pass him tools and TIG wire. Further down the row on our other side was a team I didn't know, and beside them Charlie Parker and Tank were setting up.

I was all anxiety. My heart raced, my hands shook. The equipment looked unfamiliar. They didn't call it a TIG torch in the US, had never heard that expression. In Montana the process was called Heliarc. And we didn't each get a machine, we had one power source that split at the end into two torches, like a double-headed snake.

"What the hell is that?" I asked Jaime. He nodded.

"It's a Y torch," he said. "Same power source. Means I can pass you the arc." He was experienced: this was his second job.

IN CANADA, THE welders work with fitters. The fitters put the tubes together, set the gap, get them ready for welding, and all the welders have to do is weld. In Montana, you fit your own tubes. Javier helped us rig the come-alongs, raise the panel, and set the gap. We had vice grips with pieces of angle iron welded to them that would clamp across the joint and line up the two pieces of tube so the joint was straight. We hung fire blanket between the panels to keep the draft out, because draft would blow away the argon shield and cause porosity in the weld. I didn't know any of this. It was so complicated, and everything was so crucial. Even though we had tested, the first joint was a test joint, which meant that if we blew the X-ray they would haul us out and put us somewhere else. Jaime knew a little bit, and Javier good naturedly shepherded us along, helping us fit it up, explaining things to me as we went. It took us the whole morning to set up our station and fit the first joint.

AT LUNCH I was too nervous to eat, just stood outside in the shade of the trailer, trying not to barf. I considered quitting and going home. I probably had enough money from the first week that I could buy a series of plane tickets. But this was why I'd come, what the whole adventure had been directed toward. And if I left now, what would I say to Denby? A scruffy guy with a shaved head and a long beard tied with an elastic walked across the yard toward me and asked if I had a lighter. I was sweating and couldn't catch my breath.

"I don't smoke," I told him. He produced a lighter and held it out to me.

"No really," I said. "I don't."

"Take it," he said, "you're gonna need it." Nonplussed, I took the lighter. Then he told me to go and drink a cup of water, and walked away. I went in and did what he said, downing three paper cups from the water cooler, and immediately started to feel better. Sometimes we are sent unlikely messengers.

BACK IN THE boiler, Jaime squeezed between the panels and we perched on our buckets opposite each other, a forest of tubes between us.

"Buddy likes it back there," Javier said, nodding at his partner. "Buddy just got out of jail. He likes all these tubes now. They remind him of home, right Buddy?" He laughed. "Don't ask him what he was in for 'cause he won't tell you," he continued, "but he never killed no one, did you Buddy?" Buddy said nothing. Over the course of the week I learned that Buddy had just been released from seven years in prison, where he was doing time for, among other things, drunk driving and tax evasion. I also learned that he was married, had nine kids, and on his honeymoon had taken his wife out into the swamp, where they cooked alligator together, on a spit.

"Hey," Jaime called to me, "you got a lighter?" I handed it to him.

He reached through the gap toward me and lit it next to the joint, checking if there was any draft in the tube. The flame held steady, didn't get sucked up inside, so it was safe to weld.

We tacked the tube and Jaimie covered up his side of the joint with a pair of leather gloves while I welded the first quarter. Then he welded the opposite quarter, and I welded the third, and dropped a big grape inside. That's what they call it when the root gets too hot and instead of staying in place and making a nice wedding band of weld on the inside of the joint, the molten steel melts through and falls down into the tube, leaving an icicle behind, with a droplet of metal on the end.

"I dropped a grape," I said. Jaime crouched down and shone his penlight into the gap between the tubes.

"I can see it," he said, "it's a hanger. Right where you pulled out." We had an air line and different air tools in a bucket. I took the one with the tiny zip disc and started to cut back into the joint. Stopped. Started again. I was freaking out. I had to cut into the flawed area, pick out the icicle, and reweld it well enough that it would pass the X-ray. Quickly, too, so they didn't notice. I started to panic. We discussed it at some length, then I told Jaime I wasn't sure what to do.

"The best way," I said, "I mean, the best way to fix it." I was sweating. It was like one of those dreams where you have to write an exam, and you realize it's in French, and you don't speak French, and haven't attended class all year. Javier finally pulled back the curtain of fire blanket between us.

"I hear a grinder," he said. "You ain't s'posed to be unwelding, you s'posed to be welding that puppy up."

"I dropped a grape," I said. Javier leaned over and looked inside the tube with his penlight.

"You have to cut it out," he said. "Don't cut right on the root. Cut here . . . below it. Cut a straight line, drop the icicle, then reroot it, hot." With his coaching, I made the repair.

"I'll look ya in," Jaime said. When I started welding he bent down and looked at the joint from the inside. By following the red glow, he could see where I was directing the heat.

"Move up," he said. "Up, up, to your right a little bit, OK hold it, hold it there, now move up, hold it, now move down, back a little, back, now move down . . . OK pull out." With his direction I had melted the edges above and below the problem spot.

"What does it look like?" I asked.

"Cow crap," Jaime said, and smiled. It was the first time I had seen him smile. "It looks OK, actually. It sucked back a little, but it's fused. It might be all right." My hands were shaking. "You close first," he said, "I'll watch." After I'd finished rooting my side of the tube, Jaimie looked in with his penlight again. He peered up and down inside the tube through a slot he'd left about an inch long and less than a quarter inch wide. "I think it's good," he said. "I think you made your tie-in." The tie-in is where you join one section of weld to another. If they don't melt completely together a bad tie-in can show up on the film as lack of fusion. Porosity, undercut, lack of fusion, cracking, fisheye, pinhole, lack of penetration, excessive build-up, poor alignment, cold lap, bad tie-in. On the X-ray they were innocently called "indications", but any one of them on a film could sink you. Over the course of my career I would become acquainted with them all, and learn to fix them. All of them. Jaimie closed his side and Javier pulled the fire blanket back again.

"You closed?" he asked. I nodded. "Good," he said. "It's coffee." During the actual welding, the joking stopped, the teasing and fooling around stopped. The guys got me through it, and many other difficult joints while I was learning. It was the first time I'd felt like I was on a team. It's impossible not to be part of a team when welding with a partner because the joint belongs to both of you. It didn't matter how they felt about each other, the welders worked together, combining their knowledge and skills, to make the joint. After coffee, Jaimie and I filled and capped it, not knowing if it would pass the shot.

AFTER THE SHIFT I asked Gavin Reed up for a beer.

"I love what you've done with the place," he said. The living room was empty, except for the tumbleweeds. We sat on the balcony on lawn chairs from the Everything Beautiful Thrift Store. I had a beer, and Gavin had a coke, which he carried with him. He was AA. I wondered if I'd have a job the next day.

They don't tell you the X-ray results right away. We trooped up to the superheaters, back to our spots. Day shift had completed a few more joints, and the one Jaimie and I had welded was spray-painted green. Green! Green meant we made the shot. Somehow my wise young partner and I stumbled through the next three weeks, passing most of our joints with only an occasional repair. We talked through every joint, one person watching from the inside and providing the commentary and the other following the prompts. We talked about which order to weld the tubes, when to turn the heat up and down, whether there was gas coverage, where to put the tacks. Front and back or in the tangents? It depended on what you could reach. The teams on either side of us didn't talk at all, except for Javier yelling out once in a while,

"Will y'all just weld that thing? You're not here to negotiate world peace. Stop talking about it and weld it!" We were slow but steady, and they called us the "Women and Children's Team."

EYES OPEN

We worked that Sunday, but they gave us Monday off so they could X-ray. I had just cashed my first pay cheque. Gavin asked how I was going to spend the day, and I said I'd probably do what I did most days, walk around the desert with the dog.

"You what?" he said.

"I just go for walks," I said, "walk around, look at stuff. Out by that hill, down by the highway junction." The lunchroom went quiet. "What?" I asked.

"Well... it's just...there's a lot of rattlesnakes out there," he blurted out. Charlie Parker started to chuckle.

"Do you think I could just have one day in this place without something trying to kill me?" I asked.

THE GUY WHO had given me the lighter was called Buckeye. "Whatever you do," he said, "don't go to Missoula."

"Why not?" I asked. "What's in Missoula?"

"You don't wanna go to Missoula," Buckeye's partner agreed.

"What's in Missoula?" I asked.

"Maybe she'd like to," Javier chipped in. "What do you know? Maybe she'd like Missoula."

"Will you stop it?" Frank Bender said. "Just stop it."

"What the hell is with Missoula?" I asked again. Gavin leaned in close, his voice low.

"Missoula is where…it's where all the lesbians are," he said.

"All the lesbians?" I asked. "Well howdy boys, let's go!" But at nearly six hundred miles away, it was not a practical destination for a day off.

"You could go to Little Bighorn," Charlie Parker suggested. "It's not far." This seemed like an acceptable destination to the group.

"What will I see at Little Bighorn?" I asked.

"There's a gas station," Tank said. "And some white people's monument."

"Custer's Last Stand," Frank added.

"Custer was in the Black Hills looking for gold. He was stealing the gold the government agreed belonged to the Indians," Charlie explained. "They stole the Black Hills from the Sioux."

"Custer got his ass kicked," Tank said.

"Don't go down to the Cheyenne reserve," Charlie said. "They don't want to meet you."

"Right," I said. "I'll put that on the list of places not to go to."

IN THE END, Frank and I drove to Billings. I needed to apply for a temporary US social security card, and since it was a Monday the government office would be open, and Frank wanted to buy a Brushpopper shirt at Big R Western wear.

Francis "Frank" Bender was a conservative, forty-four-year-old Boilermaker from Local 242, Spokane, Washington. He looked like a math teacher with short, parted hair, a plaid shirt, and glasses. He was a God-fearing man and an excellent fitter. And Frank had a big mouth.

"Frank's fine," Gavin told me, "He talks too much, but he's fine." In fact, he talked continuously.

Brushpopper shirts are made by Wrangler and are stiff as cardboard when you buy them. But the sparks don't burn through while you're welding. And they're out of season in Spokane, and you can only get the striped shirts in Miles City, but he thinks maybe he can find a solid-colour Brushpopper in Billings. Or maybe horizontal stripes, which would be OK, if they have his size. He was in Reno once and they had a lot of them, but nothing left in a large.

Frank didn't shut up the entire hundred and fifty miles to Billings, and he didn't shut up the whole time we were trying on the Brushpopper shirts, his narrative rising over the saloon door of the fitting room in the men's department of the Big R. He found two shirts, one with horizontal stripes, and one a solid colour, a kind of rose that I had to assure him did not look too pink.

"It's not pink," I said, as he stood in front of the full-length mirror staring at himself in a decidedly pink shirt.

"It's dusky rose," I told him.

"Not pink?" he asked, "'cause I'm colour blind. I don't want a pink shirt..."

"Definitely not pink," I said. "It's the colour of a sunset. And why would the Big R sell pink shirts?"

Frank talked continuously through Walmart as I picked out coat hangers, laundry soap, and an electric kettle. I found a coffee mug with a picture of a sombrero on it, that said "Nacho Average Cowboy," and threw a cheap lunch-kit and a can opener into the shopping cart, which Frank pushed.

On the drive home, he suddenly turned to me.

"I want to tell you something," he said. Then he started to tell me about his personal life. He had had three divorces, he shared with some pride, and the last one was messy. He had been married to an independently wealthy woman a couple of years older than himself and they were in love. Frank's complaint was that his wife had wanted too much of his time when he was at home, not that he was home much. But according to Frank, she wanted all of his attention, all the time.

"You know, when I've been out on a job for a week or two weeks or a month, and I get home, you know I don't want to have to talk all the time to my wife."

"You're probably wore out," I said. "Because you're always talking at work, and ..."

"And you know what else?" he interrupted me. "She wanted to have sex with me. All the time. And I mean ALL. THE. TIME. As soon as I got home, and then later, then every night. And I didn't want that. I just wanted some peace and quiet."

"Right," I said. "Peace and quiet."

"And you know what else? You know what she did one time? Now you tell me if you don't think this is kind of cheap. You tell me if this isn't, well, a little ... sleazy. I'm going to tell you something." Then Frank told me this story.

He was working downstairs in his workshop, building some kitchen cupboards. He had his workshop just how he liked it, and he was the only one who ever went down there. It was his place, where he went to get some peace. He was dovetailing the corners of the cupboards, setting the clamps, really concentrating. And he was happy.

"I was happy," he said. "Right? Happy."

Suddenly he hears the door at the top of the stairs open, which is weird, because no-one else goes down there. It's his wife. And she comes sashaying down the stairs, and she is completely naked. She is not wearing a stitch of clothing. On each of her breasts, covering each nipple, is a yellow stick-on Post-It note.

"And there's a word," he told me solemnly, "there's a word written on each one." Finally, Frank Bender was telling me a great story.

"And...?" I asked.

"Well, I said to her — 'just what the hell do you think you are doing?'" he said. And he told her to get back upstairs. The next day she said she wanted a divorce.

Frank hadn't seen it coming. He did not understand how his wife could have everything and still be unhappy. He'd thought it was all going well. Didn't he work steady? Didn't he hand over his pay cheque every week? Didn't he spend his few days at home mulching the grass and rehanging the downspouts? She has a nice house ... what more did she want, for Chrissake? He was bewildered.

"But Frank," I said, "what did they SAY?"

"Who?"

"The papers," I said. "The yellow sticky notes covering up your wife's nipples — what was written on them?"

"Oh." Frank said. "I don't know. I didn't read them."

"What?" I couldn't believe it.

"I didn't wait to see what they said. I told her to get the hell back upstairs and put some clothes on." He dismissed my question with a wave of his hand. "But don't you think," he asked, "don't you think that that is just a little bit ... slutty? Don't you think that that is a slutty thing for a woman to do?"

Then Frank Bender did an extraordinary thing. He paused. He glanced at me, then back at the road.

Before he started again I said, "do you want me to answer that, or do you just want to hear yourself talk?"

"No, you know. I want you to answer. You're a woman, I want to know...what...as a woman...what you think of that?" I realized Frank didn't talk to a lot of women. He talked to the clerk in the Big R, and to Wendy, the server at the Longhorn Bar and Steakhouse. But it was probably rare that Frank talked to a woman long enough that he was willing to hear anything she said. I better get my answer right.

"Well Francis," I said. "Here's the thing."

"Your upbringing as a white, working-class man tells you that you can have anything you want, anywhere, wherever you want it. There are no limits because you live in America. For the forty-four years you have walked on this earth you have been trained to fulfill and sustain your appetite in whatever form it takes: money, cars, booze, houses, greasy food, women. And you are measured by your appetite, and your possessions and property. Because in America, getting what you want is the measure of the man. And the man is hungry. America likes you hungry. It's good for the economy.

So let's talk about sex. Sexual appetite. When a man is turned on or horny or he's hitting on a woman, or he's bragging about who he screwed the night before, he is told he's virile, strong. Passionate, a stud, a Casanova. And he feels powerful. And when you are feeling sexual appetite, what do the boys say? They say Way to go, Frankie. Go get her! Nail her, Frank! And they want to know where and when and who and how many times, and did your old lady ever ask where you were?"

Frank took a breath like he was about to answer.

"Not yet," I said. "It's not your turn." He closed his mouth and stared at the highway. "When a woman expresses sexual appetite, the world doesn't say *Wow, is she ever passionate. What a stud*. The world says, *What a slut. What a sleazy, cheap, easy woman that is*. Because a woman's value isn't measured by her appetite, or her possessions or her property. She is measured by the shape of her body and the length of her hair. That is, her ability to satisfy your appetite, and her ability to be a desirable possession, a piece of property."

"You know, I never ..."

"But here's the thing," I interrupted him. "All this is obvious. It's absolutely clear. But what I don't understand ... is that here's this woman, this woman you love, and married. And you...are not a young man, you're a mature man, who has been married twice before. You didn't marry on impulse, you thought about it. You both did."
Frank nodded.

"What I don't understand," I said, "Is that this woman had a message for you. She had something to say. And you made yourself so unavailable, and you were so used to talking and not listening, and she was so desperate to say this thing to you, that she stripped naked and wrote her message on two Post-It notes and attached them to her body. Then trespassed, naked, into your sanctuary, to get your attention. And you couldn't be bothered to read the message."

Frank didn't say anything.

"You couldn't be bothered," I said, the whole story suddenly striking me as incomprehensibly sad. "I'd divorce you too."

I WILL NEVER understand the complexities of relationships. My personal life is not a testament to the enduring qualities of love, I did not marry a handsome dentist in university, have three flawless children, and create a decades-long blissfully perfect partnership. While this may have been the hope or expectation of my family, the prospect of this form of domestic life made me shudder. In my twenties, I made a series of misguided decisions that led to a sequence of terrible relationships. In my thirties, periods of being single alternated with some less horrible decisions, eventually culminating in a rich, creative partnership with a writer-musician that lasted a decade. We produced events and projects together, were part of the community, attended, and occasionally hosted, parties. But this, too, ended. I was fifty when I fell in love with someone with whom I consistently feel at ease. Optimistic, happy-go-lucky, a long-distance bicyclist with a boyish charm and a sharp intelligence, he seems unbothered by my idiosyncrasies. I continue to have high hopes.

While I do not consider myself an authority on relationships, for years I have watched men falling in love, living the dream — marriages, mortgages, kids. They pass their phones around the lunchroom with pictures of the new baby, or the birthday party, or the kids dressed up for Halloween, events they were missing while out on a job. I've seen young men — and women — put everything they had into their relationships: sincerity, devotion, hard work. But a trade where you are away all the time is hard on romance, and it's hard on families.

At the safety orientation in Alberta, we were told that the divorce rate among boilermakers was ninety-four per cent, and it is similar in other provinces. In other words, pretty much everyone. They said it was in the union contract that when new apprentices started in the trade, they had to be told this, so they knew what they were getting into. They were briefed, as part of their training, that data showed the career they were choosing would more than likely contribute to marital breakdown. So new workers entering the trade were faced with a dark choice: pursue your career, but know the odds are overwhelmingly against you having a successful relationship. But we all did it anyway, eyes open.

WHEN YOU WORK away, you are always living in a hotel, B&B, camp room, or sleeping on a friend's sofa. There's a sense of impermanence, and a cold, disconnected feeling. The anonymity of the housing, the lack of personal detail, the miraculous way the bed gets made and the bathroom cleaned while you are out. Clothes come out of a suitcase or duffel bag instead of a closet and are washed often and worn over and over. Meals are off a menu instead of created from a kitchen and shared together. Laundry goes to a service, where, for a $1.50 a pound, you can drop off a garbage bag of dirty work gear at night and pick it up the next day, clean and folded. Chores more or less take care of themselves. Which is not only convenient but necessary when you are working ten or eleven or twelve hours a day, commuting back and forth to a site, sometimes for an hour each way. There is simply no free time to take care of the details of daily living, and you learn to economize what you have and spend it wisely, on sleep, having dinner out, maybe exploring the local terrain. I used to like to go to the movies. But none of your time is spent in cozy companionship with your spouse, eating chips and watching Netflix. Relationships were limited to phone calls, and later to texting and FaceTime, maybe an occasional weekend together, if all the stars aligned. Not unlike, say, a low security prison.

ON THE WAY back to Colstrip, Frank pulled off the highway for the detour that took us to Little Bighorn. He was strangely quiet. There was a stone monument, grave markers, and rolling hills of tall prairie grass stretching into the mountains. In the distance a herd of horses travelled slowly west. I read the revisionist history on the monument while Frank walked the perimeter. We returned to the truck and started to pull away from the place where Custer had underestimated his adversaries, the Lakota Sioux and Cheyenne, and got his ass kicked. Frank still had that bewildered look on his face. I played with my camera, taking pictures out the window of the truck. He was opening and closing his mouth like a guppy, trying to articulate his thoughts.

Finally, he said, "I guess … I guess I just don't understand women."

BARBED WIRE

Four weeks into welding tubes I got something in my eye. It happens. The dust and dirt, flying particulates, people working in close proximity with air tools in a confined space, it's almost inevitable. I was escorted to the first aid room in the administration building where the first aid attendant examined me through a lighted magnifying lens.

"I can see it," he said. "I think I can get it out." He reached toward my eye with a dirty hand that was shaped like a bunch of bananas.

"Whoa, whoa, whoa," I said. "Hold on. I think I'm gonna opt for the clinic." He drove me across town to the medical clinic, where I was seen by a really smart doctor intern.

She looked at my eye and said, "Why aren't you crying?"

"You haven't said anything sad," I answered. She took out a penlight that looked a lot like ours and flashed it into both my eyes. She held my eye open and quickly swiped the surface with a swab, taking off the offending object.

"Just a minute," she said, as I was getting up to leave. And she used the light to look in both my ears, and my nose.

"Where are you from?" she asked, finally.

"I'm from BC," I said. "An island off the West Coast of Canada." The doctor nodded.

"You're not used to this climate."

"I live in a rain forest."

"You are completely dehydrated," she said. "That's why your eye wasn't tearing when you got something in it. Take a week off. And drink lots of fluids. I mean lots. As much as you can."

"I can't take a week off," I said. "I'm on a turnaround..."

"OK," she said. "Take four days."

"Two," I countered.

"Three days plus the rest of today, and if you still feel like you're drying up like a raisin, you take the weekend. I'll write you a note." She gave me a tiny tube of antibiotic ointment to put in my eye. "And drink *lots* of fluids. Juice. Gatorade. No pop or alcohol. Lots of water."

I gave the sausage-fingered first aid attendant the doctor's note and he dropped me at my apartment. Before going inside, I crossed the road to the gas station. In the driveway was a snake that had been hit by a car. They have fancy snakes in Montana, and this wasn't a little racer or a garter snake. This snake was about five feet long and the body was the width of my wrist. What the hell kind of place was this? The gas station guy told me it was a bull snake. I'd never seen one before and was amazed. I bought a gallon of water and went back to my room to lie down on the air mattress. The doctor had made me stand on a scale, I'd lost eleven pounds in just over five weeks. Dehydration made sense, and explained why I'd been so spaced out lately. Sleeping through the sunny days, working next to the steam turbines, and a diet of animal jerky, chocolate bars, and rosé. Why did I even expect to be healthy? I woke up hearing the night shift guys going down to work. Someone tapped softly on my door, and when I answered, no one was there, but there was a quart of orange juice on the stoop. When I went out later to the laundromat, there was Gatorade. For the next two days, any time I opened the door, there was something to drink, sometimes two or three things. Once, a bag of jerky. A few of them were doing it, the guys staying in the apartment block, and I never caught any of them at it.

It's always such a strange balance, being in this culture, being the one who is different, or the one who is first. Unsurprisingly, I sometimes faced hostility. But then there's this, this kindness, a bunch of guys leaving drinks on my stoop, because the banana-fingered first aid guy had gone and blabbed about my visit to the clinic.

I TOOK THAT night off and went back to work. The tube welding was finishing, jobs in all the different areas were wrapping up. The guys were talking about other work in Wisconsin and South Dakota, trying to decide where to go next. Then the furnace was complete, and we starting packing out. You start at the top of the scaffolding and walk it down, picking up everything left inside and taking it out the main manway on the ground. All the tools, materials, fire blankets, buckets ... everything had to go, and when that was done, we'd start on the scaffold itself. Local 11 was the last local on the continent to have retained a clause in their contract that said they could build their own scaffold, and tear it down. That work still belonged to the boilermakers. All the other locals had lost it in contract negotiations a long time ago.

The Local 11 guys had a system. They formed a fire line from the top of the scaffold tower to the bottom of the boiler. The guys at the top would take it apart and pass it down, piece by piece, to the next guy, who would grab it and pass it, all the way down the line. All the decking and rails, every stanchion, plank and stair tread, had to be taken apart and passed down. There was no talking, it was a serious job. Everyone aware that if someone missed a grab, a plank or railing could come down nine storeys, and hit a whole lot of people on the way. The entire exercise was aimed at not dropping anything.

They put all the locals inside, their most experienced guys at the top. A lot of the travel cards had already left the job and were headed to the next one. I opted to stay, and they put me as the first person outside the manway. That meant bending down and grabbing every piece, maneuvering it out the access, and passing it back. We did this for ten hours. At the end of the shift the foreman asked us to stay over another two. The next night we did the same thing, but for thirteen hours. Then most of us were cut loose. I had never felt so tired, or so strong.

Pete shook my hand. "You did better than I thought you would," he said. I hugged Tank, and Charlie Parker, who gave me a bag of animal jerky, "for your trip to Canada." Francis Bender gripped my hand and pumped it up and down.

"It was very nice to meet you," he said, "and I wish you all the very best."

I found my Heliarc partner, Jaime, and gave him my pocketknife.

"They won't let me take it on the plane." Jaimie lit up with a big smile. We'd had very few repairs in our welding together.

"Well, didn't we do all right," he said.

"Yep," I said. "We sure did."

WHEN HE FOUND out I was going to fly out of Missoula, Gavin offered to drive me there. He was going to see a girl in Drummond. Missoula was about fifty miles out of the way,

"But heck," he said, "Why not? I'm not doin' anything."

We stayed a last night in the rental apartments, and I got up early to pack. I dropped off the lawn chairs, air mattress, bedding and dishes to the Everything Beautiful Thrift Store. Then walked out toward the highway and whistled down the dirt road until Lucy bounded up. She came out of the neighbour's house; she had apparently permanently rehomed herself. We walked into the desert, and I carried a big stick and stayed out of the bushes.

I put all the tumbleweeds in the back of the red truck, and outside of town we pulled over so I could let them go. On the way to Missoula, we stopped to buy Flathead cherries and candy at a roadside store advertising "Ice, ATM, Bear Spray and Art." Late in the afternoon we pulled off the road to look at the ruins of an old stone jail. I was wandering around the site, poking at things, walked around a corner and there was the buffalo. He was about ten metres away, and enormous. He huffed, and turned his huge, woolly head toward me. His mane and beard were tangled, and the tip of one horn had broken off.

"Don't. Move." Gavin spoke very quietly from somewhere behind me. The buffalo gazed toward us with one big eye. "Slowly, slowly," Gavin was saying, "take a step back. Now another one." In this way we made our way, ever so slowly and walking backward, toward the truck.

"So what was that about?" I asked once we were driving.

"Well," Gavin said, "They can be unpredictable. They can charge. And that one, way out here, he's a rogue. He's probably pretty wild." I asked what he meant by a rogue. "Once a buffalo gets out, say he knocks a fence down, you can't ever get him back in again. If you manage to get him back in and close up the fence, he won't stay. He'll just use that head like a big ol' battering ram, running into the fence post until he knocks it down again. Ranchers have to shoot 'em. Or sometimes they just go rogue." I told him about the sea lion in the bottom of the dry dock, how he had the opposite problem from the buffalo. Instead of trying to get him to stay in, they couldn't get him out.

WHEN WE GOT to Missoula, I took Gavin out for sushi, to thank him for the ride. He'd never had sushi. Missoula, a college town, had a few options. So I introduced him to a big boat of sushi, and asked him to tell me about his tattoos.

"I got this one on the island of St Thomas," he said, pulling his collar down to reveal an ornate cross just below his collar bone. "Because I wanted Jesus on my chest." Gavin took his Higher Power seriously. "And this one," he said, pulling his sleeve up over his biceps, to show a surprisingly gothic heart, "this one I got in Reno, when I married my first wife," he smiled sheepishly, "for the second time." This was the wife he was in the process of divorcing. Again.

"Well, what do you know," he said when he dropped me at the hotel. "So that was sushi. I have just done something that I have never done before."

I SPENT THE day walking around Missoula, which was a strange dream after Colstrip, of art galleries and espresso bars, chic little gift stores and college students. I got my hair cut, bought a new shirt, and a soft leather handbag. There was a street art festival in the evening and I bought a strange little doll, part monster and part child, from El Salvador, with legs made from twigs.

ONE OF THE last dilemmas was that I had too much cash on hand. I couldn't open a bank account in Montana without a lot of holds and a waiting period, and it was tricky to transfer money to Canada. I had been taking my cheques to the only bank in Colstrip, where everyone seemed to know who I was, and where they had no problem cashing cheques from the power plant – everyone did it. I'd been stashing the cash in a beef jerky bag under the air mattress. The Canadian dollar was at seventy-one cents US, and when you are from another country, you don't pay income tax on the first ten thousand dollars you earn. So at the end of six weeks I had more than fourteen thousand Canadian dollars in US bills, and had to get it across the border. Technically, you are allowed to take as much as you like, but if it's more than ten thousand, you have to declare it, and the customs officials can seize it. It can take a long time to get back, and if they suspect it is from a criminal act, they keep it.

I got a travel sewing kit from the hotel, cut the seam in the back of the doll, crammed in a roll of bills, and sewed it back up. I had a package of sanitary pads, took the pad out of one of its little envelopes and threw it away, and stuffed the envelope with a wad of cash, putting it back in the middle of the package. I zipped some of the money into the lining of the suitcase, and taped another bundle of bills under the dust jacket of the novel I'd bought for the plane. I shoved a few more hundreds into the vitamin bottle, it was more or less everywhere.

In the morning, I left my welding helmet and gloves in the hotel room, combed my hair, put on some mascara, and tucked the doll and the novel into the soft leather handbag. I left early, fully expecting a luggage search. While I waited for a cab, I watched a woman trying to coax an enormous dog into a tiny car. In the taxi, a stray can of refried beans rolled around the floor. At the airport I chatted with a couple who were heading back to Canada on the same flight. The woman had her hand bandaged, she had slammed it in the car door and they'd spent the early morning hours at the hospital. When our flight was called, I followed them and we went through security together, still chatting, and again when we landed, in the customs line. I pretended to be with them. My luggage was not searched this time. Purpose of my trip? Just visiting my boyfriend. Anything to declare? Yes, I bought some make-up, this book, and this doll for my niece . . . thank you, you have a nice day too.

On the plane I dozed and dreamed of eight hundred patents of barbed wire, of the people who divided the prairies up with wires that they named "Sawtooth" and "Reynold's Necktie." I thought about these ranchers, cutting up the rangeland and defending their parcels, while their neighbours cut through the fencing at night so their animals could get to the grasslands and water. Two hundred years later the Rosebud Mining Company continues to divide the rangeland, biting into the earth's surface and cutting out swaths that are miles wide and a hundred feet deep. The dragline, the Marion 8200, is never silent, and can be seen and heard across the region, roving back and forth across the prairie, a buffalo emblazoned on the sides of the machine. I thought about the Lakota warrior known as Crazy Horse who took on the federal government and defended the Black Hills at Little Bighorn, and about the woman who was married to the axe murderer, who grabbed the hundred and fifty bucks I gave her, gassed up the car and got the hell out. I thought about the tumbleweeds, rolling themselves round at the speed of the wind, and the yellow dog who dreamed of coyotes. And I thought about the enormous chocolate-coloured buffalo, rubbing the flat plate of his head against a fencepost, until the fencepost gave way, and how he would have stepped, gingerly perhaps, over the strands of wire for the first time, then walked out on to the open prairie, lifted his head to smell something new, snorted into the hot wind, and started to run.

PART 2:

See You on the Next One

PENNSYLVANIA

"I'll just get you to put your thumbprint right there," she said, touching a spot next to my signature.

"No, I'm good," I said, which is a stupid thing to say, any time you are being fingerprinted.

"If you want to cash your cheque," she said, "you need to put your fingerprint there." I gave her a broad smile, like there had been a misunderstanding.

"I'm Canadian," I said, as though that would take care of it. "You really don't need my fingerprint."

"If you want to cash your cheque, we really do," she said. Her nametag said Candace. She had already explained the policy and wasn't going to repeat herself: I lived out of state and didn't have an account at the Bank of America, so I had to provide my permanent address and a local one, sign the cheque, show some ID, then put my fingerprint next to my signature. Even though the company that had written the cheque, one of the largest utility contractors in the nation, banked with this bank.

"You could call them," I suggested. "Call the payroll department at the site office and ask if I work there and if they wrote a cheque to me for this amount, and if today is payday." She shook her head. We had covered this. The company wasn't the issue, it was about my identification, proving that I was who I was presenting as. "Why would anyone pretend to me?" I asked. "I mean look at me. Don't you think, if I was going to pretend to be someone else, I'd pick someone,

I don't know, taller?" She did not smile, but pushed the ink pad a little closer. I told her that in Canada the only people who could take your fingerprints were the police, and that was only if you were caught doing something really bad. She didn't state the obvious, that we were not in Canada. "The fact is," I said, improvising, "I can't. I'm . . . allergic to the ink." She did not believe me. "Any kind of latex," I continued. "Rubber gloves. Condoms, sulphites, sulphates, red wine, polyester clothing, it gives me a terrible rash." She said nothing. "I can't lick stamps either," I blurted out, "pantyhose are out of the question. And you know . . . I'm allergic to beans." I had no idea where this was going. "Shellfish, nuts, cats, strawberries, chocolate, mustard, dog food . . . I swell up. My throat closes over. I should really carry one of those, you know, one of those things . . ." She sighed heavily and rolled her eyes.

"All right," she said. "All right. Just give me three pieces of ID."

IT WAS A hollow victory. It wasn't her fault, and I didn't have to be that way with Candace, so troublesome. But it irked me. That a private business, a financial institution, could require something as personal as a fingerprint, when all I wanted to do was cash my cheque.

"At home the only time you have to do that is when you've committed a crime," I whined to the guys at my table in the lunchroom the next day. "It isn't a crime to go to work. But the big banks make you feel like a criminal . . . it's no wonder all you guys are conspiracy theorists. They really are out to get you." My partner, Durland, a learned man from Noxem, Pennsylvania, leaned back in his chair, his denim overalls straining against his mighty bulk.

"And just why do you think the Bank of America wants your fingerprint?" he asked.

"Oh, I know why," I said. "The real reason. It's to authenticate the clone."

"The clone," Durland repeated.

"Ya. The one they are creating at the secret location in ... I dunno ... Florida. That's where everything bad happens, isn't it?"

"Pretty much," Durland said.

"It started in Montana," I explained. "When they told us we'd been exposed to lead and they wanted to take samples of everyone's blood. Then they gave us all donuts, free donuts, so no one complained. But don't you see? First the blood, then the fingerprint. They've already got my urine and saliva from the drug tests. It's obvious what's they're doing."

"You think they're making a clone?" Durland asked.

"Of course," I said. "Soon there will be Canadian girls who look like me welding tubes in all the power plants ... exact replicas." Durland looked over at Tommy, who was leaning his chair against the wall, his eyes half-closed. "I told them they couldn't have my blood," I continued, "I didn't have any to spare, I was using it all — the red cells *and* the white cells. I should never have given in," I added. "But they were crullers."

"I don't know how to break this to you, honey," Durland said, "but I don't think there's a clone."

"Nope," Tommy said. "They don't want any more of you."

I'D FLOWN INTO New York, rented a car, and driven eighty miles west into a cluster of towns in Eastern Pennsylvania with biblical names: Nazareth. Bethel. Bethlehem. Damascus. Zion. Rooms were scarce, but I'd found an off-season resort in Delaware Water Gap for a hundred and forty a week.

The Water Gap Inn was a two hundred-room resort hotel in the Poconos. In summers past, the place would have been booming with recreators. It included a crumbling, once luxurious old hotel, and several long, low, motel-style buildings that had been added later. My room was in one of these. There were more than fifty acres of grounds, including an unused par-three golf course, two dilapidated mini-golf pitches, a suspect-looking indoor pool, and weedy tennis and basketball courts.

I unpacked, took a nap, and went for a run along a dirt track that ran behind the hotel by the river. I turned up a path through the trees and startled a white-tailed stag. A little further, a dozen or so deer, unused to people, scattered over the abandoned golf green. On the way back, I passed a drained outdoor pool, piled high with lawn chairs. Also a tiny bandshell overflowing with chairs and leaves, and an empty gazebo.

Two guys from BC moved into the hotel, Ken and Digger. I was new to the local and did not know them at the time, but in later years got to know them as top-notch guys. Ken's son, who would have been about eight at that time, ended up being my foreman in Castlegar, years later. But they only lasted a day before they decided to move out. It was too remote, they wanted to be in town, with the rest of the crew. I didn't understand it, I craved isolation. When I asked why they were checking out they claimed the toilet paper was too thin — it was only single ply. Other reasons they gave were that there was no remote control for the TV and they didn't get their room made up every day. For twenty dollars a night you shouldn't have to get up to switch on the TV and you sure as hell shouldn't have to make your own bed, they told me. I had no idea. There was so much to learn.

They'd found a place in town, that wasn't tucked into the mountains, and recommended it, but I opted for the scenic retreat of this run-down hotel. There was the caretaker, a lonely young woman who sat at the front desk, a couple of cats, and me. There were more than sixty rooms in total, all empty but mine.

I spent two nights shaking off the jet lag and getting oriented, then drove in for day shift on Monday morning. After the safety orientation and weld test, I was shown to the lunchroom where the biggest man I've ever seen motioned me over to his table. The guys cleared a chair for me and I sat down across from him.

"Welcome to Pennsylvania," he said, opening his arms, as though the lunchroom was the entire state, in all its beauty. "What brings you here?" This was Durland Siglin, soon to be my friend. I was assigned as his partner on that first day.

Durland had always been a giant of a man, tall and broad. A few years before we met, he had been driving home from a hunting trip with a buddy and came across a tree down across the cat road. He was incredibly strong. He got out of the truck, lifted the tree, and started carrying it over to the side. His friend tried to help, but there wasn't much point. How do you help a giant? He was halfway across the road when his ankle shattered.

"Did you know that your bones get old?" he asked me, solemnly. "They don't tell you that." His friend helped him to the hospital, and he spent nearly a year recuperating, much of that time on the couch. "That's when I got fat," he explained. He was the largest person on the claim. I was possibly the smallest. Durland was a good man, and loyal. Before the first day was out, he made a point of telling me, "...because if you're my buddy, I'll die for you. And we will go together."

I HAD BEEN welding tubes in BC, working on a waterwall in Port Alice just before the call to Pennsylvania came in. All practiced up, I passed my weld test without a hitch. By the time the Canadians got there, most of the tube welding was complete. BC was known for having a good apprenticeship program, and members were highly regarded as excellent fitters, riggers, welders, and mechanics. They could still use the manpower to close up the job, so they put us wherever we were needed. Ken and Digger went up to the superheaters and I barely saw them again. I was assigned to the fabricating tent outside because no one else would confess to being able to run a plasma cutter. Durland had already been there for a few weeks. He had a worktable set up, and a couple of chairs, a clipboard where he wrote down measurements, and a radio dialled to a station that played a lot of Hank Williams and Johnny Cash.

"Do you like Hank Snow?" he asked. "He was Canadian, you know."

WE WERE WORKING on huge sections of combustion ducting that had been dropped to the ground with a crane and was being relined with stainless steel. The steel came in eight by four-foot sheets, like plywood, and was of various thicknesses. We cut it to size, and it was clipped up inside between the expansion joints. The only way to cut it efficiently was with a plasma cutter, which we had set up outside the tent with a couple of steel sawhorses. Six guys were working in the ducting. There was Tommy from South Carolina, his friend Chuck from North Carolina, and an apprentice. There was a short guy who was a flamboyant dresser they called Hollywood, because he was a folio artist and travelled to California every year to compete in sound effects competitions and work in the movies. There was also Anders, from our local, and his friend John. The demolition was almost finished, just one crew down at the far end, cutting out the old steel. A couple of guys were in the middle, measuring for new material and tacking it in. Behind them was a third crew of two guys, also measuring up and installing plate lining. The ducting was shaped like a regular square furnace vent, the kind people are always escaping through over the transom in crime movies, or where they take the grill off in the hotel room and hide the gun or the money. But in the films only the skinniest person can fit through. The duct work at the power plant was between six and nine feet high, and just as wide. People easily walked around inside and the guys had to stand on step ladders to measure out for the top pieces.

Durland and I were in the fabricating tent. Our job was to go inside, get the measurements from the fitters, then go out to the fabricating tent, lay out the shape, cut it out, and deliver it back for installation. We also made anything else that required fabricating, mostly brackets and lifting lugs. With these and cutting for two crews we stayed busy enough, but also had some down time. It was a great job, away from the smoke and noise of the main unit, not too hectic, and no one bothering us. The fall days were clear and cool, and we were able to spend time outside.

At first Durland would go into the ducting and speak with the crew. We had a set of drawings in the tent, and there were others taped up inside. They would discuss how to proceed, then he'd write down the measurements and take them back to our tent. We'd drop a piece of steel on the sawhorses and I would do the cut, and Durland would take off the sharp edge with a grinder. I'd weld on the lugs, and we'd carry it into the duct together. They were mostly manageable-sized pieces that one or two people could move around. Especially when one person was a giant.

The first time I went in to get the measurements nobody noticed me, partly because the noise was so furious, the grinders and hammers echoing around the stainless steel chamber. You had to get quite close to someone and yell to be heard. But mainly they were engaged with each other, working or talking, and either didn't notice I was there or didn't care. I finally got some measurements from both crews and went back to the tent. The third time that I found myself waiting around for them to give me the next set of numbers, I gave up and returned empty handed.

"I can't get their attention," I complained to Durland. "They're busy in there, and it's noisy. But they're also messing with me, making me wait. I didn't get the numbers." He nodded, sagely.

"Get your measuring tape," he said. "I'm gonna show you a trick." We climbed back inside through the access cut-out, and stood in the middle of the largest area, two guys working on the wall behind us, two guys talking. The trick was this: Durland held his tape measure at crotch level with his right hand, and pulled the tape out about four feet with his left. Then he angled the tape upward toward the top of the wall and started pointing at things with it, always holding it just below his belt.

"Now you do it," he said, leaning toward me. I held my tape measure in front of my fly, pulled out an arm's length of tape, and started pointing things out to him with it. "Now we just point at things and talk, and move our arms like we're making decisions about something important," he said, leaning down so I could hear him. I nodded broadly and pointed my tape up at a corner.

"From there ..." I said, "to there...and that bracket up there ..." pointing them out with my extended penis-tape.

"There's two of those," Durland said, pointing his tape at a little cut-out in the side, "and only one of those," he indicated a bucket on the ground. Suddenly I could hear him. All the power tools had stopped. The crew had stopped working and were all looking at us attentively.

"I need the measurements for this section of wall," I said, pointing my measuring-tape penis around the perimeter. Chuck climbed down off his ladder with a notebook.

"I got 'em," he said, coming toward me.

"Are you serious?" I asked Durland, back in the tent. "Really? That's all it takes? I turn my measuring tape into a penis and suddenly they're all ears?" Durland shrugged.

"They don't *know* that's why," he said, "but if you are holding the Big One, they have to listen. They can't help it."

THAT NIGHT CHUCK popped into the fabricating tent after last coffee. He said, "Excuse me, ma'am, but would you care to join me for dinner?" He was charming and good-looking, and I liked him.

"OK," I said, "but you can't call me ma'am."

"Yes ma'am," he said.

Durland pointed a big stubby finger at me. "You be careful," he said. "He may be a Democrat, but he's also a southerner. And he's married."

Chuck took me to a diner in Bethlehem where he ordered a beer and the special, without asking what it was.

"Don't you want to know what you're having?" I asked.

"Don't matter," he said. "Never quit on a Friday and always order the special. That's the best advice you'll ever get."

"OK," I said, and ended up with a home-made chicken pot pie.

Chuck told me about his wife, a hairdresser, his son who played too many video games, and his daughter, who was the apple of his eye and who he fretted over as she grew up.

Then he told me about growing up in the south, racing cars, and how he had found an orphaned flying squirrel and raised it as a pet. He'd throw it up in the air as high as he could, and at the top of the throw it would spread out its little arms, unfold its furry cape and float back down to earth.

BY THE END of the second week, Durland and I had a good system and were keeping up with the cut list. He found me a piece of I-beam, and dragged it into the tent; we had an oxyacetylene outfit and a vice, and set up a small blacksmith shop to fill in the time. The boys in the duct work were starting to weld in the roof pieces, which meant hauling them up on come-alongs, so I was welding lugs on to everything we sent out. Anders came in at one point and asked for a hook that was offset, so they could pull a piece up and turn it ninety degrees at the same time.

"Do you know how to do that?" he asked. "Do you know how to make an S-hook? How to centre it so it hangs straight?"

"I think so," I told him, solemnly.

Durland found a piece of round bar, and I used it to show him all the blacksmithing techniques I had learned. I squared the round, put in a twist, then a reverse twist, tapered one end and upset the other. I made a couple of small leaves and welded them on, finished the hook with a fishtail, making it as ornate as it could be.

"It looks a bit like a chandelier," Durland said.

"I hope Anders likes it," I said. "I really hope he does." He did. Then he asked if I could make him two more — for hanging things up in his van, which was where he was living for the turnaround. After that we had two lists, the cut list for the stainless liner, and the list of hooks and knick-knacks we were making for the crew.

CHUCK AND I had started going to a tiny bar about a mile from my hotel, because I didn't like driving the twisty roads from Bethlehem. It was called the Minisink, was surprisingly hip, and had live music. We would sit at the bar and talk about the things that made us homesick, and I would pepper him with questions about the South. I had been asking him about snakes in North Carolina.

"You ever hear of a hoop snake? Bite his own tail and roll down a hill?"

"Is that true?" I asked.

"No, it's not. But lots of people believe that. Or a joint snake? You go to pick him up or hit him with a stick an' he'll shatter, breaks up into itty bitty pieces, and when you put him down all the pieces hunt each other up and he puts himself back together and gets away ..."

"Sounds more like a Southern man," I said. He told me about the hognose and milksnake, and the black racer, a snake that could climb trees.

"He'll put a spell on a bird," he said. "Fix him with his eye and hypnotize him, so he can come in real close. And that one's true, I wouldn't lie about that." He told me about wading through the Black Swamp on a camping trip, and stepping on a deadly water moccasin, that struck him on the shin, his life saved by some heavy socks pulled up over his pant legs. On another trip he rolled up for the night in his bedroll under a lean-to and woke up with a copperhead in his pocket.

"They find their way in there at night, for the warmth," he said. "You always have to check your pockets."

DURLAND AND I usually had a long list of large pieces to cut, and I was on the plasma cutter all day, until it stopped working. It sputtered and died, a tendril of smoke curling out of the casing of the machine. It was hot to the touch. The plastic parts had turned black and begun to melt, and it was giving off that electrical ozone smell. I dragged Durland outside.

"Yup," he said. "That one's done."

"I don't know what I'm gonna do," I said, panicking. "I've melted down this machine. I've obviously overrun the duty cycle ... do you know what these things cost? Do you know how expensive those things are? I'm gonna get fired ... do you think they're gonna fire me? What do I say?" I was babbling. Durland put his big mitt on my shoulder.

"Are you done yet?" he asked. I paused and nodded.

"You are looking at this from the wrong point of view," he said. "You are a highly skilled and valued worker who came across the country to cut stainless, and this machine was not up to the task. You want to know when they will be getting a better, more capable machine in for you, so you don't have to deal with another piece of junk like this." I blinked, while it sank in. "OK?" he asked. I nodded.

When Sunny, our foreman, came by after lunch to see why I wasn't cutting, I shoved the machine with my foot.

"Well," I said, timidly, "Pardon my language, but this machine is a piece of crap. It's been cutting out for a couple of days now and today it packed in completely." Sunny shifted his focus from me to the machine. Durland nodded encouragingly. "It's garbage," I added, with more conviction. "If you want me to keep up with three crews inside, you're gonna have to get me a real machine, not some piece of junk out of someone's garage."

"That piece of junk cost twelve grand," Sunny snarled, and stomped away. Durland shrugged. At the end of the day a forklift arrived, with a big, brand new, deluxe plasma cutter, still in the box, and dropped it outside our tent.

WHERE I'D WORKED in Montana there were many opportunities to gamble, but really only one method: slot machines. They were everywhere, including the grocery store and the gas station. An aimless pastime so you could while away your time plugging quarters into a slot while you waited for your clothes to dry at the laundromat. But in Pennsylvania there was a surging appetite for gambling. Perhaps it was because actual casinos were still outlawed in 2002, but the guys bet on everything. First there was the cheque pool. Everyone put twenty dollars into the pot, which was held by the shop steward. When you got your pay cheque, you made a poker hand out of the last five digits of the cheque number. The cheques came in sealed envelopes so you didn't know what you had. So, if the cheque number was 031425, you had a run of five. I had three of a kind once but was beaten by a full house. The pot, which included all the boilermakers and pipefitters on the west side of the plant, could go to more than four thousand dollars. Almost everyone went in, because you only had one chance to play a week, so why not? Plus, it always happened on pay day.

Tommy and Chuck taught me a game from the South called bourré, and my whole table played for pocket change at lunch time. There were also card draws. In some places the steward runs these, but in Pennsylvania it was the domain of the tool crib attendant,

Benny. With a card draw, you pay to choose a card from a regular deck. Then you tear it in half, initial both halves, and give one back. When all the cards are sold there's a draw, and the person who has the other half of the card that is drawn, is the winner. While it's not a hard rule, it's understood that the guy running the draw gets ten per cent, but you can give him more. If you win the card draw and don't pay the kickback, you're considered a cheap jerk. While I had seen card draws before, Benny took it to a new level. He usually had multiple decks on the go and was selling at five, ten, and twenty dollars a card. Cut-off was Friday at noon, sharp, when the winning card was drawn, so the winner had a chance to come forward and claim the prize. The identity of the winning card was broadcast by word of mouth, so on Friday afternoons everyone was asking *What was the card*? and *Who won the pool*?

Guys would line up with wads of cash and buy multiple cards for all the draws, and also bet on whatever football pools and sports draws were going on. Sometimes Benny would be assigned a helper on Fridays to actually hand out the tools while he took care of the gambling. I never won any of the cash draws, limiting my participation to the cheque pool and the purchase of a weekly five-dollar card. At the end of the day, all the spent cards — and there would be several decks — would magically disappear. You never saw the losing half-cards on the ground or left on the tables in the lunchroom, because it was still illegal to gamble in Pennsylvania. It was like none of it had ever happened.

While I wasn't tempted to blow my cheque on a longshot at the Belmont, I could never resist the raffles. There were always weird things in the tool crib being raffled off. In Montana, it was a Case Triple X pocketknife that I had my eye on, but mine was not the lucky ticket. In Pennsylvania, the first thing up for raffle was a beautiful hatband made by one of the union brothers, out of what looked like intricately patterned beadwork that turned out to be porcupine quills. Unlike the take from the other tool crib ventures, the raffle proceeds always went to charity. The hatband was for a local youth group. Sometimes it was toy raffles, a bike or a teddy bear for the hospital. The Boilermakers are generous with charities, it's part of the union credo. So it was not surprising to have someone walk through the various lunchrooms selling tickets for whatever was on the block that week.

What was surprising was the day the guy came through with a roll of tickets calling "Gun raffle! Get your tickets for the gun raffle!" This was a popular one, and everyone lined up to buy. The next day, some of the prizes were brought in to display, and set up on a table in another lunchroom. Durland and I went over for a look. There was a shotgun, a .22 rifle, and a handgun in a wooden box that hinged open. There was an ammunition belt, and a saddle scabbard, all laid out on one of the tables.

"Raising money for your child's school?" I asked Benny. He knew me a little, and just shook his head. "Look at that handsome vest you can win," I said to Durland, pointing out an elaborate hunting vest adorned with loops for holding shotgun shells.

"Uh-huh," he said, "Camouflage. It goes with anything."

But a guy I didn't know turned on me.

"You stupid Canadian," he said. "You can't have a gun raffle for a school. And you can't enter anyhow. Because if you win, they won't let you take the guns across the border."

"I thought if I won, I would donate the guns," I said. "There's a women's crisis centre next door to my hotel. I thought I could donate them there."

"Those guns are for huntin' Canadians." He leered.

"Oh no," Tommy spoke up from behind me, "it hain't no fun to hunt Canadians, they pacifists. They don't wriggle 'round or nothin'." This diffused things because Tommy didn't usually say much. Later, he took me aside. "You stay away from that guy," he said. "He ain't right." The guy, who was from Louisiana, started throwing me the stink eye when he saw me. Then he changed lunchrooms and moved over into ours.

SATURDAYS AND SUNDAYS are double time, and if you work seven days a week it's called a ringer and works out to a couple of thousand dollars in your pocket. On the second payday, I lamented that since we were working Saturday, I would not be spending the day lining up at the bank in Mount Bethel, arguing about getting fingerprinted again.

"Honey, I'm gonna tell you something." Durland said, "and I'm gonna grab ahold of you for this one." That's what he'd say when he had something important to tell me. Then he placed an enormous paw on my shoulder, rendering me immobile until he was finished speaking.

"You don't cash your cheque at the bank."

"I don't?" I asked.

"No."

"Then where do I cash it?"

"At The Buck."

"The Buck?"

"We are going there after work."

"We are?"

"Yes."

"Why?"

"To cash our cheques." Seldom have I had a job where I enjoyed my partner as much. I still hear his wise voice in my mind when I need advice.

DURLAND TOLD ME we had to get there early, and we were walking out the gate at 5:30 sharp. I followed him to the highway and left my rental car in the Circle K at the crossroads. I climbed into his old truck and we drove a short but circuitous route that took us away from the plant, then along the Delaware River, then back up to the highway and on to the interstate. We entered one of those convoluted cloverleafs that they don't have in Canada, and exited on a side road immediately. It took us to a parking lot hidden behind a tall hedge, that was quickly filling up. Almost directly underneath the cloverleaf was a small tavern, called The Buccaneer. Known as The Buck, and also known as LeGrand's, it had no signage and was barely visible from the road. Durland had the amazing ability to do everything slowly, but with great efficiency. When working, he rarely moved fast, but always finished first and got more done than most. His regular rolling, somewhat lopsided gait covered a lot of ground, but at The Buck he moved quickly, and I had to jog to keep up. Inside he found a table, and we were joined by our foreman, Sunny, and a couple other local guys.

Durland explained that the first thing you do is order a pint of beer. Then you sign your cheque and put it back in the envelope. When the beer arrives, you place the envelope under the glass. The server then stops by and picks it up and takes it to the back room.

"What do we do now?" I asked, watching my week's pay disappear behind some swinging doors.

"You drink your beer," Durland said. Then he turned to Sunny and started talking about fishing. When the server returned, she placed the envelope back down and put a new pint on top of it. I looked around. I was the only woman. All over the bar men were sliding envelopes out from under beer mugs and pocketing them. Durland leaned toward me to speak in my ear. "Don't open it, and don't count it," he said. I slid the envelope, which was quite bulky, under the table, and stuffed it in the pocket of my Dickies. He ordered us each a Philly cheesesteak sandwich, which I had never had before.

"Never?" he asked, "Never? Well, I'd say it is about time." Then he started telling Sunny about a project we were working on, a hammered steel pot rack for his wife, whom he called The Ruth.

"Only time for two," he said, draining his mug. "The Ruth will be waiting."

ON THE WAY back to my car he explained the popularity of The Buck. LeGrand, the bar owner, put eighty thousand dollars in the safe on Friday mornings. The first forty or so people to come in could cash their paycheques, but when the money ran out you were too late. There were only a few rules. They didn't pay the change, but rounded the amount down to the nearest dollar, because quarters didn't sit so well under the beer mugs. Discretion was to be exercised, which meant you didn't talk about, look at, or count your money at the table. The staff always brought the correct amount. The customers never saw LeGrand. He came and went through the back door, driving up in a black, 1968 Mercury pickup that had been restored to its original condition. On Friday nights, he sat at his desk next to the safe, with his back to the wall, filling the envelopes. He kept a Colt .45 revolver on the desk next to the stacks of money. If there was any sign of trouble, or a dispute over the amount, the bartender, who was LeGrand's security man, escorted you out, and you were banned for life. There was never any trouble. It was a simple but effective system, ensuring a loyal customer base from all the workers hurrying to the bar on Friday afternoon. And LeGrand ended up with a full room of drinkers, each of whom had a couple of thousand cash dollars in his pocket. It was certainly less trouble, and more secure, than going to any bank.

PENNSYLVANIA WAS A sweet job, of camaraderie, card games, dinners out and lots of laughs. Sometimes it just goes like that, good chemistry and good will. All the days are fun. In the third week, I came in for lunch to find a small package at my place at the table. It was a flat square, neatly wrapped and tied with a ribbon. Someone had drawn a question mark on it.

"Looks like someone has an admirer," Durland said. We all looked at Chuck.

"Don't look at me," he said. "I ain't got no secrets."

Puzzled, I opened it. Inside was a Polaroid photo. It had been taken in a hotel room, the camera set up on the bathroom sink and facing the bathtub. It was a grungy room, with tiles peeling, but otherwise nondescript. A man was standing in the tub, his head cut off by the top of the photo frame, so he was only visible from the neck down. He was naked, with an erection, holding it in his hand. There's not much room to write on a Polaroid, but on the white space at the bottom were the words "here's a taste." On the inside of the wrapping paper, in a messy scrawl it said "you're gonna love what I'm gonna do to you – when I get you alone." I could feel my face getting hot, and put my hands flat on the table, to stop them from shaking. I slid the picture over to Durland, who turned around to look at the guy from Louisiana, but he was walking out the door.

I pocketed the picture and sat for a couple minutes, then told Durland I was going to talk to the shop steward. The shoppy was a sandy-haired guy called Bob with sad eyes and a droopy moustache. I crossed the floor and told him I needed to speak to him, immediately. He followed me outside and I showed him the photo, which we took to the office. To their credit, my foreman, general foreman, and superintendent were suitably upset.

"What the HELL?" the GF slammed his hands on his desk. "Who did this?" The sudden yelling was what set me off, and I started sobbing, further upsetting the supervision.

"This is completely unacceptable," the super said. "You tell me who did this and he's gone, fired. Right now. This doesn't happen on my site." I suppose they were unused to having a woman on the crew and were unprepared for the situation. The shop steward, feeling like he should do something, picked up the photo.

"I'll tell you what this is," he said. "This is garbage, and this is what I think of it," and he took out his lighter and set the picture on fire. I bolted out of my chair, where I had been sitting, drinking a glass of water.

"What the hell are you doing?" I shouted. "That's my evidence!" He put the fire out, but it was too late. Plastic and paper burn fast. As soon as I became angry the men settled down and turned toward me. The superintendent sat on the edge of his desk and levelled his gaze.

"Do you know who did this?" he asked. I shook my head. "Do you have an idea?" I nodded. "You tell me who did this, and I'll fire him, right now. He's gone." I shook my head again.

"I can't," I said. "I have an idea, but I can't say, because I don't have any proof."

"I don't want this guy on site," he said.

"I don't either," I answered. "Believe me." He wanted to call a meeting with the whole crew, where he would make a big deal out of telling them the behaviour would not be tolerated, but I asked him not to.

"He wants attention," I said. "He wants a big deal, and I don't want to give it to him. I don't want you to say anything to the crew. It won't make any difference to this guy, except he'll enjoy it, and it'll embarrass me, and he'll enjoy that too."

"Give me a name," the super said, "just give me a name." I shook my head. I think I even apologized. It would be so much easier for him if he could just fire a guy, the problem would be solved.

"I can't give you a name," I explained, "because I don't have any proof. And if I'm wrong, then I've wrongly accused someone. And these are my union brothers. So I can't."

AFTER THE MEETING I washed my face and crossed back to the lunchroom. The guys at my table were concerned. Chuck was upset.

"Me and Tommy gonna take care of it," he said. "After work."

"You can't," I told him.

"Oh we can, and we gonna. This problem is over."

"No, you can't," I insisted. "I can't accuse anyone, because if I've got the wrong guy, then the wrong guy gets fired. I can't do that."

"He won't have a chance to get fired," Chuck said. "We won't give it to him."

"Honey," Durland said kindly, "We all know who it is."

"That's not true," I said. "There are more than two hundred people on this site, and it could be anyone." This gave my table pause.

"Is that what you think?" Durland asked. "When you walk on to site in the morning, that there are two hundred people here, and any one of them could do a thing like this? Is that what you walk into?" I nodded.

"Every day."

This is one of the things we don't talk about, when we talk about women working in trades. We don't talk about how the maniac, the anonymous psychopath, the rapist, is out there, a monster imbedded among these good men. You could be working beside him. This is something the women always know, but the men don't think about. When you explain it to them, they are shocked. That we have to think about this, every day, every job. Every time we walk to our car after night shift. *Think of your wives*, I tell them, *think of your daughters*.

AFTER I RECEIVED the photograph, I was never alone at work. They didn't discuss it with me, but the men on my crew closed ranks. It was a long walk from the parking lot to the site tent, but when I arrived, one of them would be in his truck, waiting, and pretend we just happened to get there at the same time. If I had to go to stores or the tool crib, someone would be walking a little ways behind. If I was working in the yard, Durland would come out, or someone else. They literally kept an eye on me at all times.

"Maybe I could get an ankle bracelet," I suggested at coffee. "Or some kind of tracking device."

"My dog's got a thing on his collar," Tommy said. "Zaps him when he gits too close to the 'lectric fence. Keeps him in sight."

"Sure," I said. "Set it up."

CHUCK AND I started having dinner every night, instead of a couple times a week, and instead of parting company at the Minisink, he would drive up to my hotel and scan for unusual vehicles while I checked the room. I slept with a dresser against the door. Probably unnecessary precautions, but the problem is that you don't know whether the threat is real or not. Chuck would shrug. "Don't cost you nothing to check." I appreciated the reassurance. We had the Sunday off and on impulse I walked up to the women's crisis centre next door to the hotel. The counsellor's name was Kate, and I told her about the guy with the Polaroid, and that I was thinking of quitting. She was a strong woman and a good listener, with good advice. I left resolved to stick it out.

Three days later, Durland called me outside the fabricating tent. There were two low black cars in the distance, speeding down the plant road from the east, and a third coming in from the west.

"That looks like the po-lice," he said. We lost sight of them as they approached the parking lot. At lunch we heard that they were there for the guy from Louisiana, had picked him up right on site as he headed into his trailer at coffee. They had an out-of-state warrant for multiple rape and assault charges, and when he took off to Pennsylvania to work he was a registered sex offender in the state of Louisiana. I shuddered.

"Only time for two," Durland said, draining his pint. "The Ruth will be waiting." It was Friday night at The Buck.

"I would like to meet The Ruth," I said, on the way to my car. "Maybe we could all get together for lunch. I could take you two for some Chinese or something."

"Chinese?" Durland asked.

"Yeah."

"I have never had Chinese food," he said.

"What? Never? You've never had Chinese food?"

"I take it you have?" he asked.

"I'm from Vancouver," I said. "Shanghai noodle, Cantonese, dim sum … there are restaurants from every region of the world. You can go anywhere and get Thai food, Vietnamese, Cambodian, sushi … you've never had Chinese food? Really?"

"Nope, never." Durland was pushing sixty.

"Oh, man…you've never had an egg roll? Sweet and sour pork? Almond chicken? You've never said, 'Hey Ruth … let's run over to Scranton and grab some Chinese …?'" He shook his head.

"Not even Chinese-American?"

"Is that something different?" he asked, surprised. He pulled into the Circle K next to my rental car and I told him about some of the cuisines I had encountered on the West Coast.

"I had no idea," he said, shaking his head in wonder.

"That's settled then," I said. "You and The Ruth and I are going for Chinese food before I go back to Canada."

"I'll ask her," he said doubtfully, "but I don't know if she'll come."

THE JOB WAS starting to wind down, the combustion air liner had been fitted and the welding was nearly complete. Without much left to fabricate, Durland and I had become the organizers of the yard crew, separating the rental welding machines for different companies and getting ready to start filling semi-trailers with tools and equipment to be hauled away.

"I have been asking some friends, and our neighbours," Durland said, "and it is surprising, how many people have been."

"Been where?" I asked.

"For the Chinese food."

"You find the place, and I'll meet you there on Saturday."

CHUCK AND I spent Thursday slamming in the last couple of igniter boxes.

"There h'ain't but one way of doing it," he counselled me, "and that's the right way." We were laid off that night, as expected. The members would get another week doing pack-out, but travel cards were cut loose.

"I'm draggin' up," Tommy said happily, stuffing gear into his duffel bag. "The man can have my money." The crew milled around the lunchroom, shaking hands.

"See you on the next one," they were saying. "See you on the next one." It was like a good luck charm. It meant goodbye, good luck, drive safe, and I hope we meet again.

Anders found me on his way out and grasped my hand. "See you on the next one," he said. "See you at home."

I DROVE STRAIGHT back to the Water Gap Inn to pack and find a flight. As I left my room to get some ice, a voice called.

"Hey short britches, you got a porch for that swing?" It was Chuck. He decided to stay in town one more night instead of heading straight home, so we went to the Minisink for the special.

"Is it true it snows all the time in Canada?" he asked, "even in the summer?"

SATURDAY MORNING WAS crisp and clear, and unmistakably autumn. I packed my gear in the trunk and took my coffee maker and a cash donation to the women's centre. I didn't recognize the woman at the desk, but we wished each other good luck. See you on the next one, I thought, walking down the steps. My rental car was covered in fall leaves and I drove out of the mountains in a frenzy of colour.

I had to swing north and east to get to the address I had written down on a piece of paper. It wasn't easy to find, but it was easy to recognize, by the enormous fork and knife erected on either side of the driveway. They were silver and stood about fifteen feet tall. If you are holding the Big One, they have to listen. Durland was standing outside, with his wife. The Ruth was tall and broad shouldered, and shook hands shyly. The Buffet Supreme was the largest Chinese-American buffet in Pennsylvania. The server showed us to a booth and left us with menus that were many pages thick.

"We were surprised," Ruth said, "How many people have been." I nodded.

"You know I think it's getting more and more popular." The line at the Buffet Supreme did not go straight from the salad bar to the cash register. It was S-shaped, and featured every conceivable variation of Chinese American food. On the other side of the room was a sushi bar, where a chef whipped together various rolls at lightning speed, and at the back wall was a hamburger bar, featuring burgers, fries, and hot dogs.

"I've never seen a hamburger bar," I confessed.

"Never?" Durland asked, "Never??"

"Now the hard part," I told them. "Deciding what to have."

"The Ruth and I have talked about that," Durland said. "And we have decided ... we would like to try everything."

"I think that is an excellent idea," I said. "Go big or go home."

OTHER CUSTOMERS CAME and went, locals dashing in for a quick lunch between meetings, a table of women celebrating a birthday. Durland and Ruth were systematic, starting at one end of the buffet and working their way all the way around, sampling every item on the menu. For four hours, we drank bottomless glasses of Coca-Cola from the soda fountain, and made multiple trips with our plastic trays. I was out after round two, and sat drinking tea, but Durland and Ruth were troopers, finally making it to the dessert table. Ruth came back with a Chinese donut, an egg tart, a small slice of cheesecake, and a bowl of jello."

"I thought we could share," she said. We were the last customers in the restaurant and the closed sign hung on the door. All the staff came over at different times to say hello, and a cluster of servers stood by the kitchen doors, watching us. It was time for them to start setting up for dinner. Durland and Ruth had taken on the challenge of the Buffet Supreme with a steadfast seriousness that was admirable. They offered critiques and opinions along the way. The beef and broccoli and BBQ pork were winners.

"But you know," Durland said, leaning forward, "The Ruth did not care for the oyster." The final dish was a small plate of eclairs. When Durland pushed the plate away, the staff broke into applause. I slipped out of the booth to take care of the bill because I knew he wouldn't let me otherwise. When I came back the two of them were whispering together.

"What?" I asked. "What's going on?"

"The Ruth and I were wondering . . ." he started, "Well we were wondering if it would be OK if we took our placemats home. As souvenirs." They were paper placemats, with the Chinese calendar on them.

"I'll be right back," I said. The manager brought over our coats, and gave Ruth a little parcel: placemats, a copy of the menu, two sets of chopsticks, and extra fortune cookies.

"Well," she said. "Look at that."

OUTSIDE THE RESTAURANT my partner embraced me in a bear hug, and we shook hands, mine disappearing into his giant paw.

"See you on the next one," he said.

"See you on the next one."

MICHIGAN

A year and a half after leaving Pennsylvania, I found myself standing in front of a mirror in a room in the Knights Inn in Munroe, Michigan. I had phoned the dispatcher at the Michigan Local, 169, and asked where the travel cards were staying for the turnaround. The Knights Inn was one of two he recommended. The Best Value was full.

"Best one-star motel in Munroe County," he said. "Damn I'm glad I work in the office now." I called to make a reservation and told the desk clerk I would be staying for five weeks.

The Knights Inn was a cheap single storey with the siding painted to look like stone walls. It had fake turrets at either end, made of plywood, with little purple and gold triangular flags flapping off of them. It was the end of March and unseasonably warm, the parking lot full of pickup trucks, a river of melting slush. A couple of the guys had moved their trucks to the visitors' lot and set up barbecues in the parking spaces in front of their rooms. Most evenings, my neighbour was standing in front of his, in rubber boots, sweatpants, and a parka, nursing a Miller and flipping burgers or keeping an eye on his steak.

I was brushing my teeth. It was one of those motel rooms where there's a little foyer outside the bathroom. On one side is the bathroom sink, and on the other is a microwave and coffee maker. It's what passes as a kitchenette in a roadside motel. The lighting was incredibly good over the sink, and I was in the process of discovering that I had grey hairs. Was this even possible? I noticed one at first, then another, then another. I had had one or two before, occasionally, but this was new. I pulled a couple out and leaned into the mirror. There were more than I could count, more than I could pluck out. Damn.

I was thirty-six, the age my mom was when I was born, and she always said she felt like an older mom. Friends were having later-in-life babies. According to pop culture lore, my biological clock was supposed to be hammering away at a deafening tick-tock, but I couldn't hear it. I stared at the grey, white actually, strands, beginning to pepper my unremarkable, mid-brown, mid-length hair. I had no interest in having a child. I did have an uneasy sense that by now I was supposed to have done something — written a novel, become a radical, progressive politician, or at least a human rights lawyer. I was meant to be somewhere other than standing under a 100-watt lightbulb in a crummy motel beside the interstate outside Detroit. It was a kind of free-floating urgency, like I was supposed to catch a train somewhere and just didn't.

I dropped my toothbrush into the glass, rinsed out the French press and filled the kettle for making quick coffee in the morning. I was getting up at 5:00 a.m. for a 7:00 a.m. start. I made a turkey and swiss sandwich, filled a little plastic container with almonds, and put some fruit in a bag. I put my work clothes out on the chair: thin socks, thick socks, a clean welding hat, and turned my boots around on the heat register so they would be dry by the morning. I had a routine, and if I just stuck to it, everything would work out. A few grey hairs didn't mean I was old, not even middle-aged. I just wasn't exactly young anymore.

Then I failed my weld test. I was a bit surprised, but not really. The root just wouldn't go in. I adjusted my heat up and down, tried pushing it in with the wire, ground it out and tried again. I thought maybe it was on the wrong polarity, checked the gas pressure, adjusted the light in the booth. In the end I wasn't happy with the root, it had sucked back, especially at the bottom, dead centre. If they took a coupon from that spot it might not make it, but I wasn't overly concerned. I'd been working on the site for more than a week before they got around to testing me, so they weren't exactly desperate for pressure welders. I was welding on an expansion joint when my foreman, Cam, climbed into the air ducts. His radio kept going off. He turned it down.

"You didn't make your weld test," he said, apologetically. My stomach contracted into a small, hard ball. I felt like I was shrinking.

"Aw man," I said, finally. "I'm sorry about that. I couldn't get my root in at the bottom." I started thinking about packing my bags, checking out of the motel, and the money... this was meant to be five weeks of work. He shrugged.

"Do you want to take a plate test?" he asked. Part of my mind was still calculating like crazy, $250 a week for the room, $225 for the car...

"Plate test?" I asked.

"John heard you can run wire," he said. "We don't want to lose you and we thought if you did a flux core plate test ..." $544 last minute flight to Windsor ...

"Sure," I said. "I'd love to do a plate test." Cam pulled me off the unit and took me to the blue building with the American flag on the door.

GAS METAL ARC WELDING or GMAW, more commonly called wire feed, is a process whereby a large spool of thin wire is fed through a hollow liner inside a length of cable. Sometimes the spool is on a machine, but by the time I was in Michigan they were making big advances in the technology and a 35-pound spool of wire could fit inside a black plastic "suitcase." It was awkward but portable. You could drag it just about anywhere and set up. It was powered by a length of welding cable that ran back to the machine. Sometimes you had to go back to the power source to change the controls, but usually on field jobs the company supplied a remote-control box, so you could change the heat on the fly. The wire and the gas line run through the cable into a gun. You pull the trigger, wire comes out a small copper tip inside the nozzle, and the gas is expelled around it, protecting the weld. Wire-feed has a high metal deposition rate so a lot of weld can be laid down in a short period of time, making it very productive.

Running wire is thought to be easy, because you don't have to add external filler metal or keep changing rods — you just pull the trigger and go. The wire shoots out and melts off in the puddle. You just have to adjust the voltage and wire-feed settings correctly, keep a steady hand, and weld with the right speed and gun angle. I was OK with running wire, but wasn't making a career of it. I used to carry a slip of paper in my tool bag with the voltage and amperage settings for different positions written down, so I would know how to set my machine.

Cam gave me four plates, for the four positions, which I cut in half with a zip cut. I took the scale off the coupons with a grinder, made sure the bevelled edges were tight to the backing plates, and set the gap at 1/8". I clamped the plates to the backing with a C-clamp and tacked them together, making four test plates. Then it was coffee.

THE BOILERMAKERS AND pipefitters shared a lunchroom. It wasn't in a trailer but built right on to a level of the boiler house. They had divided off an area, built it in with plywood, and thrown more plywood down on the grating for a floor. There were portable sinks outside but no real washhouse, and instead of chairs there were benches made from planks. Pipefitters and boilermakers have an intense rivalry. According to the contracts, the work inside the confined spaces, and the first joint or flange on the outside of the vessel, belongs to the boilermakers. Everything after that, the boiler external piping, belonged to the pipefitters. There was always conflict if the work crossed over, and a perpetual argument over who got that first outside joint. So, usually, they kept us separated.

"I heard you busted out," a guy called out to me from across the room.

"What?" I asked.

"I heard you busted your tube test." He was rotund, with a scraggly ponytail coming out from under his hat, and spoke with a Southern accent. I could feel my face flushing with shame. Busting a test always makes you feel terrible.

"Yes," I said. "I did. And?"

"That's all," he said, shrugging and sitting down.

"You just wanted to let everyone know that I busted my tube test?" He grinned.

One of the guys at my table, Peter, cleared his throat and asked if we had a lot of snow in Canada over the winter.

"Ignore him," he said. "He's a pipefitter."

I WELDED A coupon on to the stand above me, in the overhead position. I always did the overhead first because it's the hardest and I liked to do it before my arms were tired. Overhead is exactly what it sounds like. The plate is positioned above your head, with the open side of the groove facing down. You have to position your body with the gun pointed up, and do everything you do in the flat position, only upside down. You fight gravity all the way, the molten metal wants to fall out of the joint, you can't get the penetration, and you are trying to see everything through a fountain of sparks that is cascading over you. My worst burns are from welding overhead.

I PUT THE root in, catching both edges, dragging the gun. I ran a zip-cut over the sides of the root-pass to check for slag, put a pass against the far edge, cleaned it with the wire wheel. I was getting "rail-road tracks," slag lines down both edges. I ground them out and welded some more, until it was done except for the cap. My arms ached.

Welds in the vertical want to slump, to collapse down. Lowering the heat makes the puddle smaller and easier to carry as you work up the joint. A trick is to tilt the plate. According to the welding code, a vertical plate can be tilted backward up to ten degrees when testing. It's not much, but enough that it helps the puddle stay where you want it. Part of my brain was still calculating the loss if I busted out the plate test as well. I was racing against the clock, and started sweating. I checked the heat and realized I was running small diameter wire and could handle it, even a little hot. I welded three quarters of the way out, then left it to cool and went back to cap the overhead. Then finished the vertical. Two test plates were complete. Inside I was disappearing, thinking: *I'm nobody now. I won't be able to answer the phone at the hotel room because there's nobody there.* That's what testing, and failing a test, does. But the flat and horizontal are always easier, gravity is on your side.

The overhead cap was a little rocky but the vertical looked great. The quality control guy shone his flashlight at it from different angles but couldn't find any undercut. I maintained an air of neutrality. Once again a job was riding on the bend test. It wasn't a good time to show emotion. After lunch I was told that my tests bent clean, and Cam put me on production in the air ducts, welding seams.

We were only working ten hour shifts in Michigan, and only five days a week, but this suited me. I'd taken the job because my mother was in Windsor, just across the border, having a hip replacement. I could go on the weekends and see her. And I had friends in Windsor, good, old friends from when I was twenty. They had moved there so their kids could get to know their grandparents.

"They have no sense of irony," I complained, over red wine, on my first weekend visit. "In Montana it was all handle-bar moustaches and pointy cowboy boots, like I was living in a trashy satire of a Western movie. And in Pennsylvania ... did you know they took four per cent off our paycheques and never said what it was for? My partner finally told me to stop asking ... because it was going to the mob."

"The MOB?" Wreford, who is Italian, raised his eyebrows.

"That's what they said. He called it protection money. On the pay stub it said 'miscellaneous dues' and it went to the union."

"You were in a mob movie," Janisse said. "Maybe you just haven't found the genre in Michigan."

THE MOST INTERESTING people on the crew were a group of travel-card boilermakers from Local 4. It was the Navajo local from Arizona and New Mexico. They had built a state-of-the-art boilermakers' training centre in Page, Arizona, at their hall, and had a reputation for being excellent tradesmen (and women) and particularly good welders. There were four folks from Local 4 on the claim, including a young woman, but they didn't mingle much, and took their breaks in a different plywood shack. I learned this from the guys at my table.

"They weren't good to begin with," the pipefitter contributed from across the room. "Terrible welders. Got all those government handouts. How come we don't get handouts to build a welding school? Hey? Well you know why..." My bench mate, Peter, was another welder and a pretty quiet guy. The pipefitter was irritating him. He told me that the Navajo had retained the mineral rights on their lands, which had proved lucrative. They had reinvested in the learning centre in Page and were rapidly gaining a reputation for being fast and proficient.

I was just delighted to see another female on the job and chatted with the young woman when I ran into her. Her name was Abey. She was traveling with her husband, her father, and her uncle. They were boomers, constantly travelling the country, going from job to job.

I LEFT FOR Windsor right after work on Friday. It had turned cold and was snowing heavily. There were long line-ups through the tunnel and I huddled in my rental car, listening to Detroit radio. Saturday, after seeing my mom, I got to spend the afternoon with my friends' kids. Simone was seven and Cyrus was four. They were game for everything and we played all afternoon. Simone was making up dance moves and showing them off, and her brother had to do everything she did. In the evening we worked on a craft project that involved popsicle sticks, sparkles, and a lot of white glue. When the kids were in bed, I stayed up with my friends and talked. I told them my doubts about work, how I sometimes found the culture too lacerating.

"At home, they said I would never make it in the trade if I didn't have a thicker skin," I said. "But I don't know how to do that."

"You don't need a thicker skin," Wreford said. "They need to stop being assholes."

Crossing back from Windsor into Michigan, the American Customs and Immigration officer scrutinized my documentation. His shirt was too tight and he had the customary squared off military haircut and matching jaw. Finally, he asked, "You're a . . . boil-maker?"

"Yes," I answered, unblinking. "You make it sound so medical."

"What?"

"Nothing. I'm a boil-maker. I make boils." He stamped my papers and handed them back, then told me to have a nice stay. I was learning to choose my battles.

THAT WEEK I had some long horizontal seams to weld, the length of the air ducts. The caps were made of three stringers, and they were not going well. Instead of three neat lines stacked one on top of the other, they looked like long worms, meandering up and down, with valleys between the passes that needed to be filled. I couldn't see it until I lifted up my helmet.

"I can't SEE it," I told Peter, at lunchtime. "There's lots of light, but I can't see where I'm going."

"Have you tried a cheater?" he asked.

"A cheater?" He rummaged in his backpack and pulled out a plastic bag with a bunch of little plastic cases inside. These were glass magnifying lenses that fit inside the welding helmet.

"You wear glasses, right?" he asked. "But your safety glasses aren't prescription? You're welding without your glasses. Try this." He slid two of the cases across the table. "That one's a seventy-five. If that doesn't work, try the hundred." After that my stringers were straight. It was miraculous.

"I can still weld," I told him at coffee. "I'm just going blind."

The pipefitter talked a lot, his nonsense forming a part of the background noise.

"Well I went in and put some ass in their face, today. Yup." He didn't even make sense. I mostly ignored him, but once in a while he would lob one in my direction to try to get a reaction. "And as soon as I get my sass money, they'll be getting even more ass in their face. Yup they'll be getting both cheeks today. I got me a date with that cute li'l thing at the diner. Don't mind if you don't see me here Monday morning, you know where I'll be."

"More like he's got a date with a grilled cheese sandwich," Peter said.

LIKE MANY OF the guys, I left early on Friday in time to cash my cheque. Letiesha was the teller at the National Bank of America on North Dixie Highway, in Munroe.

"Just place your thumbprint here, next to the amount, and I'll need two pieces of ID." She pushed over a small ink pad.

"Yes of course," I said, whipping out my thumb. "Anything you need." Had she asked for a hair sample I'd have started pulling them out for her. Blood? Which arm would you like? It no longer mattered to me if the bank had my fingerprint or if the FBI had my DNA. I was choosing my battles.

There was a dollar store next to the bank, and I bought a cheap, colourful disco lamp. On Saturday the kids and I turned the playroom into a dance club. We set up a sound system, worked on costumes in the afternoon, and had a disco party. The next morning I woke up to my friend Janisse chiding Simone.

"He doesn't like it," she was saying, as I came upstairs. "And if you keep doing it, you're going to teach him to be afraid of you." Simone, who was a person who felt things deeply, was crying.

"She's blowing on the hamster again," Janisse explained. She was being stern but I could tell she was also trying not to laugh.

"That's not good," I said, seriously.

"I know," Simone said, sobbing. "But I can't *help* it." It had been an issue for a couple of weeks. The hamster was nocturnal and spent much of the night on his wheel, then slept all morning. Simone wanted to wake him up and put him in his plastic ball, which was more fun. Knowing she wasn't supposed to pick him up when he was sleeping, she had taken to blowing on the sleeping hamster when no one was looking. She wasn't really doing anything to it, she was just blowing air.

IT WAS GETTING harder to leave my friends at the end of each weekend. Usually we worked straight through for a month or so, and I just had to get up each day and stick to the routine. But this time it was like re-entering real life every weekend, and difficult to reconcile the experience of this calm, nurturing family with the harsh reality in Michigan.

"I feel like Persephone when I have to go back," I told them, "descending into the underworld, across the river Styx."

"You are," Janisse said. "Only it's not the Styx, it's the Detroit." She shrugged. "I grew up here."

"I know it's hard," I whispered to Simone while we hugged goodbye, "but try not to blow on the hamster while I'm gone."

"OK," she said, "I'll try. And I have something for you. Hold out your hand." She pressed a tiny paper unicorn into my hand, the size of a piece of confetti. "That's so that you never forget me," she said. "I want you to remember me forever." I nodded solemnly.

"I will," I promised. "See you in a week."

THE WEATHER BROKE again and the snow had nearly melted. The air ducts were almost finished, it was Friday, and I'd been told it was my last day. My mom had gone home to BC and I was looking forward to returning as well. I wasn't having much fun with my crew. As the week drew to a close I was becoming more impatient to get going. At the Knights Inn, my bags were packed and I kept looking at my watch. The pipefitter came into the lunchroom, loud as ever.

"Did you guys see that sweet little thing out there?" He was talking about Abey. She was welding a joint on a pipe stand not far from the lunchroom.

"Don't blow on the hamster," I whispered.

"What?" Peter asked.

"Nothing," I said. The pipefitter continued, casually, but deliberately loud.

"They're no good, usually. They're lazy. They can't help it, they're born that way. But girlie — she's a fine little welder. For a Navajo. That little ..." and here he used a derogatory word for a Native American woman, "... she can walk the cup and wiggle her ass at the same time." Walking the cup is a technique that pipefitters use when TIG welding, that involves the torch cup being in contact with the pipe. Don't blow on the hamster ...

"She's not walking the cup," I heard myself saying. "She's welding freehand. She's a boilermaker." I felt compelled to claim her as a member of my trade, not his. I can't help it … I turned around on my bench. "That must really burn you, huh? Must burn your sass *and* your ass, knowing she can do your job and is taking home twice as much money as you are."

"What?" he turned toward me. "What are you talking about, Sugar?"

"Oh yeah," I said, raising my voice so he couldn't interrupt. "You know, she cooks for the crew, but her husband pays for the room. Her dad does the driving, and her uncle throws in for groceries. So she doesn't have any expenses at all. None. She banks her cheque — the whole fucking thing — and her living out allowance, and her travel money. All year. On every job." I paused and watched him doing the math. "She is twenty-six years old," I continued, "and a way better welder than you ever were. Her house is paid for, and she's got four horses. You've got two alimony payments and your truck belongs to the bank. So you …" I realized I was standing, pointing my finger at him, then I went dry. I had run out of things to say. "You can just … stick your sass … well, you know where." Peter was smiling.

"I think she's talking about both cheeks," he said. I zipped up the little purple sparkly lunch bag that Simone wanted me to take to work, and left, letting the door slam behind me.

I took the freight elevator to the ground and went into the women's washhouse. *This is so you will remember me forever.* I took ten minutes to pull myself together, then went back up to the air ducts. Shortly after, Cam climbed inside. He turned off his radio. I braced myself, again, to be fired, or at least reprimanded, seeing as it was my last day.

"I hear you had a few things to say to Sally," he said. He was smiling widely. "He complained about you."

"Sally?" I said, "That's his name?" Cam nodded.

"I told him he was in the boilermakers' trailer, and he could go eat his lunch somewhere else if it bothered him," Cam said. "I can get you Saturday, if you want it." He was still smiling. I was nonplussed.

"Thanks," I said slowly. "But I think it's time to drag up. The man can keep my money this time."

"OK," he said. "Well, thanks for helping out. You drive safe." We shook hands.

"See you on the next one."

IT WAS TIME to go. My hair was turning grey, I needed a new glasses prescription, and I wasn't changing anybody's mind. At the hotel, I packed my bags into the trunk of the little red rental car. My neighbour was already gone, and so was his barbecue. I called Windsor to tell my friends I was done, and we planned an outing to the gelato shop for the next day. It had the best lemon gelato in town, made with real lemons. I settled my bill and headed for the border.

NANTICOKE

"That's quite a cock." Lorne's eyebrows shot up.

"It is, isn't it," I said. "I saw it and I couldn't resist."

"You had to have it," he said.

"I did. I had to."

"Yes, quite a cock." He chuckled. I was holding a painting. It was on a piece of door skin, about two feet square, that had been tacked to a frame. The painting had a dark brown background, and was a head shot, in profile, of a magnificent rooster. He was white with a red wattle and comb, and was about ten times larger than life.

"It's a big one," Lorne said.

"Ya," I said, "and he has a glint in his eye." Lorne and I had met two weeks earlier. He was my foreman. The job at the Nanticoke refinery had come up suddenly. The guys at home said I was crazy. Castlegar was just about to go, then Kamloops. I would miss some of the best jobs of the season.

"But it's six weeks," I argued. "Of six tens, and the rate is better. We'll work all the Sundays."

"Ontario in February? I don't think so."

"March," I said. "It'll be early March by then."

BUT THE SPRING shut-down season was roaring to life in BC, and none of the guys that I knew wanted to go to Ontario. I wasn't expecting the call when it came, but said yes. What the hell. I packed in a hurry and booked a flight, haggled with rental car companies at the airport on my new LG flip-phone and secured a deal. Finding a hotel was harder. There were places in Hamilton, but that was more than seventy kilometres away. I found a room for the weekend at Jay's Motel. Phones didn't have easy internet connectivity in 2003 so I couldn't Google it. Jay's was going to be a surprise. When there are a thousand workers in an area for a shutdown and only one motel with vacancies, it's usually either too fancy, or too awful. Three hundred dollars a night, or bedbugs. That's the choice. Everything in between would be taken. At twenty-one bucks a night, I had an idea which it would be. I boarded the plane to Hamilton, ready to improvise when I got there.

The rental car guy at the airport matched the deal I was quoted from the place on the outskirts of town so I got a car right away, a little silver Corolla. It was always a cheap compact car on these trips, but they made it from A to B and the radio worked. My room at Jay's Motel was not as bad as I thought, but small, about twelve by twelve feet, with an over-sized fridge taking up more than its fair share.

"Do you mind?" I asked the fridge, while changing my shirt. "Do you have to watch?" The floor sloped, so there would be no playing marbles. The carpet was greasy, I would need to buy slippers. I arrived Friday night and had the weekend to explore before starting on Monday, so headed to the tourist town of Port Dover. The fish and chip shop was boarded up for the winter but there was a sweet pier to walk on, a beach, and a café.

It was that region of Southern Ontario where long roads, farms, and charming small towns full of antique stores, give way to the harder edged, more industrial areas outside of Hamilton. Dairy farms and corn fields yield to refineries, generating plants, and steel mills. I was headed to Nanticoke, to the Esso refinery.

MONDAY NIGHT WAS chaotic, with more than two hundred new hires on site who needed to be run through the extensive safety orientation and sign-on process. When a supervisor came in with a list of people who were renting out rooms in their homes, which apparently was a thing there, I took the phone number of a place in Port Dover and arranged with a woman called Sandy to move in the next day. She sounded OK, just a practical gal out to make an extra buck during the shutdown. She would be working as a fire watch at the same refinery, starting on day shift on Wednesday. I was on nights, so we'd probably never see each other. After the safety indoc, I spent the shift reading a newspaper, and napped. My welding test was scheduled for the following night.

I slept away the morning at Jay's Motel.

"See ya later," I told the fridge. "Stay cool." The new place was around the same distance from the refinery but it was only a few blocks from the town and the lake. It had a great feel. The house was an older two-story on a quiet street with a front porch and little path to the sidewalk. The living room had two comfortable sofas with crocheted blankets folded over the backs. There was plastic stretched over the windows, but the house was still draughty. Area rugs were rolled out over the hardwood floor, and one of the first over-sized flat screen TVs was set up on a stereo consul with a VCR. My room was up a flight of narrow stairs and had a view of the lake, and its own little bathroom, with a shower, across the hall. Sandy was renting out her master bedroom to another refinery worker and sleeping in the second bedroom downstairs. She seemed to have it all worked out.

"Your husband's not an axe murderer, is he?" I asked.

"Oh, did you meet him already?" she shot back. She didn't seem like a person who would put up with an axe murderer. Of the other worker renting a room she only said he was "an older guy, really nice. Quiet." He was a foreman and had already left for night shift — they started an hour earlier.

THE NEXT NIGHT I passed the weld test. I was working for Toronto Iron Works, a company that makes and erects silos, towers, and tanks. They had their own pressure welders, so I only needed to do a stainless plate test, which went fine. It was one of those jobs where they really just needed lots and lots of bodies. When a refinery is shut down for maintenance, every day that it's not running is costing hundreds of thousands of dollars. So the strategy is to hire on as many personnel as possible, man-up as many locations on site as they can, and have them work lots of hours, around the clock. They already had their key people in place, I was there as a foot soldier. It meant long days, good money, and a certain anonymity. Perfect.

My foreman was a guy who was close to retirement and seemed to know everyone. He was fluent in French and English and his crew was made up of Acadian guys from New Brunswick, Local 73. He had a lot of people, all the foremen did, and he was taking care of three towers.

"Can you climb?" he asked me. It wasn't a challenge, just a question.

"I can climb," I said.

"OK. The welding machine is up there, they won't be ready for you for a while, but you can go up and help out."

I've always loved climbing. Growing up, I spent the summers climbing the big trees around our house, and would hang out in them, with my cat, reading. I also used my third-floor bedroom window as a not-so-secret way to sneak in and out of the house at night, and had a route out the window, up over the high roof, down across the lower roof, on to the carport, then sliding down, hanging on to the fascia, lowering myself on to the brick barbecue, and down on to the back deck. But climbing trees, and to and from the bedroom window, was a pretty far cry from climbing a 120-foot reactor tower, in winter gear, with a hard hat and harness. The ladder was on the outside, and enclosed by a cage. There were inspection landings every twenty-five feet or so, so you could climb in stages, or step aside and rest. But the guys from New Brunswick didn't rest. They had grown up working at the Irving Refinery in Saint John, and this was their natural environment. They were fit and compact. They zipped up the ladder. I went last so I didn't hold any of them up, and stopped at every landing to catch my breath and settle my nerves.

At the top of the tower, four guys were inside and two were outside. The guys inside were dismantling trays and passing them out the manway where the guys outside stacked them up on the platform. I clipped my lanyard off to an anchor point. I learned later that these guys had grown up together. There were two brothers, a cousin, a nephew, and a couple of best friends, all from Miramichi. They worked in sync, as a unit, and spoke French, the outside guys occasionally shouting down through the manway, to the inside guys. From inside I could hear the distant sound of the pneumatic impact guns they were using to take off the hardware. These processing towers had a series of screen trays bolted to the inside in levels, going all the way down, and the crew was pulling them out. I hung back, out of their way. I tested the welding machine and retied it to the railing, then coiled it on the grate so it would be ready to go.

From a hundred and twenty feet in the air, you can see the whole refinery, from the flare stacks to the roads leading away toward the Stelco steel factory, Nanticoke Creek, and snowy pastures and corn fields cut into neat squares.

BY DAWN, IT was cold. We descended for the last time and took off our harnesses on the ground. There was a sea can for hanging up the fall arrest gear next to the tower. The French guys were around my age, or younger. One of them, who had been inside, turned and asked me a question in French. Then in heavily accented English.

"Where you from?"

"BC." I answered. He nodded.

"You don't speak French?" I shook my head. He nodded again and said something to the group, who laughed.

Guys were scraping the frost off their windshields, warming up their trucks, and lining up to swipe out at the exit gate. Traffic streamed out of the plant parking lot in a long line of red tail lights as dawn broke. At the crossroads, the line split, some turning east and some west. The trucks peeled off at various exits and I followed a black pickup down the turnoff to Port Dover. I had a paper map on the seat beside me with my route in yellow highlighter, and the interior light on so I could see it. The truck in front took all the turns on my map, finally pulling up in front of the little house on Gordon Street. This was the mysterious other worker who would be my room-mate.

Inside, my foreman was taking his coat off.

"You're staying here?" I asked. "Wow. What are the chances."

"We haven't properly met yet," he said, holding out his hand. "I'm Lorne. Do you want a beer? Meet you back here after the shower."

LORNE WAS A quiet, polite guy from Sault Ste. Marie. Over the next week we developed a routine after work — shower, food, and two beers each. Neither of us told the rest of the crew we were staying at the same place. Around six in the morning, after the second beer and a snack, I would go upstairs to sleep and Lorne would phone his wife, who would be awake by then. He had made this call after every shift since they'd been married, and they were about to celebrate their fortieth wedding anniversary. Then Lorne was going to retire. He and his wife ran a little hotel near the locks. They would continue with that for a few more years, then sell it. He had had heart surgery the year before and was looking forward to slowing down. He was hoping his daughter would move back.

"There's no work at home," he said. "I've been living with a suitcase in the trunk of my car for forty years. It's a suitcase local, the Sault. You're always travelling." He pronounced it *the Soo*.

At the end of that first week, I decided to take charge of the after-work snacks. Lorne had been making himself the same thing every night: bologna sandwiches with miracle whip and bright yellow mustard, one for after work and one for lunch the next day.

"You like to eat, right?" I asked him.

"I love to eat," he said, smiling. "But I don't know how to cook."

"Right," I said. "How about we do a chicken dinner tomorrow morning?" He didn't hesitate. "Sure," he said. "Let me give you some money . . ." and reached for his wallet.

"No, no," I told him. "You buy the beer. And the ice cream."

I WAS STILL on the tower crew. The wind was picking up at night now, and icy. The tower would shake in the wind, and I wondered how stable it was with all the trays taken out.

"It's like I'm illiterate in two languages," I complained, pulling a roast chicken dinner out at six-thirty in the morning. I had prepped everything the afternoon before and put it in the oven as soon as we were in, and by the time we'd showered and finished our first drink, it was ready. I'd set the table with place mats. Lorne carved, and I made gravy while the sun came up. "I mean I've never worked in a refinery before, so I don't know the drill, and I can't understand them anyway. I'm illiterate in refinery *and* French." Sandy's door flew open and she rushed out, in flannel pajamas and bathrobe, her eyes blackened with mascara, racing for the shower. She asked what time it was. Lorne looked at his big wristwatch and called that it was half past six.

"Oh my GAWD. I'm late." We heard the shower start. Moments later she dashed back into her room. She emerged in tight black jeans and a reflective parka, with her hard hat. I handed her a bag with a chicken sandwich and an apple in it. "Aw, man . . . thanks." she said. "You guys doing dinner? Cool . . . can you feed Buttercup?" Buttercup was the cat, a big, black, long-haired bruiser.

"It's Luc," I told Lorne. "He's the worst. He doesn't talk to me, so none of them do. And they all speak French all the time. I don't understand what's going on."

"Luc's all right," he said. "He'll come around. You just need a thick skin."

THAT NIGHT LORNE put me on the ground with a couple other guys, unloading trays from the crane basket, and setting aside the ones that needed repairs. I was glad to have a break from climbing, my arms and hips ached. Back at the house, I laid layers of roast chicken out on pieces of toast, and poured gravy over them. Lorne had never had an open-faced hot chicken sandwich. Sandy came in and started the coffee maker, poured herself a bowl of Cheerios.

"You guys want some candles?" she asked. "Soft music or something? Actually, that looks really good. Hey ... I got to show you this ... I did this to a cop at the bar the other night. Do you want to see my tattoo?" This was a time before everyone had tattoos. A woman with a tattoo was still a rarity. It turned out Sandy's "tattoo" was a joke, a good old-fashioned sight-gag. It was an old joke, too, but one we hadn't heard before, and after two beers and a chicken sandwich it was very funny.

"I gotta go," Sandy said. "You kids be good." We finally stopped laughing, but Lorne had a glint in his eye.

"What?" I asked.

"We should do that," he said, slowly. "We should do that to Luc. We should set him up."

Nothing happened that night.

"Well?" I asked, "Did you do it?" Lorne was setting the table.

"I didn't get a chance," he said. "We were never alone. And I couldn't just go up to him and tell him, it has to be the right moment."

"The right moment," I said, laughing. I was ladling scoops of beef bourguignon over a mound of mashed potatoes. I handed him his plate and he poured red wine into my glass. "This is a finely tuned operation. I'm glad to see you're taking it seriously."

"It has to seem natural," he said.

"Right," I said. "Because everything about this job is natural." We could hear Sandy's clock radio alarm go off. The morning paper thumped against the front door.

"I bought cake," Lorne said.

ON FRIDAY NIGHT Lorne sowed the seed, and on Saturday night I was back on the tower. I was standing at the railing, catching my breath, when Luc sidled over.

"So," he said, in heavily accented English, "you like this job?"

"I do," I said. "I like the travel, and I like the money." He nodded, sagely. He had dark eyes and nearly black hair, and was cultivating a pencil-thin moustache. Behind him, his brother Marc was standing over the job box, changing the wheel on a grinder and watching us out of the corner of his eye.

"Lorne's a good foreman," Luc said. "You stay in the same place?" I nodded.

"Yeah, it just worked out that way."

"He say you have a tattoo," he was matter of fact. I just smiled.

TWO WEEKS IN, the refinery decided to give half the crew a day off on Sunday. They were X-raying in some areas and moving cranes around in others. There was a possibility the tower jobs would be shut down for the night due to high winds. Even if we were allowed up, the cranes would be down for sure, so we couldn't make lifts. I decided to go exploring.

I drove the little rental car around the countryside, past Cheapside and Dog's Nest, past pretty farms that had their patriarchs' names painted on the barns. J. Pritt or John Peters and Sons. (*Where are the daughters,* I wondered?) I drove down to Peacock Point, took a walk in a park, and looked at the lake. I passed Smuck's Garage in Fisherville, and signs advertising the Bluewater Motel and Five Roses flour, and a diner that offered three eggs, three sausages, three pancakes, and a steak for seven dollars. A billboard encouraged me to "Play the Hiawatha Horse Park Jackpot," and I turned toward Cayuga. I needed to buy a coat.

There were nice shops, and I found a cozy coat and a pair of slippers, then went poking around a second-hand store, looking for anvils. It was run by a mother and daughter. For two weeks I hadn't spoken to anyone outside the Port Dover house, except the grocery store clerks and a bunch of French guys who wouldn't answer. I was craving conversation.

"Do you want to see the gallery?" the mother asked. "It's not open for an hour, but she will take you, show you." She elbowed her daughter. The daughter's name was Marie. She took me through the back room of the thrift store and unlocked the door that led to the storefront next door, and turned on the lights. The room was full of animals. Marie and her family were from El Salvador and Marie was a painter. She couldn't afford canvas, so she painted on anything she could find. Her main subjects were the animals from the farm where she had grown up. The first thing I saw was a larger-than-life-sized cow, painted on a wooden door. She was painted head-on, bearing down on us, one of her big knobbly knees raised in a step, her head turned slightly, she was eyeing us up with one big brown eye. Her hips jutted out behind her and her huge body rounded out on either side of her giant head. I loved that cow. Her sagging udder, the swish of her tail. There were two goats as well, each painted on half a door. There was a donkey, some ducks, and a pig. I told Marie that if I lived closer, and didn't have to take a plane to get home, I would definitely be leaving with that cow. Aside from a few tufts of grass at her feet, the cow painting had no background. No barn nor horizon, no pastoral scene nor trees or dog lying in the shade. These were portraits, pure and simple. Then Marie showed me the rooster, and it was mine.

When I got back to the house, Lorne had his feet up on the coffee table, was watching the news and drinking a beer.

"Wait until you see this," I told him, carefully peeling back the scotch tape on the brown wrapping paper. "You aren't even going to believe this." I spun the painting to face him, with a flourish.

"That," he said, "is quite a cock."

THE NEXT NIGHT I was still on the tower. Luc had started asking me about my tattoo. I had found ways to work into the crew, signalling the crane in, taking care of the landing, making sure there were enough buckets with ropes on them to hold all the hardware, tying everything off to the railings so nothing fell, organizing the job box, changing out halogen lights and redirecting electrical cords. I knew how to stay busy, and I knew how to be helpful, even though they were freezing me out of the real work. Over the next few days, Luc would pause on his way in or out of the manway, and ask about the tattoo. He wasn't exactly mean, just challenging, teasing me. Almost sneering. He made comments to the other guys about it, who laughed, and I could pick out a few words: *le tatouage. Une petite souris.*

Lorne was having a great time with it, downplaying it.

"Don't say anything to her," he would say, in French. "She's shy about it." Luc started winking at me.

"I can't take it much longer," I told Lorne, after two weeks. "It's starting to get silly."

"OK," he said. "Tonight's the night."

THE TEMPERATURE DROPPED suddenly. It was -15 Celsius. I rode in with Lorne because my car was encased in a carapace of ice. I couldn't open the door, couldn't even find the handle. He had a remote control and a block heater, could warm up his diesel while he was still in the house. It was going to get even colder over the night shift. We had switched from ten hour shifts to twelves, and everyone was worn out.

Lorne put me inside the tower, alone with Luc. We were in the bottom of the area we were working on, about a third of the way down the tower. Luc argued with him about it, in French.

"What about Marc?" he'd asked. He always worked with his brother. "What about Sebastian?"

"I need them on the other tower," Lorne said. "Don't argue, Luc."

WE WERE SITTING on our butts on the staging, our harnesses clipped off to rope lines that hung down the walls of the tower, welding on the last scallop bar ring clips. There were buckets of them. We worked mostly in silence; I was wearing a respirator and Luc was sulking because he had to work with me. He'd hold a clip to the wall.

"Tack it," he said. I tacked it. He held up another one. "Tack it." We worked this way for an hour. It was freezing inside. Everything went slowly because we both had on two pairs of gloves. After nearly two hours, Luc slumped back against the wall and lit a cigarette. I had a couple of small, square plates in my bucket, and welded stringers on one, heating it up. I held it between my hands to warm them. I offered him one, and he refused, but his hands were freezing.

"OK," he said, "gimme one." As steam rose off his gloves he said, "When are you gonna show me your tattoo?"

I ignored him. We welded on more clips.

It was more of the same after coffee, and after lunch, at midnight. Me tacking, then welding clips, Luc pestering me about the tattoo. We were all worn out. The climbing, the cold, the many, many long nights, the cramped space, the homesickness. The last part of the job was the most irritating, all the small things to be done, finishing the inspections and repairs, and welding on the "jewellery," everyone fatigued.

"Show me your tattoo," Luc said. Clearly his heart wasn't in it, he was tired too. I took the rod out of my stinger, and pulled down the mask of my respirator.

"You want to see my tattoo?" I asked, pretending to be annoyed. "Really? Really? Do you really want to see it?" He sat up straighter. "OK," I said. "Fine. I'll show you my tattoo."

Then, midway down, inside Reactor Tower Number 1, I performed a very strange, utilitarian striptease. First the welding helmet. Then the gloves. Then the fall arrest harness; the straps that go around the backs of the legs, and buckle in front, and the buckle across the chest. Free of the harness, I unzipped my oversized, company-issued, fire-retardant Nomex parka. I was slow, and there wasn't much room. Not enough to stand up under the trays, so I sat down on the grating and started to unzipper my coveralls.

"What is the tattoo?" he asked.

"It's a mouse," I told him. I unzippered down past my waist, then reached inside and started pulling up my sweater. I was wearing all of my clothes, according to the plan, in anticipation of this undressing. First, I pulled up one sweater, then another, then a thermal sweatshirt. Then I unbuttoned my jeans. I pulled down a layer of thick merino wool long johns, then a thinner layer, and finally a thin silk layer. Then back to the top, pulling up the front of one t-shirt, then another, then finally a thin undershirt, until I was nearly down to my skin. Luc stared in disbelief.

"How do you move in all those clothes?" he asked, shaking his head. I hooked my thumb over the elastic edge of my underpants and pulled them down on one side, exposing just the smallest area of skin on my hip.

"There," I said. "OK? You see it...?" Luc came closer, squinting in the dim light.

"No," he said. "I don't see it." I pulled the piles of clothes apart a tiny bit further.

"There," I said. "Right there. It's small — a tattoo of a little mouse." Luc leaned down a few inches away from my hip, squinting.

"I don't see nothing," he said. I sighed theatrically, exasperated.

"Well look again," I said. "It's right there. A mouse. And hurry up, I'm freezing." Like me, Luc wore prescription glasses, which were starting to fog up. He took them off and rubbed each of the lenses on his shirt sleeve, as though that would help. He pulled the flashlight off his belt, switching it on with a snap to see that much better, and looked again, peering into the mound of woolen clothes at the tiny patch of exposed skin.

"There's nothing!" he said. "I don't see nothing!"

"OK," I said, and snatched his flashlight from him. "I'll look." Which of course made no sense, but really nothing did. I bent over and peered at my own hip, then snapped my head up and locked eyes with him.

"Shoot," I said, "My pussy must've eaten it."

There was a long moment when he just stared at me, uncomprehending. Then the slow fog of confusion began to lift as he realized what had happened, and I started to laugh. He pulled back and leaned against the shell of the tower, his eyes widening. Suddenly his face transformed, and he started laughing too, silently at first. This made me laugh more, which caused him to laugh harder, until it seemed we would never be able to stop. The exhaustion, the climbing, the cold, the sleeplessness, all dissolved together in a fit of hysteria. We were both crying from laughing, clutching our sides.

"Stop..." I was saying, "stop..."

"You ..." he said, gasping. "You ... set me up?" I laughed harder. He suddenly let out a long, loud whoop, his voice echoing around the inside of the tower.

"You," he shouted, pointing at me, "you set me up… OH MY GOD!!" Someone's legs appeared coming down the ladder, it was Lorne. He squatted down, chuckling.

"And YOU," he said, pointing at Lorne. "You were in on it?" Lorne laughed harder.

"OH MY GOD, you guys SET ME UP…" He was shaking his head. "All those times? All those days? Oh my God…" He took off his glasses and wiped his eyes. I was trying to tuck the layers of shirts back into my coveralls and pull the zipper together. "Nobody EVER sets me up. Nobody."

We climbed up and out through the manway. Luc's brother Marc asked what all the yelling was about. Luc clapped his arm around my shoulders and answered, in English,

"She showed me her tattoo. You should see it, it's quite a mouse." Lorne grinned widely.

"Her mouse?" he said. "You should see her cock."

FOR THE REST of the job, we worked together harmoniously. My duties didn't change much, but I was included in the conversations, which were a mix of polite English and slangy Acadian French. Luc and I sat together on the job box on the last night, waiting for the crane to come and fly out the tools, the stars stretched faintly above us. He confided that he was very much in love with an aesthetician named Maya, and showed me her photograph. He intended to propose to her when he got home from the job, and he was afraid of what she might say. I told him he had nothing to worry about, that he was a good guy, with a big heart.

"Besides," I said, "if she didn't love you, she'd have already kicked you down the road." At the end of the job we all shook hands.

"You come to see us any time you're in Miramichi," he said. "We'll show you all the best things in New Brunswick."

LORNE AND I TOOK an extra day and night to get our schedules back to normal. He was going home to have some heart tests done, and his wife didn't want him driving at night. We decided to have a final dinner, with Sandy, at a regular time. As he said, six o'clock at night, not six in the morning. We mulled over a few ideas about what to have, but nothing felt quite right.

Do you like pancakes?" I finally asked.

"I love pancakes," Lorne smiled.

"Maybe Sandy has a waffle iron."

"I bet she does," Lorne said. "I'll get the beer."

FORT MCMURRAY

In the early 2000s, the retail side of Fort McMurray was run by children. The minimum age for working legally in Alberta had been reduced to thirteen years old, ostensibly for part-time jobs on weekends and after school. But kids who were eleven and twelve were lying about their age on application forms and cutting classes in grades five and six to pick up shifts. In many families, both parents worked in the oil sands, taking advantage of the boom, and would each be pulling in two grand a week, after taxes. Big money on the projects left a void in the retail sector, and businesses were offering top dollar to anyone who would put on a name tag. Minimum wage was $8.75 an hour, but McDonalds was paying $17. Footlocker was paying $21. So kids, little kids, would sign up to flip burgers and retrieve boxes of expensive shoes, and pull eight hundred dollars a week.

Finding someone to watch your kids while both parents worked twelve-hour shifts, for fourteen days in a row, was just about impossible. No one wanted a babysitter's wages, not even babysitters. So the kids got a credit card and a cell phone, a key to the house, and a threat that if they got into trouble they'd regret it. Nobody questioned the ages filled in, in childish printing on the application forms: the businesses needed workers. If the kids were working in a fast-food place, the parents at least knew where they were, that they were being fed, and there was probably someone over eighteen keeping an eye on them. Within a few years, the government recognized the shortage and expanded its temporary foreign worker program, bringing in people from overseas who would work retail for a lower wage. So eventually there was at least some adult supervision. Like everything else in the town, change was constant.

Fort McMurray was expanding at a breakneck pace. Whole suburbs were being constructed and occupied as fast as builders could build them, and huge new retail and commercial areas were spreading out from the centre. The multi-million-dollar Suncor Community Leisure Centre was nearing completion, and included courts, a running track, curling and skating rinks, an aquatic centre, climbing gym, and art gallery. North of all of this activity was the "Bridge To Nowhere," which both joined and separated the rapidly expanding city from the industrial sites that funded it.

On one side of the bridge was a city racing to keep up with itself, young families chasing opportunities for a promised "good life," and wanting to build a wholesome community where everyone had a new truck every year, went to Mexico in the winter, and the kids grew up playing hockey. On the other side of the bridge was a vast and sprawling mess of industrial oil refinery sites doggedly polluting the land, air, and water on a scale never before experienced on the planet. I wanted to go, to see it for myself, and take some pictures, naively thinking I could write about it, and expose the degradation. I went three times, and each time returned after a month or so, traumatized, bitter, and sick. The final stint involved a hospital visit, and I never went back.

By 2014, approximately 73,000 people lived in the urban service area of Fort McMurray, which is to say the city south of the river with the nice leisure centre, shopping malls, and rapidly expanding suburbs. An astonishing 40,000 people were classified as the non-permanent population living in project accommodations, which means the transient workers in the labour camps north of the river. These were two distinct populations: the happy growing families shopping at Superstore and going to swimming lessons, and the fly-in-fly-out workers who crossed the country to work new construction, upgrades, and maintenance shutdowns. They would work twenty-eight days in a row, fly home for a few days off, then do it again. I got the feeling that the wholesome family part of the city would prefer not to ever encounter, see, hear, or think about the transient-worker part. That fancy leisure centre was not for us to use. But it was difficult for a city to pretend that the oil sands workers didn't exist when there were so damned many. It was something between a poorly kept secret, and a big, messy, distasteful problem that the permanent residents wished would stay on the other side of the river.

There was friction between the two populations. Some residents viewed the fly-in-fly-out workers as a drain on civic resources, coming in to use city services like the roads and hospital, but not contributing to the economy. The temporary workers would take their fat paycheques and pay taxes in their home provinces. However, data shows that the workers from out of province actually spent between nine million and thirteen million dollars annually in the city — on food, clothing, electronics, vehicles, and entertainment. Entertainment would be restaurants and bars, the strip club, and the Boomtown Casino. In 2015, Alberta's revenue from gambling was just shy of two billion dollars.

Meanwhile, the transient workers saw themselves doing the city's dirty work, poisoning themselves as labourers and trades people, working in the trenches at the jobs the townies wouldn't take. The so-called shadow population kept the industry and economy going, paying for all those nice houses, hockey rinks, and swimming pools. Yet when they did go to town on a rare day off for a couple of hours at the blackjack table and a good steak, the reception wasn't always friendly. Talk in camp was often about whether or not the trade-off was worth it. Guys missed seeing their kids grow up, missed all the birthday parties, weddings, and barbecues. Sure, the money was good, and was welcomed back home, but you were treated like an animal, housed like an inmate, and always went home with a cough.

Of course, my sympathies lay with the temporary workers because, for a short time, I was among them. The first time I went was in 2004. I weld-tested in Edmonton at the Boilermakers' Union Hall. When I passed, I celebrated by going around the corner to the Salvation Army thrift store and buying two pairs of used corduroy work pants, for four dollars each. I boarded the Red Arrow bus for a six-hour ride north, to Fort McMurray. When I got there the bus depot was crammed with people coming and going, and I followed the crowd toward a street corner where a lineup stretched around the block. The shuttle came every hour, so I had time to haul my rolling suitcase and backpack into the Subway for a spongy sandwich and a tepid cup of coffee, before standing outside in the freezing wind. The shuttle was full, the windows fogged, and dusk was falling, so I didn't see much of the forty kilometres to Syncrude.

ONCE THERE, WE all lined up again, outside, a hundred or so workers waiting for beds. It was minus twenty-one degrees Celsius. At the counter, we were directed to stand in front of a white screen to have our photos taken, given a perfunctory run-down of the rules by a stout security guard, and handed a key on a lanyard to be worn around the neck. On the way out I was given a laminated ID card with my photo on it, looking bleary eyed and scared. I was told to put it on the lanyard with the key and keep it on at all times; you couldn't enter the worksite, or get into the canteen, or any of the common areas, without it. There were a few women in the camp then but not many. They housed us in a women-only bunkhouse at Mildred Lake, on the third floor. Most of the women in my building were bull cooks, the people who cleaned the rooms and common areas, and did the laundry.

The building was a series of portable, prefabricated trailer-like units stacked up three high, in rows. My room was eight feet by eleven, I measured it. There was brown wood panelling on the walls and one small beige curtain over the window. There was a tiny bed, slightly larger than a camp cot, with an itchy wool blanket and a thin, plaid bedspread, and faded yellow linoleum on the floor. There was a very small table in the corner beside the door, with a bare lightbulb over it, and a mirror and a towel rack, and a shelf and a soap dish bolted to the wall, but no soap in it, and no sink and no water. There was a wardrobe with a few wire hangers, and a couple of drawers. Down the hall were the floor bathrooms. One room housed a row of sinks, and a row of shower stalls. Next door was a row of toilet stalls. I slept with my flashlight under the pillow in case the power went out, and with my suitcase against the door.

It was a time when the work camps, as well as the town, were expanding so quickly the companies couldn't keep up with the demand for personnel. Temporary union cards, which quickly became permanent memberships, were being handed out in Alberta, no apprenticeship necessary. Companies were hiring whoever they could, just to get the bodies on site. Yes, people were needed to run the operations, but contractors were being paid per capita, so every worker represented a profit, even if they didn't do anything. Contractors also hoarded workers, hiring whoever they could get, with an eye to building a workforce for a project that might be coming up. *I've got 200 hundred men*, they'd say, when bidding for a contract, *right now, on site, ready to go. We can do that furnace tomorrow.* All of these people had to live somewhere.

When the camps were completely full, they would lay off half the housekeepers, to free up extra rooms, so the rooms were cleaned every other day instead of daily. Ditto the bathrooms. They ran out of blankets. They ran out of chairs. Some of the camps had jack-and-jill bathrooms, where one was shared between two camp rooms. This was a superior set-up to the institutional rows of showers down the hall, and these rooms were in high demand. When I was there, a story went around about a guy who was locked out of his bathroom by his neighbour for a long time, and complained to the security guard. When security went in, they found the worker dead, with a needle in his arm. They moved the body out around midnight, and by seven o'clock the next morning another guy was moving in.

My room at Mildred Lake faced the main Syncrude refinery. Since the 1970s when the plant and the camp were first constructed, the refinery had been expanding outwards every year, butting up to the work camp, then surrounding it. Out the small window I could see the parking lot, the chain-link fence, then refinery infrastructure — flare stacks, furnaces, hydrogen plants, towers, piping and tanks – all the way to the horizon. At night the room was still lit, from the huge sodium lights, but a woman I met in the bathroom offered to give me some tinfoil to cover it over. I was working nights so tinfoil was essential for daytime sleeping. On both shifts the constant rumble, occasional explosions, sirens, and garbled PA announcements prevented any serious sleep anyhow. The top floor, apparently, was one of the better bunkhouses to be in, since it didn't sit on the ground, where toxic sludge, sewage, and mould would accumulate under the buildings. Since it was mostly bull cooks and other permanent camp employees in my wing, they had a routine and stuck to the rules. They kept the common areas clean and didn't party, wore slippers in the hall, and were careful not to slam their doors. Three of the women I met had been there for several years, and had no other residences. Their rooms were full of plants, pictures of children and grandchildren, little shelving units with keepsakes and knick-knacks. They had made their own curtains, had rugs on the floor, and soft duvets on the narrow beds. One woman had a fifty-gallon aquarium in her tiny cell, with large, well-fed goldfish languidly swimming in circles.

It was the year Martha Stewart was sent to prison and I followed the story by reading the newspapers in the lunchroom or buying them at the commissary. I collected articles about her time in the federal jail in West Virginia, and how well she was adapting, collecting wild dandelion greens in the prison yard to add to salads. I taped her picture to the wall of my room: Martha leading a yoga class for the incarcerated. She and several inmates were lying on their backs, legs up the wall. For a short time, I thought of her as a kind of spiritual guide.

One thing camp is good for is developing a routine. Everything happens at the same time, day after day, and when all the other comforts are absent, you can lean into that predictability, one small part of a big machine. The canteen opens at 3:30 p.m. By 5:00 you'd better be on the bus, arriving at the gate at 5:30, for a 6:00 p.m. start. I used to head to the canteen early, before everyone had gone through the line and coughed on all the food. The kitchen and canteen were in a low-slung building on the outskirts of the residential blocks, and also housed a games room, and the commissary, which sold cigarettes, gum, chocolate bars, dirty magazines, potato chips, razors, toothbrushes, and towels. Anything you might need but forgot to bring. At the canteen IN door was a security guard who checked your ID and told you to take your hat off. My journal from February of 2004 said this:

The lineup stretches down the hall and nearly out the door and you wonder how many people have washed their hands as you pick up your tray and scan the array of leathery meats, lumpy chicken, soft, luminous vegetables, glutinous pastas, congealing sauces, thick white gravies, premixed potatoes as well as those in silver jackets, glistening hot dogs, sausages, sauerkraut and perogies, always perogies, even at breakfast. And you see your apprentice, that big stroppy Ukrainian kid happily ordering the Lebanese cook to load on more perogies, more sour cream, another whole plateful he sets down next to two steaks and three sausages and a huge cube of lasagna. He's twenty, good-natured, his head filled with cars and boobs and video games. He pours himself four glasses of Tang and two of milk from the machine and ploughs happily through the crowd to his friends. They use big spoons and forks and load in pork chops, bread, corn, shepherd's pie, jello, linguine, mac and cheese, fish sticks, chocolate cake, and argue about transmissions with their mouths full. A thousand guys more or less like this, eating, eating. They never get enough and they will never run out.

Video cameras in the corners take it all in and relay it back to central control. No one is worried about these guys — this is what they're supposed to do — they can't eat too much of this shiny free food. Fuel the machine. Fill it up and send it to sleep, then back to the cold and the mud in the morning, then throw money at it, girls on the weekends. Living the dream. It's the guys that don't eat at all that the cameras are worried about, the occasional wiry suspicious guys that frown and pick, push things around. Like the guy who won't eat pork, or the ones who don't eat anything from the steam table, or the ones who take soup and leave it there, or the ones who scrape the sauce off their cutlets and grimace at what's underneath, or only eat porridge in the mornings. (How the Ukrainian apprentice loves the mornings. He wakes up dreaming of bacon and sausages and steak and fried eggs, toast, pancakes, syrup, butter, cheese bread, and a plate of perogies). It's the ones who only eat from the salad bar, vegetarian discontents, obviously political, troublemakers, rabble-rousers. Or maybe they're sick and won't make it through the week. Threatening to take a leave, to go on compo, get cancer, drag up and go home. Or maybe they're drinking too much, can't keep anything down. These are the ones to worry about. The girls are bad too, fussy, complaining about the taste, the texture, the temperature, say it's fattening. Get out there and go to work, girl, forget the taste, at least there's plenty of it. Millions of people in the world would be happy to have one shot at that steam table, one chance at the wall of desserts where you can take as many pieces of pie as you want. Hell, the boilermakers shut Kitimat down one year because there was no pie in the canteen. Learn the way things work. Get your priorities straight.

THEY CALLED THE bus the "petri dish." There were actually many buses, lined up one after another, all of them full, orange school buses scaled for little children, not oil field workers in oversized winter coats and boots. They drove in a big, complicated loop around the plant, up to the axles in slush and mud, disgorging workers at various locations. By February everyone was sick, and it was a sickness that was hard to shake. The buses were wracked with coughs, nose-blowing, sneezing, and throat clearing. Anyone who wasn't sick pulled their balaclava up over their face. I zippered my parka up over that, as well, but it didn't make any difference. We were all in the same lunchrooms, the same buses, the same trailers. Once it started going around, everyone got it. It was called the "Syncrude flu." By the end of week two, I was part of the problem.

THAT FIRST TRIP, I never did any welding. They were overmanned, hiding people all over the plant, and even though we weren't needed they wouldn't let us go because there was a big furnace coming up and they wanted us there to work on it, not going off to some other site. As a travel card, I was an unknown commodity, just a body. Four of us were each given a bucket of studs — six-inch-long bolts used to bolt up manways and channel heads. Also, wire brushes and bottles of Never Seize. Our job was to brush the dirt and debris off the threads of the studs, paint them with Never Seize, find a nut and some washers the right size and thread them on, making sure it wasn't damaged or cross-threaded. When the studs were prepped they went into another bucket. It was cold, wet, boring work. All over the site they had set up small tents: structures made of scaffold, and covered in a heavy, white, tarpaulin-like material. It looked like plastic but everything had to be fireproof. These little tents had metal scaffold planks inside set up as benches, so you could sit in there and work, or just warm up. At night the temperature would drop to minus thirty Celsius.

I did that for two weeks, with an apprentice from Edmonton and two Newfie guys. When we ran out of studs to clean, the foreman told us to disappear. We'd split up into pairs, and wander the site, ducking into tents whenever we could find one with a heater. Often they were full — of all the other workers who were also hiding. The trick was not to stay in any one place too long. If a tent had too many people in it, or guys were making cots out of the planks and sleeping on them, the supervisors would bang on the walls and tell us to get moving, like rousting a band of vagabonds out of a doorway.

I had a favourite dark corner next to a hydrogen furnace that had a live steam pipe I could snuggle up with. I would lean my back against it, or lie on top of it, or wrap my arms around it, to stay warm. Sometimes, to pass the time, I would sing, trying to remember all the words to a John Prine song.

Please don't bury me, down in the cold, cold ground

Just a lonely tar sands worker, curled up singing to a steam pipe, in the middle of night.

I'd rather have them cut me up, and pass me all around

Every two hours we would troop back through a foot of muddy snow to a designated lunchroom for a coffee break, then it was back into the plant, where it was usually snowing and always windy. After five weeks of playing the industrial version of hide-and-seek, the temperature dropped again to twenty-eight below, and I asked for a lay-off.

THE NEXT YEAR I was compelled to go back. I thought I must have made a mistake, or exaggerated the brutality and loneliness of my time there, that it couldn't possibly have been as miserable as I remembered. It may have been, but I wanted to make sure, like returning to a toxic relationship because you don't remember exactly what was so lacerating. This time I flew to Edmonton, passed my weld test, and flew to

Fort McMurray. A six-hour bus ride was condensed into a forty-minute flight, the experience much improved already. This gain, however, was quickly lost when my shuttle pulled into camp. I was assigned to Millennium Lodge, one of the oldest and worst of the work camps, and there was no record at the camp that I was checking in.

"Come back in the morning," the security guard said.

"And tonight?" I asked. She shrugged. I asked politely if she would check the ledger again, suggested maybe they had spelled my name wrong, asked her to try under the contractor's name. It was known that if you were ever rude to the security personnel, swore, or raised your voice, they would kick you out of camp, and you would be banned. Which is fair enough. It was also known that they would sometimes book more people in than there were rooms, because there were inevitably no-shows: the guy who got drunk and missed his flight, or the one who'd just had enough and decided to stay home. By overbooking the camp they ensured the rooms were always full. It was also known that in this situation, where there were more workers than rooms, the desk clerk would try to provoke a fight, because if they could get you to lose your temper, they could kick you out, solving the problem of not enough rooms. It was a long conversation. I refused to move from the desk. I had nowhere to go. The last shuttle had left and there was no way back to town, and even if I could get there, there were no rooms to be had. I also knew it was highly unlikely the women's bunkhouses were full. Eventually, she got on her handheld radio, called the nightshift bull cook, and asked her to go and make up a room in one of the women's trailers. The next day I learned that it was the second women's bunkhouse, and was only half full. They wanted to turn it into a men's accommodation in order to use all the rooms, so they were trying to get rid of the women. The security guard eventually gave me a key on a lanyard. I found my room, dropped my stuff, and returned to the office, where a dozen or so guys were still lined up to check in.

"Can I have a blanket?" I asked the desk clerk.

"You don't need one," she said.

"Pardon?"

"You've got a sleeping bag. I saw it on your backpack. You don't need a blanket." The guy behind me poked my arm.

"What'd she say?" he asked, with a Newfoundland accent.

"She said I can't have a blanket because I brought my own sleeping bag."

"Come on," the guy said. "Give the girl a blanket."

"What's that then?" The question went down the line, until all the guys had heard that they wouldn't issue me one of the itchy, thin, grey wool blankets that everyone got on their bed, because I had brought a sleeping bag. Irate, they started shouting from behind me.

"What? No blanket?" "Come ON!" "Give the girl a blanket!" "Girl needs a blanket!" They weren't really fighting for me. It was understood among the group that camp conditions were already so bleak, so minimal, that if they were allowed to slip any further, the situation would be dire.

MILLENNIUM WAS THE camp that Alberta members refused to stay at. The heating and ventilation systems were rumoured to be full of black mould, and people who stayed there became sick much faster than residents at other camps, and took months to recover. It was a series of about fifty single-story, smelly ATCO trailers, with drafty windows and walls so thin you could hear your neighbour breathing. In the women's bunkhouse all the different trades were in together, and a young painter was my neighbour. Every night I was privy to the long cell phone conversations she would have with her boyfriend. We had cell phones by then, though they didn't work everywhere. Mine was a red Blackberry with a roller ball that you moved around with your thumb, and even held contact addresses and had an early version of Tetris on it. One afternoon during that first week, I cut through one of the men's bunkhouses on my way to the canteen, and could hear music. I followed it; It was coming from one of the tiny, mouldy camp rooms. Someone was playing Bach on the violin.

FOUR DAYS INTO the new year we were strung out in rows, doing army calisthenics under the jib of the Mammoet. That's the five-hundred-ton crane. It was red and had a stylized picture of a wooly mammoth on the side. I had the same drawing on a sticker on my hard hat. We called the crane by its trade name to distinguish it from the smaller one, the blue one called Bertha. There were around sixty of us gathered in the yard, arm's length apart, and Duk Sun stood at the front facing the group, holding his right arm out in front, flexing his wrists up, then down, pulling his fingers back with his other hand. Someone in the crowd counted to ten and we switched hands. At ten we switched back again. Duk yelled something no one could hear and took a wide stance. He held his right hand high over his head and bent forward, touching it to the toe of his left boot. He wore blue woolen glove liners and a fireproof toque under his hard hat. He'd taken off his standard issue Novex parka and wore a thick blue fleece zippered up over a turtle-neck sweater. We all bent forward, trying to keep up with him. Duk was sixty-six years old.

After twenty toe-touches on each side, he started a series of brisk jumping jacks. It was still too early in the day for the ground to be mushy, but the sanding truck had been by and the fine greenish yellow sand was being churned into the new snow. We were all in insulated Novex coveralls and parkas, knee-high, steel-toed rubber boots, two or three pairs of gloves, and an assortment of fire-proof head and neck accessories that exposed various areas of skin to a whipping -35 Celsius wind chill. We could barely make it up the stairwells and ladders to our jobs. Jumping jacks were ludicrous. It was my favourite part of the day, the fifteen minutes of vigorous exercise we were allowed at the beginning of the shift to warm up. Duk led the warm-up because he believed in fitness and discipline, and he thought it prevented injuries. He had learned the routine in the military, in South Korea. He worked in the rod shack on that job, and was a bright light for me, cheerful, encouraging, and kind.

I worked way out in the laydown yard on that job, in a fabricating tent, with one other guy from BC. He had liver disease and was determined to die on the job so his daughter could collect a larger settlement, but I was just as determined to keep him alive, at least for a while. He was a cranky, cantankerous, mean-spirited bully, and we grew to quite like each other, after being isolated in the laydown yard together for a month. We drank coffee and listened to the radio, and built brackets and braces and other parts that were needed. For a while I was fixing stainless trays that came out of one of the towers, TIG welding cracks. He slept a lot, and when he woke up, I made him eat oranges.

The job was OK, but the camp was not getting any better. I used to stand on the porch at the end of the trailer and watch the ravens, huge compared to their coastal cousins. There was one that flew down every day, tall as a German shepherd, with a beak as long as a thumb. He would raid the kitchen dumpster, pulling out scraps and spreading them over the snow. He would take anything he could find, except olives. He left the olives. I realized that aside from the raven, I hadn't seen an animal, or even a tree or a blade of grass, for close to a month. Every day I put in a request to be moved to Borealis, the work camp next door. This was the fancy transient worker accommodation, modelled after an American prison. We had been going over there to eat in their dining hall for our meals, because the canteen at Millennium had burned down. So we hiked through the snow and bad weather for about twenty minutes to get a cup of coffee. Two weeks in, I was ready to quit when they informed me, I was getting my move.

Borealis really was based on a design by a famous American prison designer. Prisons are big business in the US, and a lot of them looked like this: a kind of central hub, with secure little pod rooms around it, shared bathrooms, and a recreation area. It was telling that workers were scrambling to get into a facility that was originally designed as a prison, that we were considered the lucky ones. I lasted two more weeks there, but was already sick, and when they started asking who wanted a lay-off, I volunteered, along with just about everyone else.

I'M GLAD I did my stints in Fort McMurray before the bedbug infestations, apparently that's a problem now. I also missed the meth epidemic by a few years, the drug of choice was still cocaine. Weed was for lightweights and hippies, but there were more practical reasons it was unpopular. The active ingredient they drug-tested for stayed in your system too long, so if you smoked a lot of pot you had a hard time passing a urine test unless you were clean for at least two weeks. Coke, on the other hand, cleared your bloodstream in two days. If you could abstain for forty-eight hours, you could pass a piss test. Pot was smelly, took up too much space, and they were bound to find your stash when they brought the sniffer dogs through. You'd get back from your shift to find your bags packed and waiting at the front desk, and some other guy moving into your room. A slip of coke, however, could be easily taken with you on to site, in the lining of a lunch bag, or anywhere. And you never knew when you might need it. A taxi driver told me that several million dollars' worth of cocaine moved through the city each month, and it was easier to get than a pack of cigarettes, because you could have it delivered in camp. The supply was controlled by a couple of different crime groups, and customers who didn't pay were dealt with swiftly and without mercy. People disappeared, tossed off the Bridge To Nowhere in the middle of the night and swept down the Athabasca River. It was a compelling reason to pay your debts. And if you were making three grand a week, you could afford it. Until you couldn't. Workers who fell behind would hand their paycheques over directly to their dealers on payday, until their life consisted of two things: work and coke. But later on, apparently, meth took things to a whole new level, that I could only imagine.

The third, and final time I travelled to Fort McMurray, I was working for a BC boilermaker company, TIG welding stainless-steel pipe, and Loverboy was on the plane. The band was on their way to play a show at the Boomtown Casino. The airline had left my suitcase behind in Edmonton because their drum kit and keyboard took up too much cargo space. I was standing at the customer service counter, arguing with the Air Canada employee. Did he really think it was fair that I should be missing my suitcase because some superannuated top 40 band was now playing the casino circuit?

"Hey, don't feel bad," Mike Reno said from behind me in the lineup. He was well past the red-leather-pants stage of his career, and carrying an orthopaedic back cushion. "They lost some of our stuff too."

THIS TIME THE camp was Noralta. It was one of the new, fancy camps, built in an attempt to attract workers who were fed up with "the life." There was a foyer with wooden shelves where you left your boots and switched to slippers, and long carpeted hallways. The rooms were larger, had tall double beds with nice duvets, and big drawers underneath them to store things. Each room had its own private bathroom, like a hotel, and even a little TV. It was nice. It smelled like off-gassing plastic instead of hydrocarbons, but I was still glad I travelled with a vanilla scented candle.

It was a new construction job, and a mess from the beginning.

There was a lot of set-up for the first two weeks, it was night shift, twenty-five below, and a series of winter storms were blowing through, banking snow up against all of the work areas. Eventually, they set up a piping system outside, laying it out in position, on pipe stands. There was a series of nine-inch, heavy wall stainless-steel pipe joints to weld. They set up hoarding around the first joint, but there was no way to control the draft whipping through. Different welders kept trying to make the joint, unsuccessfully, and would be fired when they failed the X-ray. I was the least experienced, and therefore the last welder they were going to try on the joint. When it was my turn, I refused to weld it because they couldn't control the draft and I knew it would be full of porosity. The foreman was running out of welders. He had two superstars on their way, but they hadn't arrived yet. Annoyed, he set his crew to trying to control the wind. I walked to the edge of the work site to look at the mountainside in the distance. Sometimes the side of the hill would catch fire, a spark lighting up the bitumen that had been raked to the surface, and an eerie glow would spread over the ground. Three thin, black wolves were slinking down toward the river. I was getting sicker every day, and decided that the next day I would go into town to the hospital.

I took a cab, for seventy-five dollars. The hospital waiting room was full of people, standing against the wall, or sitting on orange molded plastic chairs that were bolted to the floor. Everyone was coughing. I took a number, like I was waiting to be served at a pizza joint, was admitted, and given a plastic bracelet. There was a young couple with a pale baby, and a snotty toddler piling up blocks on the floor. There was an old man staring straight ahead, and two teenaged girls flipping through magazines. The rest were men from the camps, trying to get some antibiotics and something so they could sleep, breathe, and keep working.

Eventually I was sent to a hallway that had been turned into an examination area by the addition of a chair and a curtain. An unnervingly handsome doctor came in carrying a stool, sat down and listened to my chest. He said,

"Congratulations, you have the Syncrude flu. Otherwise known as an upper respiratory infection." He started writing on a pad of paper. "You will take three of these — not two — every four hours with food. Understand? Are you in camp?" I nodded. "Do not return to work for at least forty-eight hours. If you can get a medical lay-off, take it. Go home and get a chest X-ray. If you need a doctor's note, see the front desk, it'll be sixty dollars, cash. Good luck." He tore off the sheet and handed it to me, picked up his stool and pulled back the screen. "Who's next?"

At the front desk I handed the nurse three twenty-dollar bills, which she flattened on the counter and put in an envelope. She sealed it and wrote "Jim" on the outside and put it in a drawer. She took out a photocopy of a pre-prepared doctor's note indicating a respiratory infection, stamped it with a rubber stamp of a signature and slid it across the counter. It was still standing room only in the emergency room.

"It seems like there's something going around," I said.

"There's always something going around," the nurse answered.

BACK AT CAMP, I called the site office to ask my foreman for a medical lay-off, and was denied.

"I'm wearing a HOSPITAL bracelet," I said. "I just came from the HOSPITAL."

"We aren't laying off any welders," he answered. "You're going to have to quit."

So I quit.

THE SNOW BLEW around the parking lot at the 7-Eleven, in little whirlwinds, so that sometimes it seemed to be falling up. They had told us in safety orientation to never go to town to cash a paycheque on a Thursday, and never go to the ATM alone, because Thursdays were payday and you were sure to be mugged. I was laid off on a Thursday, and the parking lot was full of activity. A woman wearing flannel pajama pants, a tank top, and a down jacket was struggling to push a baby stroller through the dirty snow, yelling at a man who seemed to be her dealer.

"I'm getting the money tomorrow!" she was shouting, "I'll pay you TOMORROW…" The stroller high-centred on a ridge of ice in the turning lane, and the woman abandoned it to run after the man, who was about to get into a car. A young guy picked up the stroller and lifted it on to the sidewalk.

"Hey lady…" he called after her. "Your baby?"

I HAD JUST come out of the movie theatre, where I'd watched a remake of The Pink Panther, with Steve Martin. I'd had six hours to kill before my flight left, and the camp staff told me I couldn't wait there, so I took a cab to town and went to the movies, my backpack and suitcase piled up on the seat beside me. I was standing in the theatre lobby, waiting for yet another cab to take me to the airport, eating cough candies and watching the scene outside. Inside, the theatre appeared to be run by two twelve-year-old girls, one of whom had forgotten to direct the popcorn hopper into the machine, so it was spraying popcorn into the air, and onto the floor. This seemed to be an ongoing issue, as the girls were walking around behind the counter, wading through about a foot of popcorn.

"Heyyyy… Crystal…" one of the girls was saying to the other, "didn't I saaay… put the popcorn thingy into the bin?" Crystal shrugged.

"Whatever," she said. My cab pulled up to the curb outside, and I headed for the door.

THE LAKES

It was the middle of the spring thaw when I set up the butane stove on the tailgate of my car in the parking lot of the Travelodge in Stony Plain. A few boilermakers from BC were staying there, and when the snow started melting they would barbecue in the back lot, icy water running over their boots. We sat in lawn chairs and wore sunglasses with our down parkas. In front of each parking space there was a post about three feet high. Being from the Coast, I didn't know they were 110-volt outlets for plugging in the block heaters on vehicles during freezing weather. But they worked just as well for appliances. I had a rice cooker and an electric wok, and someone else started making pina coladas with an electric blender.

I HAD STOPPED travelling to Fort McMurray, but worked in other places in Alberta once or twice a year. In 2005, I drove to Grand Prairie in the dead of winter for the new recovery boiler build at the pulp mill. Housing was at a premium, and I rented a room in the downstairs of a house at the edge of town, sharing with a woman who sold giant truck tires. It was nice to have a roommate, someone to argue over what to watch on TV. For the first night shift I sat in the lunchroom the whole time. Supervisors walked through once in a while, looking for someone, but ignored me. I sat and read a newspaper.

On the second day, I could hear the general foreman outside the trailer.

"Where the fuck is that TIG welder?" he was yelling at someone. "He's two days late for fuck's sake." He pulled open the door and strode into the trailer. "Have you seen anyone else?" he asked. I shook my head.

"Nope. But I'm here and signed up. I'm ready to work." I gave him a winning smile.

"Do you know how to make coffee?" he asked. I nodded. "Go make coffee," he said, and slammed out. Go. Make. Coffee. Well, OK then. It was Friday and twenty-five below outside, but quite toasty in the trailer. I made coffee that night, and all night Saturday, and all night Sunday. Two shifts of double time.

On Monday, I had just filled the giant coffee urn from one of the water jugs, and was putting it back together, when Dale, a guy I knew from BC, came in. The contractor worked across Western Canada, and Dale was one of their welding inspectors.

"Hey," he said, shaking my hand. "It's great to see you. We need good welders. But what the hell are you doing in here?" I indicated the coffee table, which was tidy, and well stocked with cups and stir sticks.

"I am making coffee," I said, "like I was told to."

"Like hell you are," he said. "Get your log book." Dale marched me over to the office.

"Here's that TIG welder you've been looking for, for the last three days," he told the general foreman. "She was making coffee in the lunch trailer. For ninety dollars an hour. What the hell's wrong with you people, don't you read the crew list?" The GF gave me a long, stony stare, and I stared back. It was not a great start. That job was basically an endurance test. When the temperature dropped to -25 Celsius, the main cable for the outside construction elevator wouldn't coil properly, so we climbed up ten storeys of stairs to the penthouse after every break. By the time we got up there, it was just about time to climb down again.

Later, I worked at Alpac, in Athabasca, where one of the apprentices taught me about a function on my phone called Google Maps, and boy howdy, was that a game changer, in terms of driving all over the country. No more crumpled paper maps on the seat beside me. Mostly though, when I crossed the Rockies, I worked The Lakes.

The Lakes is the region west of Edmonton where the seven coal-fired electric power stations were located. From 2011 to 2013 they were rebuilding several of these plants, were short of labour, and were paying travel money, which was unusual. I worked at three of them: Keephills, Sundance, and Genesee. The hotel in Stony Plain was sixty kilometers from the worksites, which made for a long commute. It was also very expensive, and I started looking for an alternative. The best bet seemed like a bed and breakfast in Wabamun, thirty-five kilometres closer to the plant, so I set up there. I had the main floor of the house, with a claw-foot bathtub, a kitchen, and a screened-in porch that overlooked the lake. The owner was a likeable, no-nonsense gal who was raising her granddaughter. They lived downstairs.

These jobs were better than working in Fort McMurray. I wasn't living in camp, and had my own car to get around. Most of the Alberta members lived in the area and worked that circuit every year, so I got to know some of them. The job sites were still impersonal, but a few friendly faces at the lunch table made a big difference.

By the time I started at The Lakes I had been working in BC for around fifteen years, and any sensitivities or fragile aspects of the self were either long gone or well buried. *Be careful*, the guys would say to each other, *you might hurt my feeling… and it's the only one I have left.* We worked in a physically toxic environment, with chemical exposures, extreme temperatures and loud noise, at dangerous heights, in confined spaces, over long hours. Complaining was not helpful or tolerated. There was a group pride around working in these conditions. Boilermakers are tough. You learn not to show weakness, and if you do, you are open to a wide assortment of abuses. The motto for the BC local, was *Don't bleed in a pool of sharks.* As dysfunctional as this culture was from a human perspective, it was an excellent training in thickening the skin. I no longer had any patience with people who tried to intimidate me, and for better or worse, was basically fearless. This is not necessarily a healthy place to be, and I have since learned that it is a quality shared by the incarcerated, the abused, the traumatized, and those of us who are becoming slightly unhinged.

Nevertheless, I was intrigued when one of the guys from Alberta told me not to go to the tool crib alone, because the guy handing out tools was "a bit weird."

"What are you telling her for?" one of my colleagues from BC asked. "You should be warning *him* about *her*." The guy was a bit weird, and often said inappropriate things when I went to get tools, but there were usually other people around, so it wasn't too bad. For the first couple of weeks I ignored him. When I finally did have to pick something up at the crib while I was alone, the guy became much creepier. He said something lewd, asked me where I was staying, and leered at me over the counter.

"You know," he said, "there's a way that you could save a lot of money. You could come and stay with me in my motorhome." He dropped his voice. "You could be my girlfriend."

"Yeah?" I asked. I looked at him for a long time then leaned against the counter toward him. "But if I was your girlfriend," I said, breathily, "you'd never get any sleep." He smiled uncertainly.

"No?" he asked. "And why's that?"

"Because," I hissed, "You'd be worried, that I was going to stab you in your sleep, cut out your liver, and make necklaces out of your teeth." The guy leapt backward, and I exited. Later that night, a foreman came by our table in the lunchroom, and pointed at me.

"I've had a complaint about you," he said. "Our tool crib attendant says that you threatened him. Did you threaten him?"

"Yes," I said.

"What did you say?" he asked.

"I said that, given the opportunity, I would stab him in his sleep and make necklaces out of his teeth," I answered.

"Did you?" he asked. "Well, good for you. Carry on."

THE DECADES-LONG shortage of skilled workers in Alberta had opened up room for women in the trades in ways that diversity initiatives and inclusion campaigns never had. There were a lot more women than in BC. My first time at The Lakes there was a fight in the lunchroom because one gal refused to work for another, who was assigned as her foreman, because they had some bad history. But I found it kind of thrilling to be in a place where there were actually enough women on the job to have a cat fight. At Keephills, I was partnered with a woman who was older and tougher than me, and into motorcycles, sex, hard drugs and booze. She lived completely outside my world, and by comparison, I was a nebbish, wide-eyed girl with thick-framed glasses, who brought healthy lunches. We were each other's opposite. Every encounter felt a little dangerous, but I couldn't help provoking her.

"Would you like a vitamin?" I'd ask, shaking the bottle, when she had a particularly nauseating hangover. "They're for ladies over forty."

"Fuck you," she'd say.

ONE EVENING I was late after speeding back from a dental appointment in Edmonton and had been pulled over by the police. The policeman ran my license, and seeing that I had a clean record, let me off with a warning. My work partner had had many less benign run-ins with the cops.

"First of all," she said, "who the fuck goes to the dentist when they're travel carding?"

"Dental hygiene is very important," I said.

"And second ... why the fuck would the cop let you off? You just flash them big titties of yours at him and he let you go?"

I nodded. "Yup, pretty much."

"So, what was your plan B?" she asked. "You start crying?"

"I don't know," I said. "I've never needed a plan B." She shook her head.

"Sometimes ... I don't know whether to punch you in the face, or hug you."

"Given the choice" I said, "I think I'd rather you hit me."

ANOTHER WOMAN I worked with at The Lakes was Annette. She was tall and blond and loved to chatter and have a good time. On that job, there was a group of Americans who had come up as travel cards. They were excellent pressure welders and were doing a great job, but the locals were not overly friendly toward them because they were from the USA. In fact, no one from the area would sit at their lunch table. At coffee and lunch breaks they had a card game going, playing poker for quarters. Annette was intrigued, and finally strode up to the table and asked if we could play.

"Well, sure," the guy called Bobby told her. "Just show up tomorrow with a roll of quarters."

The next day Annette had two rolls of quarters, one for her and one for me. It was a raucous, fast-paced game, and everyone would shout when the winning hand was thrown down. Annette didn't know how to play poker and spent the first couple of days trying to figure out the rules. She lost her first roll of quarters, and so did I, then I brought in two more. Even losing, it was a fun diversion, and the guys were great sports for letting us in on their game. Once in a while I'd have a good hand and replenish my pile of coins, but mostly they kept dwindling away. Annette, however, started to win. She won, and won, and when it seemed impossible, she'd bluff and win some more. She'd just shrug and claim beginner's luck. When my small stacks of quarters were gone, she'd divide a section off her huge pile of coins and slide it over to me. The Americans were baffled. She made such crazy, unpredictable moves they couldn't believe she was hustling them. Every lunch hour a crowd would gather around the table to watch the action. Different Alberta guys sat in on the game, to try to beat her, and harangued her for her unconventional play.

"That's not how you do it," one guy complained. "You can't do that ... if you've got a queen you play the queen..."

"Is that in the rules?" Annette would ask. "'Cause if it's not in the rules, I don't have to do it."

"But no one would do that ... how can we play if we don't know what you're gonna do?"

"I guess that's why they call it poker," Annette would say, smiling. She never did run out of luck and took everyone's quarters until the end of the job. By then, most of the crew was convinced she was hustling them, but she swore to me she really didn't know how to play, and just put down whatever card she felt like when it was her turn.

MY LAST TRIP out to The Lakes, I was introduced to the TIG welding foreman, Tim, as one of the experienced welders. Which just meant that someone knew me, and I could do my job. One of the rookie mistakes welders make is to brag about their abilities. Which is silly, because as soon as you think you've mastered something, welding teaches you that you haven't. Another, related rookie mistake, is to pretend you're so good that you never get repairs, because everyone gets repairs. The goal is to know how to fix them.

"YOU," Tim said, pointing. "Are you a TIG welder?"

"Yes," I said.

"ARE YOU ANY GOOD?" he asked.

"Yes."

"HOW MANY REPAIRS HAVE YOU HAD?" He was shouting, getting in my face, like a drill sergeant.

"In my whole career?" I asked, calmly. "I don't know ... forty? A hundred? I lost count around 2004."

"OK," he said, smiling, "you're a TIG welder. You're with me."

I WAS PAIRED with a large, red-faced Alberta boy who thought very highly of himself. He carefully explained how we were going to weld the joint, then said that he knew the heat he used to weld his side would be too much for me, but he would turn it down when it was my turn. When it was my turn, I had him turn the heat up, then up again, and put my root and hot pass in, in one pass. It was a show-off move that could have gone wrong, but it didn't, because one of the 359 brothers had taught me how to do it in Prince George.

"You don't want to dog-leg this thing" my partner said, realizing I had gotten ahead of him in the sequence.

"Hurry up," I said. "Let's go." On the next joint he dropped a grape in the tube, and had to stop to fix it. He lost control of the puddle, and a big gob of molten metal fell down inside. A grape is Karma. The third joint was welding a pup to a tube on a pipe stand, to extend the length. I said I was going downstairs to sharpen my bullets.

"But you're going to weld this joint," he said, "to practice." There were two fitters working with us as well, and his idea was that the three of them would stand around and watch me, trying to rattle me, as though I was auditioning.

"Why can't you do it?" I asked.

"Because I don't need to." He smirked.

"Really?" I asked. "You're the guy who dropped the grape. You can do the bench weld." And I left him to it.

THE ROAD FROM Wabumun to the power plant crosses Range Road 42 and runs through the Paul First Nation Reserve, before hitting Road 627.

"Make sure you don't hit a horse," Tim told me, one early morning after work.

"What?"

"Make sure you don't hit a horse. There are horses everywhere around here, and a lot of them loose on that road. You can get a ten thousand dollar fine and go to jail if you hit a horse on reserve land. So be careful. Watch for horses."

"I will," I said. "I don't want to hit a horse."

"Nobody wants to hit a horse."

I was stopped by animals many times, between the power station and the house. There was a beaver slowly lumbering across the road at the railway tracks, a couple of highland cattle who came looming out of the fog one night, a herd of sheep, a goat, a thin dog that I tried to coax into my car. One morning, driving back at dawn, the truck coming toward me slowed to a stop and flashed his lights. I stopped as well, and we both turned down our headlights. Dawn was breaking, and there was a low mist hanging over the country road. We waited for nearly twenty minutes while two porcupines engaged in a careful courtship ritual in the middle of the road.

Nobody wants to hit a horse. I thought about that a lot, about all the navigating that every one of us had to do, trying to find our way through tricky situations. Trying to survive. Trying to succeed. Trying to relax. Trying to get from point A to point B, and just when you start to believe you are going to make it, suddenly there are wild horses all over the road, and you have to drive through the fog trying not to hit one. I felt like that on almost every day of my career. Then very early one morning, just before dawn, just before the hour when porcupines make love, there they were. Horses. All along the grassy strip between Range Road 42 and the railway tracks. There were twenty or thirty of them, spread out for about a mile. No halters, no shoes. Muddy, their manes tangled, their eyes brightly lit with a wild look, wary, looming out of the dark, into the headlights.

NOVA SCOTIA

Each day, the union posts a list of available jobs online, and at nine in the morning, the dispatcher starts calling the out-of-work list to fill them.

"Do you want to go to Castlegar?" he'd ask. "I only have nights. Stainless welder." Or, "I've got Crofton or Kamloops. Your choice. Or if there were a lot of different jobs on the board, he'd say "See anything you like?"

Different jobs were attractive for different reasons. Longer jobs were usually preferred. Closer to home was better. There was more travel money if you went up north. Quesnel was not so good because the mill didn't like to work weekends, so there was no double time on a shut down. Camp jobs like MacKenzie and Port Mellon were a last resort. At the end of the online dispatch list, there were sometimes notes on out of province work. In November of 2017, the note said: "Any members interested in working in Nova Scotia call Mitch at Local 73." I tossed the idea around with a few pals from the local, trying to get someone to go with me so I'd have a partner. But it was too far, wouldn't pay enough, and there was other work coming up. Nova Scotia is a hard sell in November.

The map online showed the mill was in Pictou, and I started calling places to stay within a fifty-kilometre radius. Within a couple hours I got a call back from the Green Dragon Organic Farm and B&B, in Tatamagouche. This looked like a great antidote to the noisy, industrial workday — a pastoral Nova Scotia farmhouse that promised a room where the bedding was made of organic cotton fibres and the pillow was filled with flax seeds. Stephan, the owner, had a serious, deliberate demeanour that had me babbling nervously. I finally blurted out that I was looking for a longer-term rental than a regular B&B stay, closer to five weeks, and could we negotiate a weekly rate?

"We can do that," he said. I wanted to make my own meals, I told him, would need some shelf space in the fridge, and my own bathroom.

"We can do that," he said.

THE OVERNIGHT FLIGHT to Halifax leaves Vancouver at 7:00 p.m. and lands just before six in the morning. I took it so I wouldn't have to pay for a hotel when I got there, but could drive straight to the B&B. Not much is open that early in Halifax. The car rental outfit was a ways from the airport, so I took a cab there and spent an hour kicking around the frosty dawn in a seedy industrial area, with my suitcase, yawning, having spent the night watching movies on the plane.

I had found a great deal online, and for the same price as the usual little econo-car, was handed the key to a big, black Ford pickup truck. The high-tech controls were a bit of a challenge. My Honda was fifteen years old and had 340,000 boilermaker kilometres on it, so we were old friends, but this truck had something called Bluetooth and a back-up camera. I negotiated carefully out of downtown, and hit an exit to Highway 102, north toward Truro. The truck had some kind of turbo charger that ripped up the highway, and driving it was fun. All those years of the cheapest rental cars I could find, showing up to jobs in second-hand corduroy thrift store pants, eating swiss cheese sandwiches and taking the tiny bottles of shampoo from hotel rooms: I wasn't going back there. I had the feeling this might be my last travel job. I was feeling flush and confident, and I had a brand-new vehicle,

Carhartt overalls, and a new pair of Blundstone boots. The only stations I could get on the fancy stereo were an evangelical Christian one, or the one devoted to new wave music. As I careened north, I finally turned it on, and there was David Byrne:

And you may find yourself in another part of the world
And you may find yourself behind the wheel of a large automobile…

I'VE ALWAYS SURVIVED by heeding signs and symbols, and often carried tarot cards. I also believed that every job had its own soundtrack, whether it was Bob Dylan, Macy Gray, Townes Van Zandt, Prince, Patti Smith, or Skip James. In Nova Scotia there was no room in the luggage for prophesies or talismans, but it seemed that that goofy radio station was going to serve as both a soundtrack and a guide.

You may ask yourself, "Where does that highway go to?"
And you may ask yourself, "Am I right? Am I wrong?"
And you may say to yourself, "My God! What have I done!"

I turned up a winding, dirt driveway into the farm late on a Saturday afternoon. There was a charming red and white heritage farmhouse beside a pond, some big shade trees that had shed most of their fall leaves, and a flock of ducks. An old tractor with a trailer full of firewood sat outside a weathered barn. Two geese and a cat ran over to greet me. Stephan had given me instructions to let myself in. The room had its own entrance and minimal furnishings, mainly a large low bed, a little table, and a lamp. A big window looked on to the farmyard.

Stephan pulled into the driveway after dark. He asked if I wanted to go out to feed the goats. They were milling around and bleating in stalls piled high with straw. Each stall had a hole cut out of a wall above a feed trough, and one or two goats would poke their heads through to eat. As well as raising goats, running a massive market garden and a

B&B, Stephan was a photographer. He'd been at the arts centre in Tatamagouche, where he had just opened a show. That first night was windy, the windows rattled and the old house shook. I had a long, deep sleep, and woke rested, but vowed to replace the flax seed pillow. I had a day off before first shift so went shopping in town, and to Stephan's photography show. It was a beautiful series of large, black-and-white portraits of Nova Scotia farmers. Stephan sat back in a chair, his long legs stretched out under a folding table. People moved through the gallery, congratulating him.

THE FIRST SHIFT at the mill, I was hustled off with another guy to a welding shop up the road to do my welding test. Out of practice, I had failed a test a month earlier at the boilermaker's hall in Edmonton. The instructor at the learning centre was as surprised as I was, since I had tested there many times before. He showed me a practically foolproof way of putting a root in a tube, feeding the wire through the gap, and watching the puddle in profile.

"Jeez, John," I'd joked with him, "how come it took you eighteen years to show me that? Think of all the time and materials we could have saved if I'd known how to do that when I started." I spent a day practicing in the Edmonton hall, passed the test without incident the second time, then went welding in Athabasca. By the time I got to Nova Scotia, I was practiced up and finished my test in an hour. The other guy was not having such an easy time, grinding out his root and putting it back in. I went outside to stand in the sun, and reflected on the times that I had been that guy, sweating through a welding test, hoping the clock wouldn't run out, then waiting around anxiously to see if it would bend clean or pass an X-ray. It was a good feeling to be the old dog, easily making the test joint and finishing early. In Alberta, a passed weld test means you are issued a laminated ID card on the spot, printed in colour with your name and signature on it. The tickets in Nova Scotia were black ink on heavy brown paper, were printed slightly off centre, and issued from the Department of Trades and Corrections, because for some inexplicable reason the trades training program and the prison system were linked. It is by far my favourite ticket.

Back at the lunchroom, I realized that experienced meant older when they paired me up with Wilfred, who was about to retire from the trade. The rest of the guys looked young enough to be my sons. It was a superheater rebuild at Northern Pulp, almost exactly the same job as my very first travel card job in Montana. I kept having flashbacks about how everything was new then, how Javier Gonzalez had to show me how to take a grape out of a tube, and how I was nervous and unsure about everything, including how to set up my torch.

Nova Scotia and New Brunswick are both part of Local 73, so the job was full of Acadian guys. They were flinging around slangy French, keeping to themselves. They were wary of me, I could see it in their eyes. But I was wearing the right costume, the boots, the hoodie with the West Coast Boilermakers crest on the back. There were not many women in their local, but I had learned a firm handshake, and that takes care of a lot. It's a ritual, an acknowledgement that I've been here before, and so have you, maybe not in this exact ATCO trailer on this scrap of weedy parking lot, but others just like it. And now my age implies another unspoken word in this exchange: many. I have been here many times before.

Then we went up on to the unit, and the night shift was still packing up to leave. The night shift foreman tapped me on the shoulder. I turned around, and it was Luc, the guy I'd shown my fake mouse tattoo to, in Nanticoke, fifteen years earlier. He hugged me, lifting me off my feet.

"What about Maya?" I asked, "What happened? Did you get married?"

"Ah...yes we did...I have four kids now, did you know that? The oldest is fourteen..." We quickly filled each other in on our lives. Luc was regularly a foreman, well respected for his experience and skill, hanks of grey in his black hair. After seeing our reunion, the guys on my shift relaxed. "You guys be good to her," he said to my crew, in English. "She's a good welder."

BEFORE WE COULD bring the panels up with the crane, all the tubes had to have both ends cleaned with die grinders, then have rice paper stuffed inside, so there would be no draft. This was my job, cleaning tubes, making "snowballs" of rice paper, then stuffing both ends of every tube before flying the platens up into place. The panels would be lifted to the fifth floor and landed on the roof. The rigging crew would jump the rigging, move them into the boiler house, and make the second lift inside using chain falls. I asked my foreman if he wanted us to stuff the ends on the ground, or just clean them, then stuff them with paper on the fifth floor.

"Or are you going to stuff them at the top end, when you do the stubs on the header?" I asked.

"We're not going to stuff every tube," he explained. "We already have the header blocked off."

"Oh, I think we'll be stuffing every tube," I said. "Both sides of every joint. That's how you do it." He looked unsure.

"I don't think so," he said. "That's ridiculous. That'll take forever."

"Won't take as long as getting a platen in place and a crew welding it up, then realizing every tube has a draft whistling through it. Because then you'll have to cut them all out, clean and stuff them a second time, and start over, only they'll all be short. *That* will take forever." Grudgingly, he got on the radio to Quality Control. The Quality Control inspector was from Triple Nickel, Local 555. This was the local that covered Manitoba, Saskatchewan, and Northern Ontario, and the QC knew pulp mills. A lot of the Nova Scotia guys had only worked refineries.

"One of the welders, the travel card welders," my foreman said into the radio, "wants to know if we're stuffing paper in every tube. *She* says we're stuffing every stub in the header, and *she* says both ends of the tubes in the panel." He emphasized the she so everyone listening on the radio would know it was me, when the welder turned out to be wrong. I was the only she on the job. The radio crackled.

"You stuff everything," the QC guy said. "OK? All the stubs and all the tubes. Just do it the way *she* says — she's from BC. She knows how to do it." There was a pause. "OK?"

"Copy that," my foreman said, stiffly. I shrugged. I didn't feel badly for being right. He had a refinery background, I worked in mills, and I had saved him from a potential disaster. It had been a long time coming, and it was finally my turn.

FEELING GOOD, I drove back to the farm in the big black truck. It was just under fifty kilometres from the farm to the mill, which was long enough to take in a lot of new wave music, under duress. Depeche Mode, The Cure, Duran Duran, Devo. It was the soundtrack of my adolescence and I had always hated most of it, but also found it strangely nostalgic. It was bizarre to think these songs were now thirty years old, and that these artists, who used to appear in crudely coloured early videos on big screens in the club scene when I was a kid, with their tall, gelled hair and sparkly make-up, were now in their sixties. It was more bizarre to contemplate this time warp while driving a pickup truck along a lonely country road in Nova Scotia between one of the province's last working pulp mills, and one of its first organic farms. Just when the radio would become too irritating to bear, they would play Bowie or Blondie, Siouxsie and the Banshees or The Pretenders, and I would resist the urge to turn it off. So for a month I drove, cringing, for an hour each way to the dulcet tones of the Psychedelic Furs, Joy Division and New Order, then thrilling when they played The Clash, The Jam, or The Specials. This job was already strange. Why turn down the sound?

STEPHAN WAS WORKING on his laptop at the kitchen table in his farming sweater, which was full of holes. I stuffed some bread in the toaster.

"Good day?" he asked.

"Yes," I said. "You?"

"Yes," he said.

"Good," I answered. I buttered my toast and picked it up to take it with me to my room.

"I love our little talks," he said.

Stephan, it turned out, had a wickedly deadpan sense of humour, a sophisticated intellect, and a heartfelt dedication to environmental sustainability. A couple days into the job he offered me a bowl of bean soup. It was all he seemed to eat. He had grown the beans and wanted to use them, so had made gallons of the soup, which he intended to eat all winter. It was good soup, but after day two I told him it was my turn to cook and I roasted a chicken. He offered homemade beer. Within a week we were dining together, and spending a couple hours each evening swapping websites about interesting things, and discussing art projects. Stephan used spelt flour, which he kept in a large white bucket in the pantry, and I made quiche with farm eggs, and pies from frozen apples and rhubarb.

AT THE MILL the panels were all cleaned, stuffed, and rigged into place. Wilfred and I were tapped to move into the superheaters and start welding tubes.

"Game on, Kid," he said. Wilfred was a quiet and gentle man. He didn't speak unless he found it necessary, which was seldom. Just like Montana, there were pairs of TIG welders, of various levels of experience, lined up in a row. Wilfred and I were in the middle, with young guys on either side of us, who were talking their way through every weld.

"OK go up, go up, go up, circle back, OK go forward ... go forward ... catch the bottom edge ..."

"How does it look?"

"It looks OK but ... there's a fisheye where you pulled out. Grind back into it and heat it up before you go forward ..." On one side, they discussed every detail in English, and on the other, were having the same conversation in French. I remember that, I thought. I had done it too, getting my partner to look at my root from the inside of the tube, describing every minor anomaly. As I gained experience, the need to articulate everything aloud lessoned, but the narrative still ran in my head for years. Then one day, I lit up my torch and there was silence. There was nothing but the hiss of argon, and construction noise. My mind was quiet, and clear, and the welding was fine. All of the knowledge had gone into my hands. It was like typing, or playing the piano, the moment when you realize you no longer have to look at the keys to know where you are.

Wilfred had reached that place a long time ago. When we welded together, we didn't talk. We took turns, passing the torch back and forth, anticipating the sequence of events. Occasionally one of us would look inside the tube and mutter something. *Tie in's good,* or *coffee time.* But otherwise, it was quiet.

They started X-raying the weld joints right away, at the breaks on night shift. These tubes would have high pressure, superheated steam flowing through them, and any flaw in a weld joint could quickly develop and turn into a pinhole. The steam shooting out of the pinhole would drill a hole in another tube, causing another pinhole, which would drill another hole, until there were multiple high pressure steam leaks. Tubes can also crack, or blow out completely. Any fracture of the pressure boundary meant shutting the plant down for repairs, if the problem didn't cause an explosion first. Some repairs were expected on a job like this, anything around ten per cent seemed to be acceptable. But on this job the rate was much higher, more than double that. Because our rate was lower than the rest, Wilfred and I were designated the repair crew. We spent our shifts cutting into tubes that had been welded but failed the shot, finding the indications, and fixing them.

The very last tube we had to fix should have been a cut-out. Someone on night shift had welded it, and had been having trouble. According to the X-ray, more than three quarters of the joint was bad. I went to the office and asked the QC guy to see the film. He drew a donut on a paper napkin and scribbled in three large areas.

"There," he said. Those are your indications."

"Can I see the film?" I asked again.

"I'll have to walk over to the other trailer," he said. He didn't want to.

"OK."

"I gave you a drawing."

"You gave me a napkin."

"I'm kinda busy."

"Where I'm from," I said, as reasonably as I could, "we can fix anything. Literally anything. But I have to know where I'm going. I need a map. Let me take a look at the skin." I'd heard them called that by the X-ray technicians: skins. I hoped it made me sound credible. Reluctantly the guy took me over to the other trailer and pulled out a stack of brown envelopes. He flipped through them until he found the right one, and pulled out a long, narrow X-ray film.

"They're not digital?" I asked.

"Nope." At home the X-rays were taken digitally, then viewed on computers, could be magnified and enhanced, and airdropped to the welder's phone for a visual reference. The guy flipped the toggle switch on an old-fashioned light box and clipped the X-ray to it. I took a picture with my cell phone.

"Seriously," I told Wilfred, later. "It was like an episode of M*A*S*H."

WE DREW THE indications on the outside of the tube with paint pens, and both started carving out the existing cap. Fairly soon I could see patches of porosity.

"Yep," Wilfred said. "Don't go all the way through if you can help it. There's probably a draft in there." We carefully shaved away the indications and rewelded the joint. It took a long time. Overnight they shot the tube again, and this time there was just a small spot that we had missed, on my side. I carved in again, found the bubble, and fixed it.

"And if the man doesn't like that," I told Wilfred, "he can suck mine." The Acadian crews on both sides of us stopped and lifted their helmets, shocked. I couldn't tell it was because they were Catholic, or just well mannered. Or maybe they weren't used to a woman speaking that way. For a long moment, it was quiet. Then Wilfred said,

"If the man doesn't like that, he can suck mine, too. Let's go for coffee."

AT THE END of that day we were laid off, and Wilfred shook my hand.

"You are one of the old guys now," he said. "You might as well start planning your retirement." I did not yet know that in less than two years I would be leaving the trade.

"Why don't you come to Miramichi?" Luc asked, pumping my hand up and down. "The job is over. Drive up, meet my family. Meet my wife. We'll have a big party, show you everything good in New Brunswick." I told him I would visit one day, but not this time. Miramichi was in the wrong direction.

"See you on the next one, my friend."

I DROVE BACK to the farm in the big black truck, to The Smiths. I would make fish tacos on the weekend. Stephan had asked me to stay and help him with a welding project. He wanted to build a hot tub out of steel: a long, deep, coffin-like vessel he intended to get powder-coated so it wouldn't rust. I was skeptical, but he had the design and built the platform, with wooden decking around it, and had constructed benches for either end. It was going to go in the new greenhouse, so you could float in a tub of burbling mineral water, surrounded by plants.

The tub took a couple of days to weld, then Stephan filled it with water to see if it was going to leak.

"It's not going to leak," I told him. "I just put your pulp mill back together. I think I can weld a bathtub." I was going to fly to Montreal, to visit friends and have a little vacation, and by the time I got back to the Coast, it would be winter. I bid farewell to Stephan and his goats, the geese, and the cats. Then I loaded the big black truck and made my way back toward Halifax, with the radio on.

...into the blue again, after the money's gone
Once in a lifetime, water flowing underground
Same as it ever was, same as it ever was
Same as it ever was, same as it ever was.

PART 3:

Pulling the Pin

THE WOLF

I once had lunch with Garnet Rogers in Prince George while I was working there on an explosion job. I didn't know him well, but had helped produce one of his concerts, and he had stayed at our house. My dog Flash, normally indifferent to strangers, had been crazy about him, delighted that a six-foot-five alpha human would squeal at him in a high squeaky falsetto and play tug with his rubber shark. When I discovered Garnet was playing a show in Prince George at the same time I was there, I gave him a call. He suggested lunch at a Vietnamese restaurant called Thanh Vu.

"That works," I told him, "I'm staying at the motel right next door."

THE CARMEL INN is shabby residency hotel that caters to workers and people travelling on a budget. I had a non-smoking room, a twelve-foot by twelve-foot box with a queen-sized bed, a single table and chair, and a tiny kitchenette. The kitchenette featured a two-burner stove with a bar-fridge underneath it, and a sink the size of a shoebox. I could reach the kitchen counter from bed, and could just about make coffee without getting up. It featured new carpet and paint, was quiet, cleanish, and had a cheap, weekly off-season rate.

My motel room door opened directly onto the parking lot. Garnet stood on the sidewalk all tall and gangly, respectfully averting his eyes from the interior of the room because he knew, from his own travels, what was inside: a person's clothes, a bed, and absolutely no privacy. He asked for the motel's internet password, and beelined back to his van to send some stuff off on his laptop. That was another travel reality, always poaching Wi-Fi from wherever you could find it, the same way I collected those little packets of Cheese Whiz from hotel breakfast rooms.

Garnet had been a travelling folk musician for more than thirty years. He was on tour, playing a show that night in a little room above a bookstore, and I was there working an emergency job repairing a boiler that had blown up in one of the pulp mills. Over lunch at Than Vu, we talked about how our careers, which were so different, shared similarities common to people who worked on the road. We traded survival tricks, like how you can heat up a can of spaghetti by wrapping it in a heating pad and turning it on high for twenty minutes. Or how you can poach eggs in a Melita coffee maker. I knew Garnet hadn't flown in an airplane since the early 1980s, but I didn't know that he had put more than a million miles on the old Volvo station wagon he had toured in before the minivan. Literally more than one million, not kilometres, but miles he piled on, regularly crisscrossing Canada and the US playing solo shows in folk clubs, and bars, and theatres, and strange little venues in towns where people loved him. His gig that night was the room above Books & Company, all worn carpets and metal folding chairs, and ladies with handmade money aprons selling beer tickets for three dollars each. I was looking forward to it. He told me that the car, the Volvo, was still alive, and it still ran. He'd replaced the engine three times, and eventually retired it to the farm outside of Hamilton that he shares with his beloved wife. As if on cue his phone rang, and he answered immediately, completely focussed on the call. I excused myself to give him some privacy, and realized that this was another thing about the road: the sound of the person that you love most in the world coming through the phone is sometimes your only lifeline.

When I got back to the table, Garnet had ended the call and was looking out the window.

"You ever go over there?" he asked, nodding to the all-you-can-eat buffet next door. It was called the Great Wall Restaurant, only most of the letters in the neon sign were burned out so now the sign just said "eat aura."

"No," I told him, "I can't eat enough to justify a buffet."

"I never go to those places," he said. "Never. I'll always go to a Vietnamese restaurant if I can find one, never those buffet places." He paused. "Whenever I go to one I feel like I've just spent the afternoon in a third-rate porn theatre."

"You mean," I ventured carefully, "overly full yet completely unsatisfied?"

"No," he said. "More just kind of sweaty and ashamed."

When we got back, Garnet bounded forward and slid open the side door of the van.

"Look at this," he said. Inside the perfectly ordered interior were at least seven guitar cases, which I suspected contained gorgeous vintage pre-war Gibsons. A variety of amps, suitcases, plastic tubs, and bags were piled in with a mindful precision, like a big game of Tetris.

"I do it too," I told him.

"You know," he said, "I've been taking more and more stuff with me on tour, every time I go. I think that that's a reflection ... an indication ... of how much you'd rather be at home. The more you want to be at home ... you take as much of home with you as you possibly can." He slid the door shut. "Hey, how's your dog doing?"

"He's fine," I said, "he's getting older, but he's just fine."

TEN MONTHS LATER, I drove through Prince George again, on the way to a pulp mill shutdown in Mackenzie. The wind gusted fiercely, causing my cube-shaped Honda Element to bounce. It was February, snow was lightly falling, and technically, I was homeless. Since I had last been north, I had blown out my knee and had surgery, ended a relationship, moved my possessions into storage, and contracted a builder to build me a cabin in the woods, which was slated to be finished in the summer. But at that moment, I was living out of my car.

Flash the dog was at his other home, looking after his other family. He was fourteen, and had been diagnosed with a neurological condition called canine idiopathic vestibular disease, a condition that affects the balance centre in the brain. Typically it causes a dog's eyes to dart rapidly, and he would walk in circles and fall down, often unable to get up for a couple of days. The amazing part of this disorder, though, is that a dog's brain is able to rewire itself in a matter of hours, carrying information along some other route, and within seventy-two hours an afflicted animal can actually stand up and start staggering around again, making a kind of miraculous recovery. At least that's how I had come to understand the process, and that's what seemed to have happened to Flash. Within twenty-four hours of his first attack he was standing, and soon was more or less back to being his old self, though he continued to walk like a drunken sailor and sometimes looked like somebody had screwed his head on crookedly.

Mackenzie was going to be a longer job, two or three months, so I had called in advance and rented a furnished apartment. I'd packed everything I thought I would need: clothes, bedding, a stereo, books, tarot cards, yoga mat. I was carrying a complete kitchen system, devised over years, which consisted of two plastic tubs with all the dishes, utensils, and kitchen tools I could possibly need, including a grater, a whisk, and thirty-two spices. Spices were expensive in the North, cinnamon sticks eleven dollars a package. I travelled with a Crockpot, blender, rice cooker, kettle, and toaster. I carried a small butane stove, a tent, and a sleeping bag in case I got stuck somewhere, or felt like a camping detour on the way home. I preferred the water from my own well, so brought jugs of it with me, as much as I could carry, and a cooler for produce, dairy, and frozen stuff. On this trip I had two totes full of cans, bottles, and obscure organic grains and oils. Just in case they didn't carry everything at the Mackenzie general store, or whatever it was called.

I stayed one night at the Carmel, and hit the big grocery store in the morning, filling the cart with fresh vegetables and fruits, lemons and limes, ginger and garlic, anything that might linger on a northern shelf due to lack of demand. Sesame oil, tamari, tahini, quinoa, seven-grain cereal to cook in the rice cooker, organic coffee, licorice spice tea, cheeses, tortillas, and refried beans. Chicken thighs to make Vij's family chicken curry recipe for hot lunches, and a couple of packages of stew beef, on sale. I was never a dedicated carnivore, but when I was working long days and feeling depleted, I did like to make Alice Waters' beef bourguignon, the one with the orange zest and the two cups of burgundy. Which meant stopping at the liquor store for a couple of bottles of wine, and oh hell, maybe a bottle of Jameson.

By the time I'd gassed up the car and checked the tires, it was noon and snowing. I crossed over the bridge from the downtown side to the North End of Prince George under a heavy grey sky on the first of February. It was minus nineteen.

I passed the turnoff to the Northwood Mill, and headed out of town. After Prince George, there aren't any more large destination cities. If you were heading north from there, you were leaving behind all large shopping hubs, movie theatres, universities, and anything that could be described as urban sprawl. I drove without music, to the sound of the wind and the windshield wipers, the studded tires quieting as the snow began to thicken on the highway. I drove through a white landscape spotted with ravens, wondering if the ache in my recently rebuilt knee would subside or become aggravated on this job, wondering how I was going to pay for the house that was being built for me at home. And while I often worried about money, about Flash and the house, and about the future in a kind of abstract way, on this day the anxiety slowly receded as I pressed on, one of the only cars on the road heading north. I left the logging outfits and industrial sites of the northern periphery of Prince George behind, and eventually the road gave way to trees, heavy with snow, miles of them, and it became very quiet.

I was about seventy-five kilometres south of Mackenzie when I passed the wolf. He was tall and lean, trotting along the shoulder, headed south, and looked like he'd been travelling. In my mind the word *wolf* formed and hung suspended. Then I thought, a wolf wouldn't be walking along the side of the road, he'd be slinking through the forest, invisible. Fast on the heels of this thought was the next: a wolf definitely wouldn't be wearing a collar, which this one was. I kept driving, hesitant to enter into a debate with myself, alone in the car with the slow-dawning realizations that the wolf had not looked very well, that he probably belonged to someone, and that he was heading south into about one hundred kilometres of wilderness. It was already starting to get dark. I am not going to get involved, I told myself. I am not going to arrive in Mackenzie in the dark, and move into the apartment at night. I am not going to get entangled in another person's problem. No, this wolf was on his own. And then I thought of Flash, walking in circles like a drunken baby, and cursing softly, I pulled the car over at a wide spot on the side of the highway, rolled down the window so I could see, and pulled a U-turn, heading back the way I'd come.

It had not been a hallucination, or a dream of a wolf in the snow. There he was, head down, jogging deliberately along the shoulder of the road. His hips and shoulders stuck out, and he had a slow, splay-legged trot, his head hanging down nearly to the pavement. He looked ancient. I drove slowly past with my four-way flashers on, and pulled over just ahead of him at a road pullout. When he got to where I was, he stopped, leaving about twenty feet between us, and made eye contact.

"Hey Wolfie . . ." I called out, and took a step toward him. He immediately changed course and shot out on to the highway, and continued down the middle of the road, keeping a wide berth between us. Two trucks happened to swing around the corner just then, the drivers leaning on their horns and swerving on the ice to avoid the wolf in the middle of the highway. He crossed over to the opposite side of the road, trotted past me and my car, then picked his way back across and carried on exactly the way he had been going. I had achieved absolutely nothing, other than nearly getting the wolf hit by a truck.

I turned around and backtracked again, but this time I did not see him on the long straight stretch of highway. I started to panic, already too invested, and cursed more as I inched along. I'd been travelling for nine hours, and was adding time to my trip instead of cutting it down. The wolf was in a pullout at the roadside. He had his head down and was licking the icy ground, his nose bloody. I pulled far enough ahead not to spook him, but he more or less ignored me this time, looking up between eating small mouthfuls of snow. I found a jug of water, got out of the car, and called him again.

"Wolfie ... look! I have water for you ... water!" I poured some on the ground. The wolf looked my way and froze, head lifted, sniffing the air. I found a steel salad bowl in the back of the car, and walked toward him. He backed away, keeping the same distance between us. I put the bowl down and poured water into it, talking all the while about how thirsty the poor old boy must be, then walked backward to my car. He went straight to the bowl and drank, emptying it. I walked toward him with the jug and he backed up again, but this time not so far, and I poured out more water. When he was finished, he cut around the car again, leaving slightly less distance between us, and continued travelling south.

I'm in a parable, I thought, as I turned around and for a third time drove slowly past the wolf. It's a fairy tale. The wolf is either going to eat me, or turn out to be my dead grandmother. I went a little further this time, so there was time to prepare, and pulled into another pullout, one where the road crews had piled the ploughed snow into dirty mountains. I readied my pocketknife, pulled the two packages of stew beef out of the cooler, and waited.

When the wolf arrived this time he stopped and stared for a long time, more curious than wary. He was very thin, but had a thick silver coat with a ruff around his neck and beautiful blue eyes.

"I have meat," I told him cheerfully, and chattered a little bit, asking him why he was going on such a long walk, and to where. He stood patiently while I approached with the package, and I slowly placed it on the ground, one side torn open. The wolf sniffed his way over, and very quickly emptied the first package. So much for beef bourguignon. He was hungry, but stood patiently while I opened the second package, and carefully ate the chunks of beef from the ground, and then one at a time from my hand. I tried not to think about the fact that I was hand-feeding a wolf pieces of raw meat at the side of the highway in minus twenty-five degree weather. He was really an amicable fellow, very well behaved. By the time we finished the second package of meat, I had a hand on him, and started scratching behind one huge, pointed ear.

"You're just a big baby," I gushed, relieved. We were about thirty feet from my car and I slipped my hand under his collar. "Come on, Wolfie,"I told him, "you belong to somebody and it's time for you to go home." I tugged a couple of times, and he starting walking stiffly with me to the car.

The wolf stood quietly while I rearranged the back of the car. I'd taken one of the seats out at home to make more room so it was quite spacious, but I also had a lot of stuff. I piled most of it into the storage space in the back, more in the passenger's seat, and shoved stuff around on the floor by the back seat until there was a space that looked big enough for a wolf, if he squished himself in a little. Then I opened the side door and told him, "Come on, buddy, get in." Two things became clear. First, he knew about cars, and second, he was so old and hurt and tired that he was not going to be able to leap in by himself. I tried boosting him, and he didn't budge. I tried lifting one leg, but he was too unsteady. We were going to need some help.

The truck I flagged down was a new grey Dodge Ram. A woman in a light blue ski jacket jumped down from the passenger side and hurried straight over.

"Are you all right? What happened?"

"Oh I'm all right," I said, "I just can't get this ... dog ... in the car." The woman looked thirtyish, had pale skin and wore pink lipstick. Her name was Cynthia. She and her husband were headed to Prince George for the weekend.

"Is it your ... dog?" Cynthia asked.

"Um, no," I said. "I just found him. And I'm going to try to find his people." Cynthia cocked and eyebrow at me.

"He's in trouble," I explained lamely, "and he's really old and sore." Cynthia's husband, Alvaro, came around the side of their truck, zipping up a black Arc'teryx ski jacket. He had a spiderweb tattooed on his neck.

"He looks like a wolf," he said.

"Yeah, he might have a little wolf in him ..." I said, downplaying.

"A little?" said Alvaro. "That's a fucking wolf."

"It's OK," Cynthia told me, calmly. "My husband will help you."

"I will?" Alvaro looked alarmed. Cynthia just gave him a little smile and nodded her head.

"I'll take the sharp end," I told him, "you get the back?"

The wolf was heavy, and hard to get a hold of. But after a couple of tries, he seemed to decide he'd had enough of our fumbling, bent his crooked, splay-legged knees, and leapt. At the same time, Alvaro and I half-lifted, half-pushed him in, and he was in my car. I closed the back door.

"Thank you," I said, shaking hands with them both. "Thank you so much." Alvaro had a knuckle tattoo on his right hand that said R-A-M-S. He saw me eyeing it and put his two hands together. The left said T-E-I-N.

"Ah," I said, "Ramstein." He shrugged.

"They are big in Costa Rica," he explained.

"They are big everywhere," I said, and he smiled, flashing a gold tooth that reminded me of my friend Javiar, from Montana. Then I noticed that I had a wolf in my car. He had turned his head and was regarding us calmly through the back window, like a child waiting to be driven to school. His mouth was open a little so he seemed to be smiling. I started to panic.

"I don't know why I am doing this," I blurted. Alvaro put his hand on my shoulder and looked straight into my eyes, a Costa Rican metalhead in Northern BC.

"Because," he said, "you are a good person."

DRIVING NORTH WITH a wolf in your car is a strange feeling. In the rear-view mirror, his head was larger than my human head, and his ears were pressed down slightly by the roof, which is actually quite high. In such close quarters it became clear that he was massive, and that this animal certainly did have a large amount of wolf in him, and some other huge dog-like creature, and possibly dinosaur. He rode in the car sitting up, his great mouth open a little, panting, his long tongue hanging out to one side. What would happen, I thought, if he decided to attack me? He could just reach over and bite my face, and I would crash the car, and that would be that. And for about twenty kilometres I alternated between thoughts of being torn apart by a wolf while driving, and trying to banish those same thoughts, in case the wolf was a mind reader. I didn't know where he got his ideas from. But then he did an extraordinary thing. He threw back his giant head, opened his huge mouth, and yawned. An enormous, vocal yawn, and eased himself down on top of my yoga mat and red wool blanket, disappearing from sight. Soon I could hear him snoring.

This eased my anxiety considerably. By the time I got to the little store at McLeod Lake, I had a plan. I was going to take the wolf to Mackenzie, find some animal people there, rescue people or veterinarians, and get him looked after and fixed up. I'd find someone to take him. If we still hadn't found his people when the job was over in two months, I'd take him home. It would all work out.

I stopped at the general store on a hunch. It was a single building that housed a grocery store, post office, liquor outlet, and gas station. I took a picture of the sleeping wolf in my car and went in. The main store was an amazing museum of everything anyone travelling in the middle of nowhere could want. At the back was a small window, opening into the liquor store outlet, which was really just a closet filled with alcohol. A woman stood at the counter, chopping carrots.

"We're closed," she said. Behind her the door was open into her house, and the TV was on the local news channel. The prediction was for snow. The woman had her hair piled up in a loose bun and wore a plaid shirt with the sleeves rolled up to the elbows.

"I need some help with something," I said, carefully. She raised her eyebrows at me over the top of her reading glasses, about to tell me again the store was closed, but I held my phone out toward her and asked, "Do you know this wolf?"

She looked at the picture on my phone and said, "By God, that's Arlene's wolf! She's been looking for him since yesterday. Where is he?"

"He's in my car," I told her.

"Well, how did you get him ..." I raised my eyebrows over my glasses right back at her. "Nevermind," she said. "I'm gonna call her." She disappeared into the back and I could hear her on the phone.

"Arlene? There's a lady here has got your wolf. I don't know. I know, but it's him, and she's got him in her car ..." Arrangements were made for me to meet Arlene on the side of the highway, around ten kilometres north of the store. The store lady's name was Cheryl. She walked with me to the door and opened it for me.

"You need anything while you're here," she said, "you come see me."

Arlene was sitting in a small black pickup truck, idling, when I got to the spot. She climbed down and crossed the highway when I pulled over, a leash in her hand. She was an older gal wearing a black leather motorcycle jacket and a pair of flannel pajama bottoms with little Scottie dogs on them. She looked like she had left the house in a hurry, but was unfazed by being out in minus twenty-five-degree weather in her pjs. I guess you get used to the cold.

"Wake up, Wolfie," I said, opening the back door of my car. "Your mum's here, and it's time to go home." The wolf opened his eyes and blinked at me a couple of times, then creakily got to his feet and hopped out of my car. Arlene scolded him quietly while she snapped on the leash. I crossed the highway with her and helped her heave him into the crew cab of her truck.

"He's had dinner already," I told her, "but he's probably still pretty thirsty." Arlene thanked me for picking him up, and explained that someone had left the gate open, and he'd just gone off.

"What's his name?" I asked.

"What? Oh, it's Niko." She explained that Niko was seventeen years old, almost blind, and completely deaf. He had bad arthritis and liked to wander, but he didn't usually stay out overnight, and he'd never been picked up that far away before. He had travelled more than eighty kilometres.

Niko, I thought, getting into my car. Niko.

FOURTEEN MONTHS LATER, I stopped in at McLeod Lake again on my way to Chetwynd to work at the gas plant. Cheryl was there, looking the same, sleeves rolled up to the elbows. I bought a six-pack, and asked if she remembered me.

"I'm the person who found Arlene's wolf," I said.

"Oh yeah," she said. "I remember."

She paused, "You know he's gone now."

I nodded. I'd thought he would be.

"When did that happen?" She couldn't really remember, but she thought it was the previous spring, because her husband had to take the backhoe up to Arlene's to dig the hole. At her mention of the backhoe, a lump formed in my throat, and I couldn't speak. It was unexpected, and I concentrated on the beef jerky display, which was surprisingly elaborate, until my eyes stopped swimming.

I did not ask how Niko had died. I think if it had been on the highway, she would have told me, but she didn't say. So I didn't ask if he died in his sleep, or wasted away, or if it was a compassionate bullet. I was pretty sure he didn't go the way Flash left last fall, lying on the grass in the sun outside of the vet's while I stroked his face and fed him liver bars, and told him what a good boy he was, the Best Boy in the Whole World, while the good Dr. Bella injected a magic serum into a vial attached to his leg, and the life slipped out of his eyes. No, Northern dogs don't leave the world that gently.

"Oh," I said, no sound coming out. I cleared my throat and tried again. "At least she had a body to bury." Cheryl nodded, studying me.

"You know, she's got another wolf-dog now," she said. "A puppy." I nodded.

"A puppy. Nice. A puppy."

"He's young," she said. "But this one's going to be big. You can tell."

THERE WAS A certain soundtrack to the drive North. I usually started with the radio, then after Chilliwack the highway is crossed with multiple high-tension power lines, and the reception cuts out and never quite recovers. I liked CDs while I was travelling. I might begin with Richard Thompson's record, Sweet Warrior, or something by Martha Wainwright. Driving in and out of the art deco tunnels north of Hope, the music might change to Martin Simpson, maybe his strange, heartfelt rendition of Boots of Spanish Leather, filled with longing and impossible to sing along to. As the tunnel highway gave way to the cut of the Fraser Canyon with sheer cliffs on both sides of the road, I might navigate to Vic Chesnutt's reedy harmonies picking through Little Ceasar. At Spence's Bridge I usually stopped at a coffee shop with a perpetual waitress who had painted-on eyebrows, and north of there the landscape would relent, becoming gentler, a little more rolling. David Francey might cheer me up into the Cariboo, and from there the cowboy music would sneak in. Townes Van Zandt, or Emmylou Harris when she's singing something creepy.

WHEN I LEFT the store at McLeod Lake the last time, it was dusk. I put the beer in the cooler, opened a package of teriyaki-flavoured beef jerky, and put on Night Drive, a live version of a powerful, spell-inducing track by Garnet Rogers. It's a song about a very long drive, and it's about missing those you love, those you've left behind, and those who have gone to spirit. I drove that evening through the softly falling snow to Garnet's haunting electric guitar progressions, and the car was full of ghosts. The track segued into Northwest Passage, it started raining, and my various worries began to dissolve. Puppy, I thought, suddenly. Big, soft, puppy.

THE MONEY BOX

Chetwynd appears to be an ordinary town, but it is not. It is one of those Northern towns where you get the sense that people are determined to make a life, to create a community, and if any conveniences are lacking, they will be invented or improvised. There are many young families, and there are hotels that house transient workers, like me, who have come to work in the gas plant.

There are features of the town that are perfectly ordinary, such as a beautiful new recreation centre with a gym and a pool. There is a trail network that branches off at the top of Nob Hill, just before you get to the water tower, but it's a little hard to navigate in winter because it's so steep the trail turns to a slick of ice. There's a schoolyard down by the river, and a light aircraft runway, and a walking path that extends the entire length of town, parallel to the highway. The walking path is one of the most popular amenities in town, and is paved to accommodate baby strollers, wheelchairs, and bikes. It is flanked on either side by wide swaths of well-tended grass, which separate pedestrians and cyclists from the highway, and it is upon these boulevards that you can get an up-close look at the feature that renders this town extraordinary: chainsaw carvings.

There is a large monument in downtown Chetwynd declaring the town the "Chainsaw Sculpture Capitol of The World." It is a controversial claim. Hope, BC, likewise boasts the title of "Chainsaw Carving Capitol of The World" with equal pride. Global context seems to be important to this art form. Hayward, Wisconsin hosts the Lumberjack

World Championships; Ridgway, Pennsylvania's Chainsaw Carvers Rendezvous claims to be the largest such gathering in the world; Mulda, Germany, holds the Husky World Cup; and, Toei, Japan, has established the World Chainsaw Art Competition. Clearly, regional credentials just don't make the cut.

The annual Chetwynd International Chainsaw Carving Championship has been steadily growing in popularity, attracting artists from around the globe to this northern village of three thousand residents. The contest takes place over four days in June, which, in 2014, also happened to be the last weekend of the maintenance shutdown at the Pine River gas plant. This meant that the town, which had been inundated for weeks with boilermakers, pipefitters, and bricklayers, was now also accommodating dozens of chainsaw-wielding artisans. I did not attend the festivities, as I was working nights and sleeping in the daytime, but I heard them, the distant buzz of Husqvarnas seeping through my earplugs and penetrating my dreams.

The gas plant is forty-five minutes west of town on the company bus. We were working 11s, which, with the bus, made for a long day. It didn't leave much time to clean up, eat, make lunch for the next day, and sleep. With laundry, banking, and shopping, there wasn't any downtime, and on night shift sleep was of poor quality and in short supply. After four weeks without a day off, workers were wandering around town in a daze. Driving was dreamlike, and I would hear myself telling the grocery clerk, *I'm sorry, I'm working the night shift. What did you say?*

Adding to the dreaminess was the fact that the town was permanently populated by a hundred and fifty enormous, varnished chainsaw sculptures of unlikely subjects. Too large to fit in a car, let alone the baggage compartment of an airplane, the results of the competition did not travel home with their international creators. So Chetwynd had installed the pieces along the streets and boulevards, turning the entire community into an outdoor gallery. There was a permanent collection spread all over town, and during the competition, their population doubled. They adorned the sidewalks and graced the boulevards, like some kind of phantasmagorical conference of monsters. We sleepwalked through the streets among carvings of enormous serpents, Japanese warriors, cowboys, and sports heroes. Yetis and leprechauns appeared overnight.

AT THE END of week four, I had a night off, and was drifting around in my car, running errands. I turned right between the moose and the rearing Pegasus, drove up the hill, then left at the life-sized horse and cartoon cowboy, into the IGA. I bought groceries, looped around the giant octopus embattling a sailing schooner on the way to the ATM, and made a quick stop at the drugstore for vitamins, parking in front of two copulating humpback whales. On my way to buy a six-pack of Stella at BJ's Liquor Emporium, I passed the nine-foot pumpkin-headed scarecrow, and the two battling (or possibly copulating) griffins outside the tourism office. I planned to celebrate my night off with sweet, salty, high-calorie food, and bad detective shows, so my last stop was to pick up an order of ribs from the local steakhouse. I rounded the corner next to the giant Buddha, and turned onto the highway, noticing as I did, that there was money all over the road.

I turned the corner slowly and was positive that it was real money. I continued on toward the steakhouse, and parked between the cougar with the treed bear cubs and one of the hockey goalies. The steakhouse was in a prime location so some of the best carvings were right outside, including one of my favourites, a huge inverted alligator. I loved the criss-cross texture of his back and his wry, alligator smile. When I paid for my ribs, I asked the server where the RCMP station was, and was told it was up the hill, just past the sasquatch cuddling the little forest creatures. I found the station, by a couple of giant frolicking rabbits, but the door was locked. I pressed the button on the little speakerphone and no one answered. I was tired. I wanted to go back to the hotel room and watch cop shows and eat ribs. Instead, I drove back the way I'd come to see if the money was still there, or if someone else had picked it up.

I drove slowly past the larger-than-life crucified Jesus, and pulled into a parking space right at the end of the row, between the Buddha and the other goalie. This was the better of the two goalies, unpainted, with his glove hand extended over his head, about to pluck a slapshot out of the air. The money was still on the road, change mostly, including quite a few one- and two-dollar coins. A couple of people walked across the crosswalk, but both were texting and didn't notice the pavement shiny with silver. Why me? I grumbled to the Buddha. He was large and well made, laughing beatifically, and holding an orb high above his head with one hand. A dragon reared up and peered over his shoulder. My ribs were congealing in their cardboard box.

I climbed out of the car and walked on to the highway. When there was a break in the traffic, I started scraping the change together into a pile with my feet, then scooping it up and putting it in the pocket of my hoodie. The story came together when I found the money box, upside down in the grass at the edge of the road. It seemed someone had stolen the metal cash box from a local business, pocketed the paper, and thrown the incriminating box with the change out the window when they hit the highway. Thinking I could at least rescue the box and try to get it back to its owner, I flipped it over. The little plastic tray was still inside, along with a set of keys, and a large, disorganized pile of five, ten, twenty, and fifty-dollar bills. This changed things. I shoved everything into the box, including the change, and quickly made a last scan, gathering up a few more stray quarters and nickels, and a fifty that had blown up against the Buddha's stomach. It started to rain. I closed the box, jogged to the car, and locked myself inside. Sleep deprived, I was sitting in my car in a strange town, surrounded by monsters and gods, with what was most likely a stolen box of money on the seat beside me. I took off my hoodie, threw it over the box, and drove back to the hotel.

As casually as possible I ambled across the lobby, a greasy takeout bag in one hand, and a suspiciously square package wrapped in my damp sweatshirt in the other. I asked the desk clerk if there was a non-emergency number for the RCMP and she jotted it down. Up in my room I locked the door, pulled the blinds, and pondered the box. What is with people? I muttered, crabbily. A year ago on the same stretch of highway I had found someone's wolf, and now this. Why can't people keep track of their stuff?

I CRACKED A bottle of beer, using the TV remote as an opener, sat down at the desk and counted the money. There was $1487.85. Not bad for a day's take, but not great for a robbery. There were also the keys, and some paper notes from someone called Carrie, that said things like "$5 dish soap, Carrie." Or, "$76 4 tips, Carrie." Carrie had apparently been taking cash out of the box during the course of the day and replacing it with these scraps of explanation. Carrie might be in big trouble for this box finding its way on to the highway, and then into my hotel room. I imagined the note she would write in her loopy, girlish handwriting: "Fired for losing money box, Carrie." There was also a receipt from a propane company for a one hundred-pound bottle of propane, made out to someone called William Victory, of Wild Bill Enterprises. Scrawled across the receipt were the words "Paid Cash." So. It seemed someone had paid the propane bill out of the cash box too, and the propane belonged to Mr. Victory. This was almost as good as a cop show.

The RCMP officer's name was Brian. I'd left a message that I'd found a box of money and wanted to return it and he phoned back within minutes. He offered to come by and take care of that for me, right away. For some reason, I wanted someone else there when he arrived, so I called the only person I could think of who was staying on the same floor, my foreman, Nigel.

"Can you come to my room right away?" I asked.

"Um, why?"

"Because the police are on their way here and I need a witness."

"I meant why me?"

"You were my last resort," I said, "and I don't want to be alone in a hotel room with a police officer and a pile of money. Why do I have to explain everything?" I hung up the phone and used the end of my fork to flip the cap off another bottle of beer.

WHEN NIGEL ARRIVED, I was kicking back on the spare bed in pajamas with a pile of rib bones in the box beside me, drinking a Stella. I introduced him to Brian, a trim, unassuming RCMP officer standing at my desk counting out piles of cash.

"What's going on?" Nigel asked.

"I found a box of money, and I'm trying to give it back," I explained. "Do you want a beer?"

"No, thanks," Nigel said. "Hey, does he know about your record?"

"He hasn't asked."

"I guess he hasn't run your name," Nigel said, thinking he was funny, "or he wouldn't have come up here by himself."

"You're not really helping," I said.

"So ... you found this money, and you're giving it BACK?" he asked.

"Yeah."

"Well how much is it?"

"Around fifteen hundred."

"Well that's just stupid," he said. "Why didn't you keep it? That's what he's going to do ..." He nodded toward the officer.

"You know what?" I said. "What's stupid was thinking that you'd be helpful. You can go. I think Brian and I can handle it."

"Do you know how many hookers — and how much blow — you can buy with fifteen hundred bucks?" he asked.

"Not that many, I don't think," I said, getting up to usher him out.

"So my standards are slipping," he said. To his credit, officer Brian ignored us.

"What did you do with the bag of coke?" Nigel asked, as I steered him toward the door. "You're keeping that, right?"

I made officer Brian write me a receipt for the money, and before he left, I showed him the bill for the propane bottle. I pointed out that the money box could very likely belong to the individual called William Victory, and since I had done most of the leg work for him, maybe he could just find that person and return it. I'd learned that term from the cop shows: *leg work*.

"Yeah, I know Bill," he said. "I'll get back to you on this."

And that was that. I slept for about twenty hours and went back to work the following evening. During my night off, Nigel had made sure that the story got around, especially the part about how stupid I was, trying to return a box of free money. Different people approached me through the day to confirm the facts, and either agreed with him, or told me that I had done the right thing. But there was no right thing, it wasn't my money. The guy's name was in the box.

Officer Brian called my cell phone at lunchtime to tell me that Bill Victory was "Wild Bill," an older gent who ran the trailer park with his wife, just to the west of town. A number of our guys — boilermakers — had parked their rigs at the campground and were living there for the shutdown. Predictably, we called them the "Trailer Park Boys." As well as the trailer park, Bill and his wife ran Wild Bill's Burger Wagon, a fancy, silver food truck that he had built for the chainsaw carving festival. On the day I found the money, Bill had left the box of cash on the fender of the burger wagon and driven away. When he turned the corner on to the highway, it must have flown off and opened, spilling the money. One of the trailer park boys, Big Steve, took me aside and told me that Bill and Joyce were really nice people, and that Bill was having some health issues.

When I got back to the hotel early the next morning, there was a bouquet of flowers on the little woodgrain coffee table. Beside the flowers was an envelope, with a gift certificate for the Red Dragon Chinese Restaurant, and a stack of lottery tickets inside. As well, there was a thickly embossed card, with a picture of a horse on it. Someone had written: *Thank you so much for finding and returning the money. It was from our burger wagon*. Please stop by and say hello before you leave, the burgers are on us. It was signed Joyce and Bill.

THE NEXT DAY I took Chinese takeout for lunch, and when I got around to checking the lottery tickets at the drugstore, one of them was good for a hundred bucks. After the job, as I pulled out of town for the last time, and drove past the carved effigies of serpents and sea creatures, owls and foxes, crucified Jesus and the upside-down alligator, I was comforted. It was good to know that if I was ever in Chetwynd again, I had burger credit at Wild Bill's, and I waved to the giant, laughing Buddha.

SULPHUR

The liquid natural gas plant outside of Chetwynd is one of the slums of the refinery industry. It's a sprawling mess of conduits, liquid sulphur lines, and piping of all diameters that carry product, steam, water, and gas. The design appears to be largely unplanned, with sections added on haphazardly. The main components of the plant are called "trains." There is Train A, Train B, and Train 3. The people who named them didn't have much respect for the alphabet. Each train consists of a huge industrial building that houses the tanks, stills, and condensate towers that are essential to the production, processing, and purification of liquid natural gas. To the west are some smaller tanks, a warehouse, and the pipefitters' shop. To the east, the heavy lines leave the buildings of each train and snake out across the middle of the plant into an area called A-B Sulphur. This area is dangerous because of frequent gas leaks or, as the industry calls them, emissions. Unlike working in the pulp mills, we don't carry escape respirators at the gas plant. The reasoning is is that the gas is so strongly concentrated and moves so swiftly that it will kill you long before you ever get your escape respirator out of the pouch on your belt and into your mouth. So mitigating safety hazards is more a matter of trying not to be at the wrong place at the wrong time.

The gas travels in pockets. There are all kinds of chemicals floating around that will make you sick, one of the big ones is H_2S, hydrogen sulphide. In its solid form sulphur is bright yellow, but H_2S is a colourless, and therefore invisible, gas. It is highly poisonous, corrosive, flammable, and explosive. It smells like rotten eggs, and if you get a whiff of it — a whiff that's not so strong that it kills you — the best thing you can do is run away. There are windsocks stationed around the plant and everyone keeps an eye on them. You don't need a weatherman to tell which way the wind blows.

Because some areas of the plant are so dangerous, we were instructed in our indoctrination that during the shutdown we would not be permitted to cut through the trains to get to our work areas unless we had been specifically cleared to do so. This clearance would be indicated on the permit that each crew had to obtain prior to commencing their tasks. I was on night shift, and every night we lined up with the rest of the crews at one of the three permit shacks and waited for the operators to meet with our foremen and fill out the hot work, confined space, and other required permits that would allow us to get to where we needed to go. Sometimes we waited from 6:30 p.m. or so, right after the toolbox talk, until after midnight. So for half a shift we would wait, loitering with the rest of the trades, outside the permit shack. A tremendous amount of time was wasted in this manner, and patience wore thin. After a crew received the permits and was cleared to enter a work area, the workers would start down one of the long roads between the trains, trudging to their stations. Because of the no shortcuts rule, everyone had to walk the long way around. Sometimes, by the time you got to your station, assessed the job, walked to the tool crib, and got back and set up, it was almost last coffee. Just enough time to make the long walk back to "Trailertown" for a fifteen-minute break. Then back to the job location to work for an hour or so before the end of shift.

"I don't know why they call it working," my young partner, Mathew, said. "They should just call it walking." It was true that people seemed to spend more time walking than working. Except the supervision. They had bikes.

The foremen, the general foreman, and the superintendent all had brand new black Supercycle Classic Cruisers from Canadian Tire. It was the least expensive adult bike in stock, running at $169.99 and our company had purchased twelve of them. They were a single gear bike with a chain guard and coaster brakes, and were outfitted with baskets that clamped onto the handlebars, which seemed like an excessive luxury. The baskets enabled people to carry clipboards, boxes of hardware, and small parts around as needed. The day-shift foremen were issued the bikes, and at cross-shift their night shift counterparts would take them over along with the clipboards.

Some of the supervisors were more used to riding larger bikes, noisy Harley Davidsons, and the idea of actually pedalling a bicycle was met with skepticism at first, the objection being that it lacked a certain machismo, or, as the complainants might say, made the rider look "gay." The convenience, however, of not having to walk twenty kilometres a day around the site quickly won everyone over. Even the baskets, initially discarded for their inherent gayness, were quickly reinstated. The bikers modified their rides, peeling off the factory decals and painting them flat black, and applying stickers of skulls and flames to the frames.

THE DAY AFTER the bikes were issued Mathew and I were standing outside Trailertown enjoying paper cups of weak coffee when our handlebar moustached, pot-bellied, Harley-Davidson-t-shirt-wearing foreman pedalled by on his Supercycle Classic Cruiser. He had decked it out with the requisite dollar-store flame stick-on decals, and he, or someone else, had added pink flagging-tape streamers that whipped off the ends of the handlebars in the breeze. Mathew shook his head.

"That is so ..." he lifted his hands and formed ironic air quotes around the word " 'gay'." That's the difference between the twenty-five-year-olds and the fifty-year-olds: the older guys would have said it for real. So we were making progress. Sort of.

The bikes were not only embraced by our supervisors, they were coveted by the ordinary workers. It was hot and dusty, and we resented the trudging, often laden-down with tools, from the trailer to the permit shacks, the shacks to the work areas, the work areas to the toolcrib, and back to the trailers, four times a day. I had had knee surgery earlier in the year, and my bicycle envy was stronger than most because walking was slow and painful. I watched the guys pedal by and harboured a dark and growing resentment. Then I started to plot how I was going to get a bike.

Shortly after the bikes were issued, my foreman gave me a job in the fabricating shop, making repairs to some stainless-steel trays. It was a TIG welding job, so I needed a machine and a table. The shop had been colonized by pipefitters, who normally would have grumbled about sharing the resources with a boilermaker, but I adopted an air of aggressive good cheer which, combined with the immunity I sometimes enjoyed by wearing my hair in pigtails, seemed to confuse them long enough for me to set up in the back. The trays were intermittent. Mathew would bring some by when he pulled them out of the tower, and I would fix them. When I was out of trays I wandered in the boneyard, where I found the dead bicycle pile. A tangle of decommissioned bike parts was stacked next to the scrap metal bin. Thrilled, I found a reasonable frame and two wheels that weren't flat or bent, and dragged them back to the welding shop. Mathew dropped a couple of trays on my table and eyed the bike frame.

"I could help you with that," he said.

"Really?" I felt a wave of affection for Mathew. It turned out his favourite thing was building mountain bikes. I took the wheels off the old frame and Mathew put the new ones on, set the brakes up, tightened the chain, and even found a kickstand. It was a ghastly, horrible thing, my bike, and I was jubilant. Just before quitting time I parked it in an empty sea can and sprayed it with the only paint I could find, which was bright yellow.

BACK AT THE hotel, I dreamed of the bike, of coasting down the gravel roadways, streamers whipping off the handlebars. The next evening, as soon as our toolbox talk was over and my crew was headed to the permit shack to wait for paperwork, I headed to the sea can. Mathew was already there.

"I've got something for you," he said, and held up a wire basket. It was bent and rusty, but it was a basket. He found some hardware and bolted the basket on to my handlebars, and I touched up the frame with yellow paint.

"It looks good," he said.

"What if someone wants to steal her?" I asked.

"They won't," he said. "It's yellow. It's too gay."

"I'm calling her Sulphur," I said, and took a big black Sharpie, and wrote the bike's name on the yellow frame, in a flowing script.

I couldn't wait to take Sulphur for a spin, and soon was tooling around the plant like a champ. My welding helmet and chipping hammer fit in the basket, and I rode with great purpose, as though I had to get to where I was going fast, to make a critical repair. It was the first time I'd been on a bike, other than in the gym, since my surgery. My knee loved it. During the first two weeks of the job, while I was walking, I had always been the last one to arrive in my work area. The last to coffee, the last to the bus, limping slightly, pitiful. With Sulphur the whole world changed. I cruised around the trains, under the overhead coolers and between the stills. I stood up on the pedals when riding uphill and learned to skid the back wheel sideways a little when I stopped. I rolled down the hill to the main sulphur tank and parked ostentatiously on the roadside, using the kickstand, while I was welding out a nozzle on the roof.

Suddenly I was strong and mobile again, and I was part of the team. I was the only one with a bike, and my crew tolerated this special privilege because they had gained a runner. I was happy to hop on my bike and run the errands that we normally took turns with, slogging up the dusty hill on foot. Need a crescent wrench?

"No don't get up," I'd say. "I'll just nip over to the tool crib and get you one." Dead battery in the radio? "I'll go grab one from the office," I'd say, thinking always, *on my bike*. I'm not sure they did, but I imagined that my crew also held me in slightly higher regard because I'd turned the pipefitters' fabrication space into a chop shop and built myself a ride on company time. Some of my colleagues who weren't on my immediate team were not so tolerant.

"How did you get a bike?" an apprentice sneered as I coasted past him.

"I'm blowing the boss," I called back breezily, over my shoulder. I was invincible. I could say whatever I wanted. I turned the local slang on its head. I was blowing the boss on my gay bike.

When the chain came off, which it often did, I'd just pull over and fiddle it back on to the sprocket. It was while doing this that the superintendent pulled over on his newish black Supercruiser.

"Where did *that* bike come from?" he asked.

"I dunno," I said, wiping grease on my coveralls, which, along with my boots, had been over-sprayed with bright yellow paint.

"You don't, eh?" he said, looking pointedly at my yellow boots. I shook my head, and he climbed on his own bike and pedalled away.

FOR THE FIRST week I had Sulphur I parked her at the end of the shift in the sea can with a hand-printed cardboard sign propped against her that said "WET PAINT." The idea was that anyone who found her and was desperate enough to ride a yellow bike probably wouldn't be willing to sully his coveralls with wet spray paint as well. After a week or so I found the sign on the floor of the sea can and the bike facing the other way, which meant someone on dayshift had been riding her. I became fiercely possessive after that, and started parking her in the darkest recesses of an abandoned warehouse across from the lunch trailer. Back at the hotel I worried that I'd show up for work and she'd be missing, or trashed and thrown back on the dead bike pile next to the metal bin. At the start of each shift, after the toolbox talk, I'd hurry across the road to the warehouse, a little fearful that she wouldn't be there. But every time she was, bright in the beam of my flashlight, and I'd experience a little thrill while I walked her out, pretending she was a high-strung racehorse.

NEAR THE END of the job, after I'd been riding Sulphur for nearly five weeks, she went missing. We'd been working long days and hadn't had a day off in twenty-six shifts. Everyone was tired and edgy. We were waiting for our permits and I'd walked across the road to the operators' building to the bathroom. When I got back, she was gone.

"Where's my bike?" I asked the guys. I tried to stay calm, thinking they had maybe hidden her on me as a prank, but they genuinely didn't seem to know. I walked casually away, like it didn't matter, until I saw Mathew.

"I can't find her," I said, beginning to panic. "Sulphur. She's gone." Mathew took the situation seriously, and acted as my agent, asking a couple of the other trades if they'd seen the yellow bike that was propped against the water tank. I paced, agitated. Mathew came back after talking to the sheet-metal guys.

"Those guys say they think one of the brickies took it," he said.

"What?" I asked. "WHAT??" I went over to the group of sheet-metal guys and peppered them with questions. They were more or less in agreement that one of the bricklayers had taken Sulphur from the water tank and gone for a little spin up and down the road. They hadn't noticed what happened next. I looked over at the group of bricklayers. They weren't subcontracting for our company but were local guys working directly for the plant, which meant I didn't know any of them. Bricklayers, generally, are big, strong, easy-going guys whose lives are ruled by quiet precision, straight lines, and perfect contours. Many seemed to be Irish, and I think of them as soft-spoken, kind, and serious, with big hands. But on that day, I was furious. I wanted to kill them.

"Yeah," Mathew said, later. "You really lost your shit."

WHEN I HAD confirmed that a bricklayer had taken my bike, a stranger, no less, I headed over to their group and stood on a little step so I was almost as tall as some of them.

"HEY!" I said. "Which one of you motherfuckers has been assing up my bike?" The buzz of conversation around the permit shack stopped. The workers moved in a little, to see what was happening. The bricklayers seemed confused. I picked one at random and said "Yeah, I'm talking to you . . . motherfucker. Where's my bike?" The guy I'd singled out started to bristle, then looked behind me at the little group of boilermakers, who were my crew. When I glanced back, they were sort of smiling and scowling at the same time. Unlike bricklayers, boilermakers are not known for their even tempers and easygoing ways. They are mostly known for being foul-mouthed and a little crazy. They might be up for a brawl, not in my defence, but just to break the monotony. The guy I was challenging slowly turned and looked at another guy, giving him up. Then they all looked at him. This fellow was in his early twenties, about half my age, and had freckles and sandy-red hair. He turned around and walked a little way away, then pulled Sulphur out from behind a propane tank. He wheeled her over to me.

"Sorry," he said, handing her over. "I didn't know it was yours."

"Yeah?" I said, "Well, thank you." I wheeled my bike away and the boys turned back to their conversations. There wasn't going to be a rumble after all.

THERE WERE NO repercussions for my behaviour, there never are. In any other job there's a chance you'll get fired if you call someone a motherfucker but in my job it happens all the time. It's just part of the culture, a kind of short hand. On the upside it cuts out a lot of verbal frippery; you can get straight to the point and everyone knows what you mean. After years of taking offence to the local patois, I had started using it, and found that by doing so I could render certain idioms meaningless, or at least ridiculous.

I didn't mind appearing to have lost my mind, going toe to toe with a stranger who was a foot taller than me and half my age. It happens. I didn't mind being caught out using vulgar language; that happens often enough too. What I did mind was that I hadn't used it consciously. I had just been mad, had misplaced the thread, and that made me an asshole. But more than anything, I minded that the encounter made me feel old. The bricklayer who handed back my bike was polite, and I felt like some sort of archaic, redneck throwback as I took it from him. *We don't talk like that anymore,* he seemed to be saying. *I'm not really like this*, I wanted to tell him, *I'm not part of the problem*. But it seemed the younger generation was already carrying the torch. The culture had been evolving for the better, and I had failed to keep up.

When my foreman asked if I wanted to stay on for another month to install several thousand stainless anchors inside one of the vessels, I declined and said I'd take the lay-off. I was sore and tired and my nerves were shot.

"Let the young ones do it," I said. "I'm going to take the summer off."

AT THE END of my last shift, I gave Sulphur to Mathew. She was a little small for him, and the colour was wrong, but he said he was going to take her back into the shop and do some mods. The chain was constantly coming off by then, but he'd found a better one, and a newer sprocket. He said he thought he might lengthen the handlebars and chop the frame, turn her into a low-rider. He was going to paint her flat black and get some flame stickers from the dollar store, and maybe some real streamers for the handlebars.

"Yup," he said, "That's going to be one sweet ride."

SOURDOUGH

The Camelot Court Motel in Prince George was originally built and decorated with an Arthurian theme in mind. The sign out front still featured a knight in chain mail and a similarly outfitted horse. But despite its aspirations to the sovereign class, the Camelot was a dive. Decades of service as a low-end residency hotel had stripped it to its essence: cinder block walls, polyester bedspreads, and decaying woodgrain furniture. The live-in manager was a well-liked person who had two English bulldogs, Duke and Paige, which had some sort of bulldog foot problem that made them very smelly. Not all the rooms had kitchenettes, and none of them had air conditioning. But the Camelot was popular with some boilermakers because you could back your truck right up to the door, and it still had rooms you could smoke in. The boys called it the Cameltoe.

Across the highway was the big grocery store. During my only ever stay at the Camelot, I ran across the street to pick up a loaf of their surprisingly good sourdough bread, and ended up in line at the bakery, behind a woman who was shopping with her son. He was around seven, had straight-cut bangs and round eyeglasses. He was trying to talk to his mother while she was trying to shop. The sourdough was still warm, plump round loaves sitting in rows in plastic bags on the big rolling rack. The mother picked one up.

"But WHY?" he asked her, in the way of a child who has asked a parent something many times, and not received a satisfactory answer. "WHY do they call it SOUR dough?"

"I told you," his mother said, "I don't know." They lined up at the bakery counter.

"But there must be a reason why," he insisted.

"Here," she said, handing him the sourdough. "You can use the slicer." The bakery had a slicing machine that customers could use. You unwrapped the bread and put it in a little rack, then pressed a button that fired it up. You could watch the bread slide down the rack at an angle until it engaged with multiple slicing blades, which sawed through the loaf. Then it popped out and landed in another little rack at the bottom, perfectly sliced, ready to go back in its bag. For this curious child the slicing machine was a big deal, and he hopped from foot to foot in the line, as though he was waiting his turn for a ride at a theme park. I got in line behind them with my own loaf of sourdough. A bakery employee pushed a cart of rye bread out on to the floor and the boy stepped in front of her.

"Why do they call it sourdough?" he asked.

"I dunno," she said, maneuvering her cart around him. He sighed. The line moved forward. He turned to his mother.

"There must be a reason," he said again. The mother checked her phone. The customer in front took his croissants and moved on. The boy had his loaf out of the bag and pushed it up over his head into the slicing rack. He pushed the button. Nothing happened. He pushed it again. His mother pushed it, still nothing. A baker came over and told them that the machine wasn't working.

"NOOOOO . . ." The boy rolled his eyes toward the ceiling and groaned. Then he darted forward and grabbed the corner of the baker's white jacket.

"WHY do they call it SOURdough?" he demanded.

"What?" the baker asked.

"The BREAD," the boy said. "Why do they call it SOUR dough?"

"Um, well," the baker stammered. "I'm not sure. I guess because it tastes kind of . . . sour?"

"But WHY?" the boy wailed. The baker turned to the mother.

"You can use our slicing machine, if you want. Just give me a minute, I can do it for you. I'll be right there." He disappeared into the back with her bread.

"Why do they call it sourdough," the boy muttered to himself, "why do they call it sourdough," a mantra, trying to invoke the answer. I was still in the line-up behind them, and heard my own voice say, "It's because of how they make it." His head snapped up.

"What?" he said.

"The sourdough," I said. "They make it differently from other kinds of bread." His mother was giving me a warning look, but I kept going. I was trying to help, passing the time while we waited for the baker, who showed no signs of reappearing.

"How do they make it?" the boy asked.

"Well," I said, "It's a different kind of leavening agent."

"What's leavening?" he asked.

"It's what makes the bread rise," I said. "You know all those little air pockets in the bread? Those are formed by little bubbles in the dough when it's still raw, then when you bake it they turn into those air pockets. You get them from adding a leavening agent to the dough when you are mixing it up."

"It's an AGENT?" he asked, his eyes widening.

"Well, not a SECRET agent," I said. "Usually it's yeast, which is the same thing that makes the bubbles in beer. But sometimes it's soda. It's a chemical reaction in the dough."

The boy nodded. His mother checked her phone again and leaned over the counter looking for the baker.

"But what about the SOUR dough?" the boy asked, urgently, sensing his time was running out.

"Well," I said, "sourdough doesn't use yeast. It uses a live culture instead."

"It's ALIVE?" he asked, and peered at his own round loaf.

"Yes," I said. "You have to feed the culture once in a while, and keep it within a certain temperature range, and you can take off little bits of it and put it in your bread dough and it will make it rise. And the sourdough culture has that sour taste. That's why they call it sourdough." I smiled, explanation over. The baker came out and we all paused while he put the loaf of sourdough through the slicing machine. As he was putting it back in the plastic bag, the boy turned back to me.

"Now hang on," he said. "What do you mean it's alive, and you have to feed it?"

"Well," I said, "you keep it in a jar in the fridge, or in a crock on the counter. And you feed it flour and sugar and water and it eats that stuff and it grows." The boy started hopping up and down.

"You mean it's really ALIVE?" he asked.

"Well, it's not alive like an animal," I said. "I mean it's not ... it's not a mammal, with a heart and everything ... I mean it's not like a PUPPY ..."

"But it's ALIVE ... what IS it?"

"It's ..." I was struggling. "It's a kind of goo, it's got microbes in it or something, microscopic creatures ... it's a culture ... a colony of tiny animals so small you can't see them ... it's ... it's a GOO, made out of flour and sugar and water, and it keeps growing as long as you look after it."

"How long does it live?" he asked.

"Oh," I said, "it can live a long time."

"HOW long?"

"Um ... some, I think, some sourdough cultures are more than a hundred years old." He looked at me incredulously, as though nothing could possibly live that long. His mother kept trying to take his hand and drag him out of the store, but he twined his arms around a bread rack, gripping it so she couldn't pull him away.

"Thanks," the mother said to me.

"A hundred YEARS?" the boy asked. I nodded.

"Yep. As long as you feed it. That's how they brought it across in the covered wagons."

"WHAT???"

"When the settlers first came," I told him. "They didn't have any yeast or any other way to make bread, but some of them had brought sourdough culture in a jar from Europe, and they carried it with them across the country in the covered wagon. Drawn by horses. They used to sleep with it in their beds to keep it from freezing during the cold prairie nights. The most important thing was to keep the sourdough alive. Because as long as the sourdough was alive they had bread. If the sourdough died, the people would starve, or get some sort of awful malnutrition disease, and the children would die." I was hoping my enthusiasm would make up for the inaccuracies in my story. The boy now had a death grip on the bread rack.

"It's time to GO," his mother said, trying to take hold of his arm.

"Hang ON," he told her, then summarized, speaking quickly. "So let me get this straight. It's a kind of wet goo made of lots of tiny creatures, so small you can't even SEE them, and it lives in a JAR on your counter, and it's ALIVE. And you FEED it with sugar and flour, and it has to DRINK when it's thirsty so you give it water. And it acts like a secret AGENT in your bread, and it has MICROBES that make the air bubbles before you bake it. And it can live for more than A HUNDRED YEARS..." He was jumping up and down. "...and they brought it across the ocean from Europe and carried it in the BED with them, across the whole COUNTRY, in a covered wagon pulled by HORSES and if it died all the PEOPLE died too?"

"Yep," I said, "pretty much, that's it. And it's the sour taste of the goo, that's why they call it sourdough." The boy nodded at me.

"Thank you," he said, releasing the bread rack.

"Can we get some?"

"What?" she asked.

"Some SOURdough," he said. "Can we get some?" The mother turned back to me, and smiled sarcastically.

"Like I said, thanks for that." she said.

"Can we get some SOURDOUGH?" the boy asked again. "I'll look after it. I'll feed it and everything."

"Sorry," I called after the mother. "Look . . . can I buy you a goldfish or something? Maybe take his mind off it?" The mother took the boy firmly by the hand and marched him out of the store while the boy chattered, using large hand gestures. I imagined them going home to a big, messy house, with a thousand ongoing projects, a shrine dedicated to this boy's insatiable curiosity.

The baker handed me my sliced bread, and I headed back to the Camelot, Guinevere of Sandwich.

ACID TEST

WARNING: This story contains language that may be offensive.

My first field job with Local 359 was at Harmac, in Nanaimo, working inside the Kamyr digester. It's a vertical vessel, twelve storeys tall, that is used to cook the black liquor in the recovery boiler process line. Another welder and I rode up the outside of the tower in a construction elevator, a yellow cage that slides up and down on a temporary track attached to the vessel. At the top, we got into a little, steel man-basket and were lowered 135 feet down inside the tower on a cable. We were told to hold tight to the middle bar on the basket and make yourself small going through the hole at the top. The basket was only big enough for two people, and was lowered down on a tugger, which is a kind of winch. The basket swung and spun, all the way down to a staging platform. On the platform we got out of the basket, and gouged stainless-steel plates off the inside walls. There was a large fan on the top hole, but it was ineffective. Then the fan stopped working and the vessel filled with smoke. We realized our radio wasn't working either, and communication with the top of the tower had been cut off. We waited a long time, until someone noticed, then watched as an object was lowered down through the hole on a rope. It was a handheld radio. My partner untied the rope and pressed the button.

"Would someone please get us the fuck out of here?" he said.

Another time during the same job, I was at the top, maintaining radio contact with the guys inside, watching down the hole, and signalling the tugger operator. Halfway through the shift, the tugger stopped working because the generator that powered it ran out of fuel. I had two men stranded a hundred and thirty-five feet down a hole, inside a confined space for nearly an hour, while the apprentice ran around trying to find fuel for the generator. None of these things should have stopped working: the fan, the radio, the winch, the generator. Any one of them could have had serious, if not fatal, consequences. Near the end of that job, I was gouging inside again, and my welding cable came apart at one of the connections, about fifty feet in the air. The bare end, alive with 450 amps of current running to it, swung languidly back and forth. If it touched the winch cable and arced out, that cable would be compromised, in danger of breaking under load, and we would have had no way to get out. I called up on the radio to the apprentice:

"Break the welding cable at the top, OK? Copy that? Don't pull it up — disconnect the power to the welding cable on the outside of the hole... and tape the live end. Then we're coming up." The entire job was terrifying, from start to finish. The man-basket isn't used to lower workers into digestors anymore, it's too dangerous. Now they erect scaffolding inside, with stairs, and install proper ventilation systems, and good lighting.

Years later, we were trading stories in the lunchroom about our first jobs. When I told that story, Craig said, "They put you down a digester in a man-basket on your first job? They should never have done that, put a green worker down there. That was a mistake. Or else they were testing you." Deliberate or not, it had been a test. On the early jobs there were many tests.

NOT LONG AFTER the job at Harmac, I took a call to go to work at Canexus, the chemical plant that's snuggled into a nook on the north shore of Burrard Inlet, just east of the Iron Workers Memorial Bridge. I had been welding rollover pipes on dozer boats at the shipyard in North Vancouver, and helping with the conversion of a friend's sixty-foot steel tugboat into a live-aboard. I was house-sitting for some friends in North Van while they were in Spain, so had a place to stay. When the tugboat job ended, I took the job at the chemical plant.

The plant made liquid chlorine, but it also processed sulfur products, including hydrogen sulfide, and sulfuric acid. There were huge tanks of liquid chlorine on site, enough to poison thousands of people on the North Shore with chlorine gas, and take out a good section of Burnaby as well, if there was ever an explosion. A significant leak would mean a massive cloud of poisonous gas settling over the city, then drifting toward Burnaby Mountain. I was edgy just being there, and kept thinking about earthquakes.

It was a small crew, four of us, crammed around a table in one half of a little ATCO trailer and the foreman's office at the other end. The trailer wobbled on uneven wooden blocks at the edge of the parking lot. It was winter and dark when I arrived at six in the morning, and dark when we left at five in the afternoon. I was still very new to the trade, and didn't know anyone there. My strategy was to keep my head down and fly under the radar. I'd brought a book to read at the breaks, *Life of Pi*, which had just come out.

When I got there a middle-aged guy with greasy hair and restless eyes was pacing the room. He was solid, with big arms and gnarled hands. He talked fast and loudly, telling stories in which he was always the hero, interrupting himself with a laugh that was half bark and half bray. When the coffee cauldron gurgled to a finish he poured a paper cup of coffee and sat down across from me.

"So," he said. "Are you married?"

"Oh, here we go," another guy said.

"I just asked if she was married. So are you? Are you married?" I didn't answer. "So what, you're not talking to me? You're not going to answer? I don't see a ring." He studied me. "You don't look like the married type."

The other guy reached across the table and we shook hands.

"I'm Kurt," he said. "I'm the shop steward. It's nice to meet you. If you have any issues, you come and talk to me OK?"

"If I have any issues?" I asked, raising my eyebrows. He rolled his eyes.

The guy sitting across didn't miss a beat.

"So do you have a boyfriend? Are you shacked up? Do you live together? Is it an open relationship? Hey? Do you have some kind of arrangement 'cause I know you must be away from home a lot." He paused, "Tell me, do you like to fuck?" That was the first time I met Bo.

MOST OF THE welding in the chemical plant is stainless steel, not carbon. They use stainless piping systems to move the finished products around because it's less reactive and less likely to corrode, but it is harder to weld. You can get regular steel to flow in any direction when it's molten by directing the heat where you want it to go — liquid steel goes to the hottest point. But stainless is trickier, especially in any position other than flat. You have to get the amperage just right, and the rod angle, and you have to weld fast. The slag forms a solid crust over the bead and will suddenly crack and fly off as the weld cools, burning the welder, sticking to her skin. But if you're good at it the result is a flawless, flat, shiny weld. If you're not good at it, the slag doesn't pop off easily, has to be chipped, and the weld is a lumpy, droopy line of goo, filled with slag inclusions. I was new and didn't have a stainless ticket, so spent most of that job as a helper, going up in the man-lift with my partner, Francois, and taking down pieces of scrap metal. We unbolted flanges and replaced gaskets. I'd never been in a chemical plant before, was wide-eyed and nervous, trying to keep track of what was going on, trying to help when I could. It was loud, the roads narrow and crowded with construction vehicles there for the rebuild as well as those used in normal operations. The whole plant stank of chlorine, and we worked in respirators, communication restricted to Francois's accented voice muffled by the rubber mask, and his eyes.

On the second day Bo was in the trailer when I arrived, and sat down with his steaming cup of coffee as soon as I did. He leaned across the table.

"Maybe you're a lesbian, yeah, that must be it. Tell me, do you like to fuck other women? Are you one of those dykes that hates men? You seem like you could be a lesbian. I think you probably are one. She's a lesbian," he announced to the room. "She likes to get it on with the girlfriend. Hey? Is that right? You got an old lady? So do you use dildos or what? Vibrators? Or maybe threesomes? My old lady is into threesomes. She likes to get it on with another broad while I give it to her up the ass..."

On day three he was quieter, staring at me across the table. I took out my novel, like I did at every break, and tried to read. It was a cold day in early March. Bo waited until I took out some lip balm.

"So what's that for?" I didn't answer, and looked at my book. "Are you lubing up?" he continued. "Look, she's putting the lube on. Lubing her lips. You know what that's for, right, you know why she's doing that? It's because she's getting ready to suck my cock." He leaned in close. "I know you think about me. I know that's what you think about when you get home... sucking my cock... and that's what you're thinking about right now, while you're lubing up those lips..."

KURT AND FRANCOIS occasionally tried to settle him down, or left the room in frustration. The apprentice sat silently in the corner, next to the coffee machine, relieved, I suppose, that he wasn't the target. The guy they called Lil Pecker, however, was bitter, and enjoying the sport. He was Bo's audience and admirer, and on the fourth day he joined in.

"I've said it before and I'll say it again," Pecker said, "the biggest fucking mistake we ever made in this local was letting women in, and the next biggest mistake is that we let in welders."

"Welders are idiots," Bo responded. "Who would want to be a fucking welder? It's just a tool in the toolbox."

Kurt asked to see me outside. He had been my partner the day before, patiently explaining the piping system, showing me how to maneuver the man lift into a tight space. Outside the trailer he paced.

"You know you don't have to take that," he said.

"Actually I think I kind of do," I said. "You know how it is." Kurt shook his head. He told me I could complain about Bo if I wanted to, that he was out of line, and I could put a grievance into the union.

"He shouldn't get away with that, it's bullshit. And I'll back you up." His concern surprised me. I told him I couldn't make the complaint. Because I was still on probation, I wasn't a full member and didn't want to make any waves. But also, Bo was trying to provoke me into action.

"I know what this is," I told him. "I've been here before. It's a test. The only way I win is if he gets nothing back from me."

"OK," he said, "but I want you to know that you don't have to put up with that. You can come and talk to me."

EVERY DAY BO ramped up the hazing, taking it to a new level, surprising everyone, including himself, with the breadth and scope of his own obscenity. I soon lost the ability to read, but pretended to, bracing my forearms on the table so my hands didn't shake, and moving my eyes down the page, counting lines, then slowly turning the page in a plausible imitation. I drank paper cups of black coffee scalding hot, the way he did, then crumpled the cups and threw them in the bucket.

After three days of interrogation about my personal life, to which I didn't respond, Bo moved into the third person, commenting on everything I did. The lip balm, the book, what I wore, the scars on one of my arms. At five days he just started talking generally about things he thought would offend me: stripper girlfriends, prostitutes, threesomes, sex acts with animals. He told a long story about how he ran into two women who were "bisexual lesbians" and how he had a sex date with them on the weekend. There followed a long, speculative description of how he intended to have sex them. He described the women as "youngish."

"I mean let's face it," he said. "I'm not going to fuck anything that's my age." Moments later he contradicted himself.

"Oh, you want to fuck the old ones," he said. "Fuck them when they're forty because they're grateful. They act like they're never going to get it again." I counted lines and turned pages.

After the fifth day I started treating myself after work, buying little gifts to compensate. A little stone coaster at a gift shop in West Vancouver. The next day, two pairs of wool socks. Then takeout from a Thai restaurant on Lonsdale, a huge extravagance.

On day seven, Cooper, the shop steward on night shift, asked to see my outside. He asked if Bo was saying mean or provocative things to me.

"Not really," I said. "I mean no worse than he usually is."

"Because Kurt said he was asking you if you were a lesbian and all this stuff and you don't have to take it." I was touched by his concern. I told him I was going to stay the course and ride it out. My plan was to do nothing.

"That's impossible!" Cooper said. "But it would drive him crazy, that's for sure."

BY THE EIGHTH day I was angry. The fear had transformed into a slow, smouldering rage. It had become a battle of wills. What nerds lack in power they make up for with stamina. Around the same time, Bo started to get bored with the sport, and branched out into other topics. It was as though by enduring him for more than a week without displaying any visible cracks I had earned a kind of reprieve, and by the ninth day he was ignoring me completely. He started talking about other things, engaging more with the other guys. He'd bring it back and try to offend me when he thought of something, but his heart wasn't in it. I relaxed into the shadows, like the apprentice, counting lines and pages. Then he started talking about his divorce. About his ex, the stupid, worthless cunt, who took him for $535,000.

"Stupidest thing I ever did was marry that bitch," he continued. "It was nine years of misery, and in the end I had to pay off the stupid cunt. Five hunnerd and thirty-five grand. Can you believe it? It would have been cheaper to have a hunting accident, just blow the bitch's head off. A high-speed lead injection. Bullets are cheap. Would have cost me fifty cents for the bullet."

"You don't want to use a single shot," Pecker contributed, "or a small calibre. That would be execution style. That would be too humane. The idea is to blow the top of her head right off."

"Yeah that's right," Bo agreed, "take the whole top of the skull off so you can't even recognize the body." He paused. "The thing to do, would be to make her wear a hat with antlers on it and shoot her in the head at close range. I'll just tell the cops I thought it was a deer." They laughed. "Or just leave her there. It's an accident, right? Stupid cunt shot her own self in the head. Or just get rid of the body, she disappears. Would have been a fuck of a lot cheaper. That's what I shoulda done. I know guys, guys who do that for ya. Get rid of a body. That's what they do. And I mean it'll cost ya but it wouldn't have cost five hunnerd and thirty-five grand..."

There was a pause as he came to a break in the rant. I put my novel down and looked up from it very, very slowly.

"Hang on a minute." It was the first thing I'd said to him in nine days.

"Yeah?" He zeroed in on me.

"You say you were married?" I asked.

"Yeah. Yeah I married the bitch."

"How long were you married?"

"Nine years."

"How much did you say the divorce settlement was?"

"$535,000."

"You were married for nine years, and when you divorced you paid her $535,000?" I confirmed.

"That's right."

"I wouldn't go to the movies with you for that," I said, and went back to my book. Kurt was smiling.

"I'd call that a burn, Bo," he said. Bo got up and left the trailer, slamming the door. Outside we heard him laugh, long and loud, something between a bark and a bray.

I only saw him intermittently after that; we were not on the same jobs together very often. I liked to travel and took jobs out of town, where I'd receive living-out money, and Bo lived in the city and took the jobs closer to home. Sometimes years would pass when I didn't see him.

But after that, he was always friendly, saying "Hey, Peachy . . ." and slapping me on the back like we were old friends. I was wary as ever, knowing he could flip in a second. One time he came up to me, belligerently and posturing, clenching his fists the way he did when he was looking for a fight.

"I heard you called me a narcissistic sociopath," he said.

"With no conscience," I added. "You're welcome. Most people just say you're fucking nuts." He barked out that laugh.

Well in that case, thank you. I accept the compliment," he said.

YOU HAD TO treat him carefully, avoid him completely in certain moods, and never back down. Since I was small, and a woman, I didn't pose any physical threat to him so I didn't feel any real danger in return. I was just another anomaly to him, another freak in the sideshow where we went to work.

"Peachy, we all have one thing in common here," he told me once. "We all sat at the back of the class." I suspected he liked people who stood up to him, and also that he liked being insulted by women. I tried to oblige when I could.

Years after I passed the acid test at the chemical plant we worked together again, at the Chevron refinery.

I made a point of sitting beside him at the lunch table, leaning in closer than would be comfortable and saying, "Good to see you, Bo." The best way to keep him at bay was to get too close.

"Peachy!" he said on that first day, "this is going to be fun." He told me that he was going to haze every person in the room. He would start at the back, at the furthest table, and work all the way down to our table, abusing each person in turn to see who he could crack. It was just for kicks, for his own amusement. Every day he assessed his next victim.

"What's wrong with your skin?" he'd ask the kid with acne. "Is that some kind of syphilis? I hear you can get that if you're having sex with immediate family members..." It was a kind of stream of consciousness, improvised monologue. "Did you go down on your sister last night?" It was a catch-22. If they stood up to him he would destroy them, and if they didn't, well, he would still destroy them.

Slowly he worked his way around the room, picking off his targets one by one, occasionally eliciting a short skirmish before his victim would storm out of the trailer.

"That's another point," he'd say, beaming. He went easier on the older guys that knew him. "Hey Bernie... you still screwing your mother-in-law?"

"Fuck off, Bo."

"I think I should get a half point for that. I mean I've fucked his mother-in-law. It's not like she's choosy."

I REALIZED PART way through the exercise that if the job lasted long enough he would indeed get all the way around to our table, and I knew I would not be spared. When he was a table away, picking off a foursome of apprentices one by one, I started writing my script. It was concise, with short, pointy sentences I'd be able to remember under pressure. Mainly straightforward insults and name-calling, just bizarre enough to throw him off kilter. I practiced it when I got home, in the shower, and in the car driving to and from the job. When the inevitable day arrived, I was apprehensive, but well rehearsed. Standing in the fire with him was the only option I could think of to deal with Bo. First thing in the morning, as the two foremen took their place at the front of the room to lead the toolbox talk, he fixed me with his reptilian stare, his eyes hardening.

"Sorry kid," he said, "nobody here gets out alive." I decided to go for the pre-emptive strike.

"Suck my cock you fat bag of shit," I opened. He raised his eyebrows in surprise.

"Oh yeah?" he said. "Fatter than you? 'cause you're pretty fa—" I interrupted him.

"Fatter, stupider, uglier, with a face like a rhino's ass and the personality of a plastic bag." I took a breath while he let loose a torrent of obscenities, and I countered with my own catalogue of filth.

"What the hell is this?" one of the foremen asked. He'd been just about to start his daily safety talk when the firestorm broke out.

"You're just another liberal slut-bag who doesn't belong here..." Bo volleyed.

"You're a psychotic, power-obsessed douche-canoe..." I countered.

We continued in the same vein for a couple more minutes, over-talking each other with increasing volume until we were both out of ammunition. Then Bo looked at me calmly.

"Well, I'll give you one thing, Peachy, you do know how to defend yourself." He stood up, stretched, and headed outside.

"I need a smoke."

"What the hell WAS that?" the foreman asked, again.

"It was nothing," the other foreman answered, reading his clipboard. "They were just renewing their vows."

AFTER OUR FIRST skirmish, at the chemical plant, I wasn't afraid of Bo. I figured if he was going to kill me he would, and if he was going to let me live there wasn't much he could do to me that hadn't happened already. For his part, I think I was a steadying presence, didn't hesitate to say what I thought, and neither posed a threat nor acted like a victim. If I had food, an orange or a cookie, I always offered him one and he would accept. In this small, unremarkable transaction, lines were drawn that defined us in that moment as allies more than enemies. I was just another anomaly. I was like him.

There were occasions when I was even glad to see Bo. When there was a weird vibe on site, or someone from another trade was acting aggressively, or engaging in verbal horseplay with me. It didn't matter what differences he'd had with another member, there was an us and a them. He was a psychopath, but he was our psychopath. If the enemy was outside the trade and he crossed one of us, he risked Bo's wrath. One time in Crofton, the safety officer for the mill approached while I was tacking in some tubes.

"You look sore," he said.

"What?"

"I said you look sore," he repeated.

"I'm not," I said. My fitter, Steve, gave me a puzzled look.

"You should come down to the first aid room, and I could give you a massage," the mill guy said. Then he leaned in closer, his voice breathy, "I give really good . . . massages."

"Yeah?" I said. "OK. And we can review the sexual harassment policy while I'm there. Why don't you get started without me." Steve, who was a small guy, took a couple of steps toward him.

"Or," he said, "you could just fuck right off." First aid guy sauntered away. "That was weird," Steve said.

"It was, wasn't it," I said. "I mean it wasn't just me who thought so?"

"No, no," our apprentice concurred. "That was super weird." They thought I should report him, make a complaint. But while we were discussing it, Bo stepped out of the elevator. I had a better idea. I called him over.

"How would you like a massage?" I asked.

"Sure Peachy," he said, without hesitating. "Where do you wanna go?"

"Oh not from me," I told him. "They're giving free massages down in the first aid room." Steve told him what had happened. Bo lit up.

"Oh yeah," he said, nodding. "I could really use a massage. I'm sore all over." He stretched, farted, cracked his knuckles. "He can start on my ASS. I'll go down right after coffee." He laughed.

I DON'T KNOW exactly what happened in the first aid room because I wasn't there, but my understanding is this: Bo barged in after coffee, red-faced, sweating copiously, breathing heavily, clenching and unclenching his fists, cracking his knuckles, and generally acting like a maniac. "I HEAR YOU'RE GIVING OUT FREE MASSAGES," he snarled, pacing the room, spit flying. "WHERE DO YOU WANT ME TO UNDRESS?"

The next day he was laid off. I didn't see him for several months, but when I did, I thanked him.

"Oh no, Peachy," he said. "The pleasure was all mine."

THE LAST TIME we spoke was back at the refinery in Burnaby. I was renting a room in a friend's house off Commercial Drive. It was February and bitterly cold, and I was riding my bicycle back and forth to work, pulling eleven-hour night shifts. I'd leave and return in the dark, but loved the ride, labouring up the Burnaby hill as people were going home to dinner, then careening down the icy pavement at five in the morning, heading home to a hot shower. I was determined to keep it up until it snowed. About a week into the job, Bo was hired on. He was in the trailer when I arrived, sitting on a metal folding chair, his gut bulging in a torn black t-shirt over his belt buckle. Dark stains spread under his arms and across his chest. His thinning hair, combed straight back, retained the tracks of the comb. One corner of his mouth lifted slightly in a permanent scowl.

"Peachy!" he said. "Look at you — you're so thin ... you're gonna disappear!"

"I know, right?" I said. "First time I've seen my dick in ten years." Bo laughed loud and long. A few weeks later he was dead.

Stories about him persist: The time he was travel-carding in Ontario, working up a tower with a crew of locals, and defecated in a bucket because he didn't want to descend the hundred feet of ladder to the ground.

"You're an animal," his work partner said, appalled.

"No I'm not," Bo replied. "An animal wouldn't have used the bucket." There was the time he offered a female welder a ride to a job, drove wildly, dangerously, for hours and refused to stop at a bathroom, until she was in agony, finally pulling over in a wide-open area with no cover.

"OK," he said. "Go ahead." Then he watched and laughed while she squatted, humiliated, at the roadside. The time he kicked through a piece of half-inch plywood with his motorcycle boots to escape a burning vessel; the time he vaulted over a turnstile at the airport and drop-kicked an ironworker who had been saying "disrespectful things." Acts of violence both obscene and occasionally heroic, retold alternately, and sometimes simultaneously, with disgust and admiration.

THE JOB AT the refinery was his last. He had entered a spiral of mental illness from which he couldn't recover, a tailspin of hallucinations, until he turned his violence inward, taking his own life. The news was met with shock, nostalgia, a few older guys who mourned the passing of an era, and a number of people who said they were glad he was gone. I heard it from a welder who had known him for twenty-five years. I asked if he was sad about it, and he paused for just a moment.

"Nope. I'm really not. You?"

I shook my head. "Not at all."

THEY SAY THAT wherever you find the monster, you will find the child, and where you find the child there will be the monster. Because the two look after each other. All the violent men I've known have been a mixture of these two things: on the one hand extreme destructive impulses, cruelty, sometimes remorse but often none. At the same time a kind of happy-go-lucky naivete, and no understanding of the consequences of their actions. Bo had that childlike, casual disregard for others, but what I appreciated about him, in a way, was the purity of his evil. His complete lack of balance, or any redeeming quality. He was the essence of toxic masculinity, undiluted. He was an abyss.

He was by no means the only one. There were others who carried different shades of the same darkness. Boilermaking thrives in the dark. It's a trade that takes place in confined spaces, places where you have to get special permits to enter, test the air to see if it's breathable, enter by crawling through a hole in a steel tank and shimmying along a plank until you get to the thing you are going to repair. And welding is a trade that requires you to wear a special helmet that blocks out all the light, and no one else can look at you while you're working or they risk damage to their vision. You cover up to protect your skin.

It's not an occupation that requires finely tuned social skills. What is valued? Endurance. Fearlessness. Ingenuity. Strength. The ability to assess a task that appears to be impossible, and get it done. If you have most of these attributes, it could be a good fit. Manners were not required. They didn't matter, and neither did the abuses or injuries inflicted on each other. How is it possible to spend an entire career swimming against this undercurrent of violence? It was all just part of the same big, filthy, toxic backdrop, along with the smoke and the noise, the poisonous chemicals and long hours, against which we were living our lives. It's the deal you make, and sometimes there are monsters.

I WOULDN'T TAKE YOU WITH ME

I would never take a woman with me out on the high iron. Lawrence told me that at Harmac while we were partnered together on the blowdown tank. He was an ironworker who worked with us as a permit, then later joined as a member. He was an excellent welder and seldom spoke. He was slight and wiry and nimble as a cat. He always wore the heel-less ironworker boots with his cuffs tucked and taped up, and a black hoodie with the hood pulled well forward, shielding his face. At work he wore the hoodie under his coveralls, and under his welding helmet. His face, when you could see it, was always dirty, like a child's. He just blurted it out. He finished burning a rod, lifted his welding helmet and delivered his line: *I would never take a woman with me out on the high iron.* It was the only time he'd ever spoken to me, a statement of fact. He wanted me to know, I suppose, that that's where he drew the line.

I knew what he meant. If you're an ironworker welding structural steel, walking the I-beams twenty, or thirty, or forty storeys up, you need to be able to trust your partner. You don't want to be out there with just anyone. You want to know your partner is capable, doesn't need looking after, isn't going to walk out to the end of a beam and freeze. And you want to know that person is capable of saving your life, if necessary, because it might be. Lawrence had worked the high iron for years as a younger man, before fall protection was mandatory. He didn't have to brag, the fact that he was still alive said enough.

Fortunately, we were not working on a forty-storey building, walking out on a nine-inch I-beam. We were welding out the transition of the top of the new blowdown tank, which is only about twenty feet up, and we could get to the top by climbing a few levels of scaffold. The tank was shaped roughly like a giant acorn, with sides that sloped inwards from the top down. At the top of the wall sections was the transition weld, where the sloped roof joined the tank. I was welding while standing on the scaffold, and Lawrence was crouched on top of the tank, welding a seam that couldn't be reached from the platform. I could tell it wasn't personal, he just wanted me to know. He'd weld jet rod with me, but walking the high iron was out.

"That's OK, Lawrence," I said, "because there are lots of places I wouldn't take you either, so we're about even." We finished the shift in silence.

THE NEXT DAY the sky was clear and blue when we climbed up on the tank and started welding. Jet rod is a fast-moving fill rod with a heavy flux and a high deposition rate. I hadn't used it before. The rods were long and awkward and you had to move quickly. Lawrence had welded miles of it in his life, and when I asked, he gave me a quick lesson. It completely changed the way I was handling it and my welding was suddenly much better than the day before. Then out of nowhere he spoke.

"Where?"

"Where what?"

"Where wouldn't you take me? You said yesterday, there were places."

"Oh," I said. "Well, I wouldn't take you to the opera."

"I wouldn't go to the opera," he said.

"That's why I wouldn't take you. I don't think you'd like it."

After first coffee we climbed back up on to the tank.

"Where else?" Lawrence asked.

"Where else what?"

"Where else wouldn't you take me?" He seemed genuinely interested. He knew he wouldn't want to be with me twenty storeys in the air, but he hadn't considered that I might also have no-go zones for him.

"I wouldn't take you to the ballet," I said. Lawrence scowled.

"I wouldn't go to the ballet."

"I know." We welded for a while longer.

"Where else?" I took off my helmet, unsnapped my respirator, and started cleaning it with some alcohol wipes.

"I wouldn't take you to a library, because you'd be bored. I wouldn't take you to a night school cooking class, or to yoga, because you're shy."

"Do you go to those things?" he asked.

"Yes."

We welded.

"I would not take you to an art gallery," I volunteered, "where there was, say, a retrospective of French impressionist paintings, but I would take you to a sculpture garden."

"What's a sculpture garden?" he asked.

"It's . . . a park, or a public place, like a garden, and there are giant sculptures displayed, sometimes by one artist and sometimes different ones. They can be bronze, or steel, or stone, whatever. You just . . . walk around the park and look at sculptures. There's a big one in Central Park. In New York City." Lawrence studied me for few seconds.

"I'd go to that," he said. I nodded.

"They're cool."

THAT'S HOW THE rest of the week played out. We would weld, then discuss the places where I would or would not take him, and he would tell me whether or not he'd go. Usually I had it right.

"I would take you to a dog show."

"I'd go to a dog show."

"I'd take you on a bird count. Where you spend the day looking for birds and recording what you saw."

"I'd do that."

"I wouldn't take you ice skating. I wouldn't take you with me to try on shoes. I would take you to ride a miniature train. I would not take you on a Ferris wheel." While we were at work the world became neatly divided into places where Lawrence would go with me, and places where he would not.

"I would take you to a punk rock show," I said, on our third day on the tank, "but only one of the old-style ones, in an abandoned warehouse or somewhere. Not a nightclub."

"I'd go to that."

"I wouldn't take you to a jazz improv show or a new music concert."

"I don't think I'd like that."

"I'd take you to a poetry reading," I said, "but only if it was in a bar. Not a cafe." Lawrence looked doubtful. "In a really crummy part of town," I added, "and I wouldn't make you stay for the whole thing."

"A bar?" he asked.

"Twenty minutes, tops. Then you're free to go."

"I'd go to that," he said, decisively. "If it was in a bar."

"I wouldn't take you to a fancy dinner party where your place setting had more than two forks ... but I would take you to a Moroccan restaurant." Lawrence paused, frowned.

"I don't know about that," he said.

"Seriously?" I asked. "This is the deal breaker? I thought for sure it would have been the poetry reading."

"That's Africa, right?" he asked..

I nodded. "North Africa. On the Mediterranean."

"What's the food like?" he asked.

"It's great," I said. "There's ... um ... lamb, or you can order a big, hot delicious stew with whole pieces of chicken in it, and vegetables, with spices, and preserved lemons, and olives ... and sometimes it's cooked in this clay, chimney-shaped dish called a tagine, so it comes out really tender and flavourful." After a long moment, Lawrence nodded.

"I would try that," he said.

ON THE FOURTH day we finished the tank, and our seam was going to be X-rayed overnight. Lawrence, who hardly ever spoke to anyone, was waiting for me at the end of the shift, outside the trailer. We had started walking out of the mill to the gate together. A couple of guys were watching, from the smoking area.

"Where are you two love birds headed off to?" one of them called out. Before I could answer, Lawrence turned around, and called back.

"We're going to a dog show in a sculpture garden, dinner at a Moroccan restaurant, and maybe a poetry reading after. In a punk rock bar." He kept walking, smiling a little. I shrugged.

"I just let him decide," I said. "It's easier that way."

THICK SKIN

Prince George was where I learned to swear, and if swearing is something you need to learn to do, it's as good a place as any. It's the main city in the north of the province, home to three of the nation's largest pulp mills: Intercon, PG Pulp, and Northwood. Locked in the Interior, surrounded by mountains, with sub-zero winters and black fly summers, it is a place of great extremity. I always had the feeling that the Northern mills were where the big dogs played, with more capacity, more danger, and a general sense that you could get into more trouble, both on and off the job.

The mills weren't the quaint, oceanfront facilities in picturesque tourist towns on Vancouver Island, where I was from. In Nanaimo and Campbell River you could go salmon fishing on your day off. In Crofton you could spend it on Saltspring Island, buying homemade soap and having a reiki treatment. In Prince George, the guys mostly seemed to go to the strip club, get in fights and end up in the drunk tank. For several years in a row the city held the dubious title of "the most dangerous city in Canada," and was the murder capital of the nation. I was told repeatedly by colleagues not to walk around alone at night, advice I did not heed.

Because of the three mills, I travelled to Prince George once or twice a season, and always felt comfortable there. I loved the riverfront parks, bike paths, cottonwood trees, bears, and foxes. There's a terrific train museum, and one of my favourite bookstores, Books & Company, that used to hold concerts upstairs. I even found a yoga class to attend.

THE YEAR OF the explosion job, an ignitor lance came loose and fell into the recovery boiler, piercing a tube. The water from the tube reacted with the liquid smelt bed of the recovery boiler, causing an explosion, and the whole thing blew, ripping apart the corner seams and twisting huge sections of tubes. We replaced most of it that year. Not long afterwards, there was the clinker job, when a nugget of salt cake the size of a Volkswagen came down from the superheaters, and fell to the bottom, crushing the floor. We were there for months. Living the dream.

BC boilermakers were known for being super well skilled, having an excellent apprenticeship program, and being badass. Scruffier, louder, more foul-mouthed, and generally more inclined to hijinks, no topic or commentary was off limits, and in the early days I found it hard to take.

"You need to have a thicker skin," I was told.

"Why do I need a thick skin?" I'd ask, "Why can't you just act like a human being?" The answer to that question turned out to be complex, and has taken years to unpack.

BOILERMAKING HAS ITS own vocabulary – the names of tools and processes, the anatomy of equipment – but it also has a language, a dialect that separates those on the inside from the uninitiated. Every occupation has its linguistic shortcuts, its identifiers. But boilermakers have a specific, recontextualized social slang. For one thing, there is an inordinate amount of language that references genitalia. If I had a dollar for every time I've heard someone mention cocks, balls, dicks, asses, assholes, pussies, and cunts, while I was at work, I could retire. This is the hard liquor of small talk, the stuff that takes getting used to. As rough as the dialect is, it has its uses. It quickly establishes social order, a hierarchy, in a dangerous environment. It dispenses with personal sensitivities. It's designed to toughen you up, to thicken the skin. As the hard hat sticker says, "If you can't stand the heat, get the fuck out of the boiler."

WHEN I WORKED in the creative sector, inclusive, respectful language was valued, and reflected the work we were doing. When I became a welder, misogynist and homophobic epithets were common parlance. I didn't like it, but for the most part was unable to say much, especially in the beginning.

There have been attempts by external administrative bodies to expunge sexist language from the workplace, under the guise of making it a more welcoming place for women. These efforts usually fell short, and often had the opposite effect, identifying the women on site as targets who were disrupting the status quo. Realistically, one woman on a site with four hundred men is not going to effectively redesign a deeply embedded cultural vocabulary, even if she wanted to. Her objections will have no impact, and are likely to trigger a protracted group hostility that can be career ending.

I have always loved language and have been fearless in it. To move in language is to swim. It is flight. At its best, language is wide open, a wondrous and free commodity, like water. Like snow. I didn't always buy the argument that rewriting workplace jargon would create a safe and welcoming space. Words make up the script, and aren't as harmful as the thinking behind them. That's not going to change by regulating the dictionary. When someone consistently used misogynist language, he was self-identifying as misogynist. This was useful information to have if I had to work beside him for a night, or a week, or a month. I liked to know where people stood. The futile task of trying to cleanse a vocabulary was not going to change anyone's mind.

Sometimes, the only political statement I was able to make was to show up every day. To be present, to set an example by being there. Being present over time meant trying to get along. I put in long shifts, worked in close quarters, sat in lunchrooms, rode the bus, made small talk, and lived at work camps, with hundreds, actually thousands, of male colleagues. Most of them were good guys, and over the years I got to know and care about my union brothers, and sisters. We watched each other grow up, form relationships, have babies, get married, and divorced. As cliché as it sounds, we shared successes, and personal tragedies. I learned who was having an affair, who was in trouble with the law, who had a secret habit, and who knocked up the babysitter. I knew whose kid had just won a scholarship, or was being scouted by a hockey team, or had just come out as gay, or was making it big as a singer in Nashville. We were all in it together.

But along with the good guys were some who left their goodness at the gate. They were different people at work than they were at home. And they were right; you did need to have a thick skin in the trade. Vulnerabilities were tenaciously attacked. You don't bleed in the shark pool.

I was surprised to discover that a thick skin is something that can be learned. Being immune to injury, to some degree, was a necessary quality in the trade. It indicated to other people that they didn't have to worry about you, that you could take care of yourself. It also meant that you could say what you really thought, which was liberating. Communications were direct, and the usual social conventions didn't apply. Interactions were straightforward and authentic, and revealed a startling variety of interests, eccentricities, and quirks. Underneath everything, there was a surprisingly tolerant micro-culture.

When other women were on the job it made a remarkable difference. One other woman, and you are no longer the freak, the anomaly. You have an ally. Three or more, and everything changes. We can no longer be isolated or targeted in the same way. It becomes an undeniable reality: there are women here. Someone has to organize a second bathroom.

While the number of women I've worked with has steadily increased over the tenure of my career, there are still very few in positions of authority. Notable exceptions were Kate, one of the best welders the local has ever had, who made superintendent. Jane was regularly a foreman at the refinery, and Willow broke into Quality Control as a welding inspector. I can't think of any others, even though the women I've worked with were, without exception, extraordinary.

I am asked, constantly, what it's like to be a woman working in heavy construction. I have many opinions — political, social, and psychological — that circle around this topic, and I try to refrain from expressing them. Opinions are less interesting to me than actions. I will say, that the process of creating room for oneself, as a woman in this environment, can be slow and difficult. And sometimes, it is easy. I am reminded of a time when Wendy and I were tacking I-beam supports under a boiler in Prince George, with two young fitters. One of them told the other to move the beam over just a cunt hair. He then remembered both his welders were women, and apologized for his language.

"You know, I've never really known how much that is, a cunt hair. Like, as a unit of measurement, how big is that exactly?" I asked Wendy.

"Just a sec," she said. She took off her gloves, unbuttoned her coveralls, reached inside and rummaged around for some time, then pulled out a single, invisible "hair." She held it out to me with a flourish and a big smile and said, "the width of that."

"Oh," I said, leaning in and making a show of examining it closely, then taking it from her. "So a cunt hair's not very much at all, it's like, a tenth of a millimetre." Our fitter blushed.

OUTSIDE THE TRADE, it's acknowledged that profanities are toxic, and they are used sparingly. At work, it was fit in, or fuck off. We worked in the rough embrace of a sprawling, unruly, dysfunctional family, with lots of alcoholic uncles who used filthy language. But women kept showing up.

When I joined the local there were around seven hundred members, and seven were women. A few others had come before, but not many. Some men were supportive, some didn't care, and some thought allowing women on the job was a terrible idea and would cause all kinds of upheaval, from sexual entanglements, to industrial accidents, to communism. Men were going to have to take down their pin-up girls, clean up their language, and make room. Some of these changes started to happen, but not because of the women. They happened when gender politics hit the mainstream, and corporate clients realized that a visibly sexist culture could damage their profile.

Twenty years ago, there was an overt territorialism, a desire to keep well-paid trades jobs exclusively for men, and to keep women out. It wasn't articulated that women were a threat. What was said, was that we couldn't do the job. That we weren't strong, or smart, or technical enough. To make sure the argument proved out, knowledge and opportunities were withheld. And if we were going to insist on being there anyway, we better be able to handle every aspect of the job, including the cock talk. These days, younger women tell me this is not their experience.

"I don't know what you're talking about," one apprentice told me. "The guys have always been cool with me." This is about the best thing that I can hear, because it means my time wasn't wasted.

"That's good," I said. "Now make sure you get the promotions you deserve. Accept a position of leadership. Be a foreman. You should be carrying a radio before you're forty." Women who work in the trade still face barriers and abuse, and an avalanche of filthy language, but expectations of conduct seem to be changing, and employment equity policies are actually enforced. We are a more culturally diverse and inclusive workforce than twenty years ago, and I have faith in the new people coming into the trade, the young women and men. They have grown up online, raised on a bounty of information, and live in a much larger world than their parents and grandparents.

Harassment in the workplace based on race or gender makes less sense to them. Having women in the apprenticeship class is normal now. Women in trades organizations are gaining visibility. Some of the positive changes in the workplace culture are thanks to a younger, more in-touch executive at the union hall, where, it should also be noted, positions of power are still exclusively held by men.

IT WAS ON the explosion job in Prince George that a foreman knelt down beside me while I was welding and whispered, intimately, into my ear:

"If it had been up to me, you'd have been fired weeks ago. This is no place for women."

"If you don't like your job," I said, "you can go and work in a flower shop."

PRINCE GEORGE IS a city of contradictions. Heavy industry and natural beauty. Decidedly working class, there's also a university, a theatre, and some good restaurants. There's a right-wing, Catholic, new age health food store, where you can buy a crucifix with your probiotics. When I went to vote at the elementary school during a federal election, a hooker was flagging down trucks across the street at ten o'clock in the morning. It's a city that taught me a lot about my trade, about people, and about the weather. I was always happy to pass the last campground, cross the last bridge and pull into town, and almost, but not quite, sad when it was time to leave.

The cottonwood trees self-seed in the gravel bars in the middle of the rivers, and after they bloom, the parks are filled with the blowing fluff from their seed pods. You can ride a bicycle around the perimeter of the city, following the rivers, if you aren't afraid of bears. On the east side of town, for a five-dollar donation you can tour the train museum, and ride the miniature railway through a network of antique logging equipment. There is a park there, that floods occasionally, beside the river, which is the first place I ever saw a fox, sly and red, so thin that when it turned away it seemed to disappear, transforming into a shadow.

May 22

Cut the side of the bullnose loose, gouging the membrane that attached it to the side wall. Gas alarms going all night so evacuations. String lights blowing breakers in the boiler, making everyone crazy. In a confined space when it's dark it's DARK.

WE HAD A colleague that Charlotte called the Clean Welder, because his coveralls, remarkably, were never dirty, no matter where he spent his workday. He went to the same Chinese-Canadian restaurant every day after work, sat at the same table, and had two or three things that he always ordered, in rotation.

"Can you imagine?" Charlotte asked, "always going to the same place, having the same thing?" I could imagine it, and how this synthesized familiarity was comforting. The proprietors recognized him and greeted him warmly, brought the kind of beer he preferred, and engaged in the same social routine every night. He knew what to expect. He could relax. His evenings were without anxiety.

May 23

Blew holes in the old bullnose so we can hang the rigging. Laid out cut lines for four tubes on level 7 where they will be removed and a header put in.

I AM INTERESTED in the Jungian idea of the shadow, that part of the consciousness that is left unexpressed. Not evil, not the dark side, but the parts of the self, as James Hollis puts it, "...that I find troubling, that are contradictory to my values, that are counter to my intentionality."

"Jung thought that in order for an individual to make successful passage into middle life, it was necessary to make an appointment

FIELD NOTES

Small goats browsed at the side of the road. A barn owl loomed out of the dusk, glowing rings around his dished-out eyes. A sign warned of badgers crossing. Sage-covered foothills rolled down to the highway giving way to a pastureland sprinkled with white-faced cattle. Black Angus calves picked their way unsteadily toward a creek. A sign advertised chainsaw carvings in front of a scrubby field dotted with creatures carved out of logs. The Coquihalla was closed because of an accident, so I was driving to Kamloops the long way. I pulled into the gas station in Boston Bar. Outside on the notice board was a card, advertising black Russian terriers for sale, taped above a picture of a somber looking young man in the middle of a pack of black dogs of dubious parentage. A second notice offered a gold dredge with a new motor and pump in perfect shape for two thousand dollars, if I called Wayne.

It was just before midnight when I pulled into the Hospitality Inn. A printed sign said "Ring After Hours," and an arrow pointed to a button that I pressed. A woman with a silver beehive hairdo, moccasins, and pink satin pajamas came to the door.

"I'd just about given up on you," she said.

THE HOSPITALITY INN is on the side of a mountain in upper Kamloops, on Columbia. There's a two-storey building, and a single storey, both built in the 1980s. I had a primo room in the single story, which had sliding doors that opened on to a grassy area on the side of the hill. From there, a panoramic view of the city below, then the river, then the mountains.

May 17

Gouged out forty feet of skin casing without nicking any feeder tubes. We're taking the external casing off to expose the tubes and thickness test them, to see if the walls have thinned out. The noise and toxic smoke keep the fitter and apprentice away — it's a sweet pocket of solitude. They wait out on the roof until I'm done, and when they come in to lay out the next section I go out. There's a great view from the roof. Beyond the chip pile, the reservoir pond, the river, the rolling hills, the city, the mountains, the stars.

IN KAMLOOPS, CHARLOTTE taught me that you have to do one thing outside of work every day, even on night shift. You have to get up, get dressed, go out into the world and do something. She would go to a movie, or a restaurant, or shopping for a project at home. Charlotte had been welding in the union fifteen years longer than me. She was an inspiration, always cheerful, with a let's-get-to-it attitude and didn't take any nonsense. I didn't have the "do something every day" rule, but I tried to eat healthy, drink water, and find a yoga class when I was out of town. There was a nice yoga studio in Kamloops, near the college, and we started going in the afternoons, a couple days a week. Other days we'd drive downtown and look in the shops, to break the monotony of just working and sleeping.

May 18

Still on demo, removing membrane and skin casing in the bullnose. Stayed over to help land a buckstay on the one below in the tight space between the waterwall and the staging. Some hot slag fell into my jacket and burned my chest. Quick thinking apprentice soaked me with water

from the squirt can. Expected wet T-shirt jokes but there were none kudos to him for putting out the fire. He saved my skin.

THE TIME RIGHT after work was a favourite time, because there a whole twelve hours before I'd have to do it again. Back in the c semi-subterranean room, I'd turn off all the lights but one, pull latches across the door, put out the "do not disturb" sign, shower, make a cup of tea. Then do nothing but look at the view and down as the sun came up.

May 20

10 hours lying on my back under the inside of the bullnose, wel stiffeners in overhead so they can demo and lift the side wall out.

PSYCHOLOGISTS WHO STUDY rituals say they provide struc to one's life, and a sense of belonging, and it was always the s habits that defined my parameters, that kept me from coming a The customs varied from place to place. In Montana, it was a gla rosé in the bathtub after shift. In Port Alice, it was tarot cards. T kinds of vitamins, different creams for hands and face, a handf pistachio nuts in a blue Melmac bowl. Sometimes it was watching same cop show at the same time every night, sometimes James H videos about Carl Jung. In Michigan, I listened to *Purple Rain* at volume in the rental car every day while driving from the hot the power plant, and never told anyone. In Wallula, I always dra Corona in the shower after shift. I kept myself sewn inside a rou of small movements. I get homesick, and repeated rituals proc the illusion of home, no matter where you are.

with the shadow," says Hollis, on YouTube. I like this very much. Instead of the dour, thirty-year doldrum that lacks both the energy of youth and the wisdom of age, Hollis makes middle life sound like a trip, preceded by a fun lunch date. It's the word *passage*, as though you are about to board an ocean liner and embark on an exciting sea voyage. We hear people talk about facing their demons, or embracing the dark side, but Hollis says "...make an appointment with the shadow." As though you can just pick up a phone — an old rotary dial phone — and call her up: "Hello Shadow? What are you doing on Wednesday at 4:15?"

May 27

Less hot work and more rigging. Piece of the new bullnose, 8 ton section of tubes, moved on to the ground under the boiler. Our job is to mouse it — send a half-inch cable through looking for blockages. Discovered they'd stuffed it with rice paper before QC had signed off, so had to get the snowballs out with an air lance, then water...

THERE'S A WEBSITE featuring thrift-store paintings that have had monsters added to them. Originally it was a couple of young artists who would search thrift stores for oil paintings or watercolours, usually landscapes. Pastoral scenes of the English countryside, or mountains and lakes in the Midwest. Then they would carefully paint in various monsters. The idea was to use the same colours and textures of paint so the paintings were not visibly altered. They would just become a pastoral English village ... with a cyclops standing in a doorway. Or a pristine glacial lake, with strange fish creatures flying in the clouds.

One of the things I liked to do while working away from home, is page through magazines and find images of animals or objects, cut them out and insert them into the hotel room art. They needed to be small and of the same colour palette, incongruous content only noticed if someone actually looked at the art. Of course no one does that, looks at the art in hotel rooms. I've never received an irritated phone call from a hotel manager, asking me if I'd glued a tiny picture of a horse into a scene of skyscrapers, or placed a little elephant among a herd of cattle. Hopefully some future guest or cleaning staff person will enjoy a little surprise.

May 29

Welding at ground level — pads on tubes and the bullnose so pressure parts — a bunch of bored riggers hassling me. Fred putting his hands in front of my eyes while I'm grinding. Jerry tapping my shoulder and disappearing, someone shaking the jig, hiding tools, changing the polarity on my machine. Pecker took apart my die grinder and hid the pieces. It was sport for most, no one seemed to have a personal beef except him. He told the apprentice I was "taking work from some man."

"So where the hell is this guy?" I asked the apprentice. "Because I'm getting tired of doing his job for him ... when's he going to show up?"

Bonaparte is the general foreman. He was in a hurry to get the lugs welded on, and asked why I wasn't welding. When I told him his riggers were holding me up, he freaked out and chased them away. Later, Pecker approached me in the yard.

"I don't hate you," he said. "I just don't think women should be here." In other words, it's not personal, he just hates women.

"I don't care what you think of me," I answered. "Just stay the fuck out of my area."

SOMETIMES THAT'S WHAT it feels like at work, like I'm slipping little animals, or small monsters, into the landscape. I say things and don't recognize myself, things that come straight out of the shadow.

June 5

Welding screen tubes. It's excellent. The other welders are so young, so happy and fun. My apprentice is puppyish. My fitter is Clive, of the porn-star moustache. I make everyone on the crew figure out their porn star name. It's the name of your first pet plus the street you grow up: Max Rippen. Mike Divine. Daisy Shamus. Porky Penn. And Lulu Bridgeport

IN KAMLOOPS THERE have always been mice at the plant, lots of them. They scurry around the yard, so many that raptors circle overhead at dusk and hunt there, and owls come in when it's dark and swoop under the precipitators. We could never understand why there were so many mice at Kamloops, until they decided it was time to bring new crew trailers in. When they hooked up the old ATCOs to take them away, hundreds of mice poured out of them. It turned out there was a colony living in the unused forced-air heating vents that ran through the bottoms of the trailers. The heat had been switched to electric baseboards years earlier, and the mice took over, packing the air ducts. For years we had been eating our lunches on top of a mouse megalopolis.

June 20

Last night we fit the last pieces of mesh screen into the bullnose instead of skin casing. It's a sealed bullnose so no welding on the inside.

CHARLOTTE ALWAYS GOT us to go out to lunch. Indian, Mexican, or some little place downtown. Frank was staying in the same complex that I was, only he was in the part that was having the roof replaced. When a sudden, fierce rainstorm came on overnight, all the guys on the top floor were flooded, and Frank got it worst of all, the rain washing in a sheet of water down the inside of his window.

"I've got a water feature in my room!" he said, beaming. I don't remember where we went, just that we had lunch, a small group, den-mothered along by Charlotte. Her son is our foreman. On the last job, he laid her off on Mother's Day.

"You're laid off," he said.

"You can't do that, I'm your mother," she answered.

"I just did. You're laid off."

"It's Mother's Day. You can't lay your mother off on Mother's Day."

"See you on the next one."

These social occasions and miniature field trips were instrumental in allowing my work persona to join with my real life. For a long time it was easier to keep them separate, then time passed, and it was impossible. Assimilation, Jung calls it. The joining of disassociated aspects of the psyche, in striving toward wholeness. "Healing of the psyche," Hollis says, "always comes from the shadow."

June 21

Dry squeeze on Sunday night. Bonaparte tells us to take an extra 15 minutes for lunch — the mill is so appreciative. Wow. 15 minutes. And how many thousands was his bonus?

AFTER THE LAST shift on any job, the night before I drove home, I would pack the car for a quick getaway in the morning. Then I would put on my one good shirt, some earrings and a ring, comb my hair, and go out for dinner at the best restaurant in town. In many pulp mill towns this is not as indulgent as it sounds. The Victorian Steakhouse in Port Alice, for example, has yet to achieve its first Michelin star. The rib place in Chetwynd is OK, and on "Wing Wednesday" you can get a pound of wings for five bucks. There's a private room made to look like a giant wooden barrel that people can sit inside.

In Kamloops the best restaurant is The Brownstone, a former bank in a brownstone building in the heart of the old downtown. It is small, quiet, elegant, with a serious wine list. The menu features duck, elk, and Arctic char, and there are usually one or two exquisite specials. The wine glasses are oversized and thin walled and always the right temperature. The wait staff are courteous, professional, and smart. They ask if I would prefer to sit by a window. They don't want to be my friends. They don't ask how "that first bite is tasting" when my mouth is full. It's a place where I take my time, ask questions about the food, and order carefully. I tip well, and they forget me immediately as soon as I leave. I appreciate the Brownstone very much. Especially the forgetting.

GOOD ALTERNATIVES TO BAD MOTELS

"Do you hear that?" Hal asked. "It sounds like a cat. You can go through anything now, any kind of weather." He was talking about the metal studs in my new winter tires while we took a test drive around the block. Hal had been looking after my car for more than 300,000 kilometres. Many times I had called after reaching my destination in bad weather, and left a message: *I'm in Grande Prairie*, or I'*m in Castlegar. Tell Hal he saved my life again*. From the garage in Nanaimo, I drove north on the Island Highway, stopping once to phone and ask where the hubcaps were, and learned there aren't any when you buy studded tires. My old Honda Element was just a machine in winter, no stylings.

Campbell River was a blur of slush, the gas station a brief respite, icy rain slapping the shoppers around. When I got out to fuel up, the wind pulled the door out of my hand, bending the hinge. I sprinted to the store through the sleet to buy all the necessary things: carrots, apples, shampoo, nuts, Band-Aids, crackers, Polysporin, cheese, sardines, tiny bottles of mustard and mayo, celery to keep me awake on the road, orange juice, yogurt. It was the same for every job, and I always meant to make a list. Way up in the ceiling struts of the store, small birds darted around, chirping. They weren't trying to get out, they lived there. I had with me a small wooden birdcall, and when I twisted the metal pin, it squeaked and chirped. The little brown birds flew down and perched in the aisles around me while I looked for mouthwash. St Francis of A Superstore.

THE BIRDCALL IS one of the things I carried in my pocket while travelling, along with a round stone, a knife, a lead bullet, and a tiny plastic poodle. Talismans that protected me, from exactly what I was never sure, but they kept the monsters at bay.

Vitamins, rice cakes, beans, bread, oranges, walnuts, organic frozen burritos, and the rest: health food and personal hygiene items all mixed up in the buggy together. I would not do well in a food insecurity situation. Not because I needed all the things, but because I needed to choose, assemble, and organize them, to know they were there. I needed the system.

I had taken the seats out of the Element, welded a frame together and cut a piece of plywood to make a bed in the back of the car, and everything fit under it, in big drawers: the cooler, portable kitchen, camp stove, work gear. A memory foam mattress, plush duvet and pillows made for a cushy option in case I needed to sleep at the side of the road. I slept in the car a lot. On ferries, car camping in Manning Park, or naps along the Cariboo Highway. It was a good alternative to bad motels. No one would know I had a pile of tools tucked away under the paisley duvet. I just looked like some girl glamping.

So much rain. I backtracked to the highway past the wedding dress shops, diesel engine repair mechanics and fish smokers. Past the crappy, two-storey hotel on the corner advertising weekly rates, strippers, and a steak sandwich special, hanging on despite the chain motels advancing from every direction. Good for you, crappy corner joint, serving the needs of fucked-up alcoholics for more than sixty years.

FIELD NOTES

Small goats browsed at the side of the road. A barn owl loomed out of the dusk, glowing rings around his dished-out eyes. A sign warned of badgers crossing. Sage-covered foothills rolled down to the highway giving way to a pastureland sprinkled with white-faced cattle. Black Angus calves picked their way unsteadily toward a creek. A sign advertised chainsaw carvings in front of a scrubby field dotted with creatures carved out of logs. The Coquihalla was closed because of an accident, so I was driving to Kamloops the long way. I pulled into the gas station in Boston Bar. Outside on the notice board was a card, advertising black Russian terriers for sale, taped above a picture of a somber looking young man in the middle of a pack of black dogs of dubious parentage. A second notice offered a gold dredge with a new motor and pump in perfect shape for two thousand dollars, if I called Wayne.

It was just before midnight when I pulled into the Hospitality Inn. A printed sign said "Ring After Hours," and an arrow pointed to a button that I pressed. A woman with a silver beehive hairdo, moccasins, and pink satin pajamas came to the door.

"I'd just about given up on you," she said.

THE HOSPITALITY INN is on the side of a mountain in upper Kamloops, on Columbia. There's a two-storey building, and a single storey, both built in the 1980s. I had a primo room in the single story, which had sliding doors that opened on to a grassy area on the side of the hill. From there, a panoramic view of the city below, then the river, then the mountains.

May 17

Gouged out forty feet of skin casing without nicking any feeder tubes. We're taking the external casing off to expose the tubes and thickness test them, to see if the walls have thinned out. The noise and toxic smoke keep the fitter and apprentice away — it's a sweet pocket of solitude. They wait out on the roof until I'm done, and when they come in to lay out the next section I go out. There's a great view from the roof. Beyond the chip pile, the reservoir pond, the river, the rolling hills, the city, the mountains, the stars.

IN KAMLOOPS, CHARLOTTE taught me that you have to do one thing outside of work every day, even on night shift. You have to get up, get dressed, go out into the world and do something. She would go to a movie, or a restaurant, or shopping for a project at home. Charlotte had been welding in the union fifteen years longer than me. She was an inspiration, always cheerful, with a let's-get-to-it attitude and didn't take any nonsense. I didn't have the "do something every day" rule, but I tried to eat healthy, drink water, and find a yoga class when I was out of town. There was a nice yoga studio in Kamloops, near the college, and we started going in the afternoons, a couple days a week. Other days we'd drive downtown and look in the shops, to break the monotony of just working and sleeping.

May 18

Still on demo, removing membrane and skin casing in the bullnose. Stayed over to help land a buckstay on the one below in the tight space between the waterwall and the staging. Some hot slag fell into my jacket and burned my chest. Quick thinking apprentice soaked me with water from the squirt can. Expected wet T-shirt jokes but there were none, just kudos to him for putting out the fire. He saved my skin.

THE TIME RIGHT after work was a favourite time, because there was a whole twelve hours before I'd have to do it again. Back in the dark, semi-subterranean room, I'd turn off all the lights but one, pull both latches across the door, put out the "do not disturb" sign, shower, and make a cup of tea. Then do nothing but look at the view and wind down as the sun came up.

May 20

10 hours lying on my back under the inside of the bullnose, welding stiffeners in overhead so they can demo and lift the side wall out.

PSYCHOLOGISTS WHO STUDY rituals say they provide structure to one's life, and a sense of belonging, and it was always the small habits that defined my parameters, that kept me from coming apart. The customs varied from place to place. In Montana, it was a glass of rosé in the bathtub after shift. In Port Alice, it was tarot cards. Three kinds of vitamins, different creams for hands and face, a handful of pistachio nuts in a blue Melmac bowl. Sometimes it was watching the same cop show at the same time every night, sometimes James Hollis videos about Carl Jung. In Michigan, I listened to *Purple Rain* at full volume in the rental car every day while driving from the hotel to the power plant, and never told anyone. In Wallula, I always drank a Corona in the shower after shift. I kept myself sewn inside a routine of small movements. I get homesick, and repeated rituals produce the illusion of home, no matter where you are.

May 22

Cut the side of the bullnose loose, gouging the membrane that attached it to the side wall. Gas alarms going all night so evacuations. String lights blowing breakers in the boiler, making everyone crazy. In a confined space when it's dark it's DARK.

WE HAD A colleague that Charlotte called the Clean Welder, because his coveralls, remarkably, were never dirty, no matter where he spent his workday. He went to the same Chinese-Canadian restaurant every day after work, sat at the same table, and had two or three things that he always ordered, in rotation.

"Can you imagine?" Charlotte asked, "always going to the same place, having the same thing?" I could imagine it, and how this synthesized familiarity was comforting. The proprietors recognized him and greeted him warmly, brought the kind of beer he preferred, and engaged in the same social routine every night. He knew what to expect. He could relax. His evenings were without anxiety.

May 23

Blew holes in the old bullnose so we can hang the rigging. Laid out cut lines for four tubes on level 7 where they will be removed and a header put in.

I AM INTERESTED in the Jungian idea of the shadow, that part of the consciousness that is left unexpressed. Not evil, not the dark side, but the parts of the self, as James Hollis puts it, "...that I find troubling, that are contradictory to my values, that are counter to my intentionality."

"Jung thought that in order for an individual to make successful passage into middle life, it was necessary to make an appointment with the shadow," says Hollis, on YouTube. I like this very much. Instead of the dour, thirty-year doldrum that lacks both the energy of youth and the wisdom of age, Hollis makes middle life sound like a trip, preceded by a fun lunch date. It's the word *passage*, as though you are about to board an ocean liner and embark on an exciting sea voyage. We hear people talk about facing their demons, or embracing the dark side, but Hollis says "...make an appointment with the shadow." As though you can just pick up a phone — an old rotary dial phone — and call her up: "Hello Shadow? What are you doing on Wednesday at 4:15?"

May 27

Less hot work and more rigging. Piece of the new bullnose, 8 ton section of tubes, moved on to the ground under the boiler. Our job is to mouse it — send a half-inch cable through looking for blockages. Discovered they'd stuffed it with rice paper before QC had signed off, so had to get the snowballs out with an air lance, then water...

THERE'S A WEBSITE featuring thrift-store paintings that have had monsters added to them. Originally it was a couple of young artists who would search thrift stores for oil paintings or watercolours, usually landscapes. Pastoral scenes of the English countryside, or mountains and lakes in the Midwest. Then they would carefully paint in various monsters. The idea was to use the same colours and textures of paint so the paintings were not visibly altered. They would just become a pastoral English village ... with a cyclops standing in a doorway. Or a pristine glacial lake, with strange fish creatures flying in the clouds.

One of the things I liked to do while working away from home, is page through magazines and find images of animals or objects, cut them out and insert them into the hotel room art. They needed to be small and of the same colour palette, incongruous content only noticed if someone actually looked at the art. Of course no one does that, looks at the art in hotel rooms. I've never received an irritated phone call from a hotel manager, asking me if I'd glued a tiny picture of a horse into a scene of skyscrapers, or placed a little elephant among a herd of cattle. Hopefully some future guest or cleaning staff person will enjoy a little surprise.

May 29

Welding at ground level — pads on tubes and the bullnose so pressure parts — a bunch of bored riggers hassling me. Fred putting his hands in front of my eyes while I'm grinding. Jerry tapping my shoulder and disappearing, someone shaking the jig, hiding tools, changing the polarity on my machine. Pecker took apart my die grinder and hid the pieces. It was sport for most, no one seemed to have a personal beef except him. He told the apprentice I was "taking work from some man."

"So where the hell is this guy?" I asked the apprentice. "Because I'm getting tired of doing his job for him ... when's he going to show up?"

Bonaparte is the general foreman. He was in a hurry to get the lugs welded on, and asked why I wasn't welding. When I told him his riggers were holding me up, he freaked out and chased them away. Later, Pecker approached me in the yard.

"I don't hate you," he said. "I just don't think women should be here." In other words, it's not personal, he just hates women.

"I don't care what you think of me," I answered. "Just stay the fuck out of my area."

SOMETIMES THAT'S WHAT it feels like at work, like I'm slipping little animals, or small monsters, into the landscape. I say things and don't recognize myself, things that come straight out of the shadow.

June 5

Welding screen tubes. It's excellent. The other welders are so young, so happy and fun. My apprentice is puppyish. My fitter is Clive, of the porn-star moustache. I make everyone on the crew figure out their porn star name. It's the name of your first pet plus the street you grow up: Max Rippen. Mike Divine. Daisy Shamus. Porky Penn. And Lulu Bridgeport

IN KAMLOOPS THERE have always been mice at the plant, lots of them. They scurry around the yard, so many that raptors circle overhead at dusk and hunt there, and owls come in when it's dark and swoop under the precipitators. We could never understand why there were so many mice at Kamloops, until they decided it was time to bring new crew trailers in. When they hooked up the old ATCOs to take them away, hundreds of mice poured out of them. It turned out there was a colony living in the unused forced-air heating vents that ran through the bottoms of the trailers. The heat had been switched to electric baseboards years earlier, and the mice took over, packing the air ducts. For years we had been eating our lunches on top of a mouse megalopolis.

June 20

Last night we fit the last pieces of mesh screen into the bullnose instead of skin casing. It's a sealed bullnose so no welding on the inside.

CHARLOTTE ALWAYS GOT us to go out to lunch. Indian, Mexican, or some little place downtown. Frank was staying in the same complex that I was, only he was in the part that was having the roof replaced. When a sudden, fierce rainstorm came on overnight, all the guys on the top floor were flooded, and Frank got it worst of all, the rain washing in a sheet of water down the inside of his window.

"I've got a water feature in my room!" he said, beaming. I don't remember where we went, just that we had lunch, a small group, den-mothered along by Charlotte. Her son is our foreman. On the last job, he laid her off on Mother's Day.

"You're laid off," he said.

"You can't do that, I'm your mother," she answered.

"I just did. You're laid off."

"It's Mother's Day. You can't lay your mother off on Mother's Day."

"See you on the next one."

These social occasions and miniature field trips were instrumental in allowing my work persona to join with my real life. For a long time it was easier to keep them separate, then time passed, and it was impossible. Assimilation, Jung calls it. The joining of disassociated aspects of the psyche, in striving toward wholeness. "Healing of the psyche," Hollis says, "always comes from the shadow."

June 21

Dry squeeze on Sunday night. Bonaparte tells us to take an extra 15 minutes for lunch — the mill is so appreciative. Wow. 15 minutes. And how many thousands was his bonus?

AFTER THE LAST shift on any job, the night before I drove home, I would pack the car for a quick getaway in the morning. Then I would put on my one good shirt, some earrings and a ring, comb my hair, and go out for dinner at the best restaurant in town. In many pulp mill towns this is not as indulgent as it sounds. The Victorian Steakhouse in Port Alice, for example, has yet to achieve its first Michelin star. The rib place in Chetwynd is OK, and on "Wing Wednesday" you can get a pound of wings for five bucks. There's a private room made to look like a giant wooden barrel that people can sit inside.

In Kamloops the best restaurant is The Brownstone, a former bank in a brownstone building in the heart of the old downtown. It is small, quiet, elegant, with a serious wine list. The menu features duck, elk, and Arctic char, and there are usually one or two exquisite specials. The wine glasses are oversized and thin walled and always the right temperature. The wait staff are courteous, professional, and smart. They ask if I would prefer to sit by a window. They don't want to be my friends. They don't ask how "that first bite is tasting" when my mouth is full. It's a place where I take my time, ask questions about the food, and order carefully. I tip well, and they forget me immediately as soon as I leave. I appreciate the Brownstone very much. Especially the forgetting.

GOOD ALTERNATIVES TO BAD MOTELS

"Do you hear that?" Hal asked. "It sounds like a cat. You can go through anything now, any kind of weather." He was talking about the metal studs in my new winter tires while we took a test drive around the block. Hal had been looking after my car for more than 300,000 kilometres. Many times I had called after reaching my destination in bad weather, and left a message: *I'm in Grande Prairie*, or I'*m in Castlegar. Tell Hal he saved my life again*. From the garage in Nanaimo, I drove north on the Island Highway, stopping once to phone and ask where the hubcaps were, and learned there aren't any when you buy studded tires. My old Honda Element was just a machine in winter, no stylings.

Campbell River was a blur of slush, the gas station a brief respite, icy rain slapping the shoppers around. When I got out to fuel up, the wind pulled the door out of my hand, bending the hinge. I sprinted to the store through the sleet to buy all the necessary things: carrots, apples, shampoo, nuts, Band-Aids, crackers, Polysporin, cheese, sardines, tiny bottles of mustard and mayo, celery to keep me awake on the road, orange juice, yogurt. It was the same for every job, and I always meant to make a list. Way up in the ceiling struts of the store, small birds darted around, chirping. They weren't trying to get out, they lived there. I had with me a small wooden birdcall, and when I twisted the metal pin, it squeaked and chirped. The little brown birds flew down and perched in the aisles around me while I looked for mouthwash. St Francis of A Superstore.

THE BIRDCALL IS one of the things I carried in my pocket while travelling, along with a round stone, a knife, a lead bullet, and a tiny plastic poodle. Talismans that protected me, from exactly what I was never sure, but they kept the monsters at bay.

Vitamins, rice cakes, beans, bread, oranges, walnuts, organic frozen burritos, and the rest: health food and personal hygiene items all mixed up in the buggy together. I would not do well in a food insecurity situation. Not because I needed all the things, but because I needed to choose, assemble, and organize them, to know they were there. I needed the system.

I had taken the seats out of the Element, welded a frame together and cut a piece of plywood to make a bed in the back of the car, and everything fit under it, in big drawers: the cooler, portable kitchen, camp stove, work gear. A memory foam mattress, plush duvet and pillows made for a cushy option in case I needed to sleep at the side of the road. I slept in the car a lot. On ferries, car camping in Manning Park, or naps along the Cariboo Highway. It was a good alternative to bad motels. No one would know I had a pile of tools tucked away under the paisley duvet. I just looked like some girl glamping.

So much rain. I backtracked to the highway past the wedding dress shops, diesel engine repair mechanics and fish smokers. Past the crappy, two-storey hotel on the corner advertising weekly rates, strippers, and a steak sandwich special, hanging on despite the chain motels advancing from every direction. Good for you, crappy corner joint, serving the needs of fucked-up alcoholics for more than sixty years.

The road wound past the Elk Falls Mill and the sign to the contractors' parking lot where I was not stopping. The rain turning to icy snow and the road treacherous. Five hundred kilometres to go, and north the only direction. What was I forgetting? The only time the road was really visible was in the headlights of oncoming cars or the bright eyes of animals on the move, but who would be out in this weather? The snow was horizontal, the last daylight slipping away, and cell signal was discontinued. You are now out of the serviceable area.

OH, THESE LONG scenes of driving, these hours giving way to measured distance, tricks to the eyes and swirling snowfall. The stretch between Sayward and Woss was always a bastard; if it wasn't like this it was fog. The guy in the pickup in front was skating around, too light in the back end, but I crept miles behind him on studded tires, the twin sparks of his taillights trolling through the black grey frozen winter crappy night.

There was a new gas station just outside of Port McNeil and cell service was restored. Hello? Hello are you there? The manager of the B&B advised me to take my time, the road off the highway was slow going in bad weather. Thirty more kilometres of snowstorm highway, then thirty-six on the crazy, winding forest road. Mice ran through the headlights. It was very dark. Somewhere on the left was the lake and the clear-cut, and to the right, more trees, more snow, animals, the rest of the mountain, and then the sea. Switchbacks slashed through the mountain and signs warned of logging trucks that didn't stop. The road finally opened up to the village.

The managers of the B&B, had waited up for me. They were new to town, young kids, unsure if they would stay, but giving it a shot. They showed me the driveway, perpendicular, like backing down a pyramid. Everything is in extremity here. This is the hall, furnace room, stairs, living room, kitchen, your bedroom, the other bedroom, bathroom, jet tub, another bedroom, fireplace... You're kidding, this place goes on forever. Then they were gone, and I unpacked the car.

CONSTRUCTION ON THE pulp mill started in 1916 and in a couple of years it was producing seventy-five tons of lumber a day and had started making pulp. A townsite next to the mill was cleared, and fifty houses, a hotel and a boarding house were constructed, then wiped out by a landslide. During one of the later expansions, part of the mill was built on top of the old cemetery, causing some of the dead to become agitated and start haunting the mill. Between the cemetery spirits, First Nations ancestors, some dead loggers, and mysteriously murdered travellers, the streets of Port Alice are lousy with ghosts.

I SLEPT AS long as I could, preparing for night shift, and in the late morning took a little walk. Everything was the same as the last time: the bank, the Greek restaurant, the liquor store with its weirdly excellent selection of single malt (apparently one guy in town kept requesting good Scotch), the little grocery store where everyone stared if they didn't know you. Alice, you sweet gas station of a town, all starstruck and miserable, boasting one of everything, even a laundromat.

Behind the mall was the hotel where most of the boilermakers stayed. It was the worst accommodation we have ever had, whole buildings that had been condemned, suddenly reopened to house transient tradesmen during the shutdown. It was held together by sticky linoleum, greasy shag carpet, and the nesting materials of silverfish. An apprentice had a photograph of his bed, so broken that the middle sagged down and rested on the floor, like an exhausted hammock.

There was a golden eagle that spent his days in the top of a large fir tree beside the greening, slimy swimming pool. Golden eagles are handsome birds, and rarer than bald eagles, and will stand sentry wherever there is a large colony of rats. The rats were the main reason I had booked the B&B. I do not stay in that hotel. And I do not eat in the hotel restaurant, since observing an uncovered ice cream bucket of raw chicken breasts being used as a doorstop for the kitchen door.

IN PORT ALICE, it rains. It was raining as I drove to the mill, parked on the muddy roadside and trudged down to the trailer. Some of the boys were outside, under the overhang, smoking. We shook hands. The lunch trailer was narrow and sloped, the floor spongy under the peeling linoleum, with just enough room for four folding tables. A tattered picture of a centrefold from a twenty-year old magazine was taped to the woodgrain panelling. John and Tommy Hill were there, and I put my lunch kit on their table, far from the ailing microwave, and poured a paper cup of watery coffee. The brothers were legendary welders, and had taught me a lot.

"Well?" I asked. "Are you ready for the ghost?"

Tom gave a little smile.

"We'll see," he said.

Not many people liked working in Port Alice because the travel money was minimal, the road long, and the amenities few. Only six hundred and sixty people lived in the village, and there wasn't much night life. I'd always thought it was charming. But strange things happened in this town, terrible things. There always seemed to be a story about a cougar dropping out of the trees and attacking a local, who inevitably wrestled with the giant cat before fighting it off with a buck knife. He'd be a hero for a few weeks, his picture featured in the North Island Gazette, showing off his stitches.

If you wanted to golf on your day off, you could go to the local course, where you were given a short safety orientation, informed of the muster point and location of the wind socks, and issued an escape respirator, which you were required to have on your person at all times. The golf course butted up to the mill, and the sudden gas emissions had been known to waft over, dropping golfers to their knees on the seventh green.

This is the mill where the wall came down. An entire, four-storey wall, part of the old power boiler house, crumbled and collapsed one night. Full of asbestos, it filled the air with fibres and the crew was evacuated. It happened during a dinner break and no one was hurt, but everyone filled out asbestos exposure reports, and some guys refused to ever go back to the site after that.

I've never seen a ghost in Port Alice, but the Hill brothers have encountered the apparition that haunts the fourth floor of the recovery boiler several times. John swore that while he was welding someone was standing behind him, leaning on him, and watching him weld, and when he lifted his helmet and turned around, no one was there. His brother was convinced that the ghost was changing the heat settings on his machine. Over the years, they developed a relationship with the ghost, whom they thought was basically harmless, and had a pretty good sense of humour. It would play tricks on them, hide things, and generally act spooky. Lizard Smith saw it once, and refused to go up and work on that floor again.

Some people think the ghost is one of the workers from the Chinese cemetery, and others think it has something to do with the Nazi door castings. On the older part of the mill is a tank recycled from post-World War II Germany. Swastikas are cast into the manway doors. When you go there for the first time, if you ask about them, someone will take you over and show you.

"Can you believe it?" The guy who showed me shook his head. "This is Canada..."

"Ya," his friend said, "but it's Port Alice."

ONE OF THE reasons I liked the mill is because I got to weld tubes. The contractor had their steady guys, like the Hills, who went where the contractor went. But not being a popular destination, it was hard to attract the superstar welders, so Port Alice sometimes had to settle for the second string. I used to say I played centre ice for the third line: I wasn't a top scorer, but I did my job and could usually make a few shots, when they used me.

The year of the big boiler rebuild, we replaced all four walls. There was a track saw, like a chop saw turned on its side, that ran along a track, cutting a straight line right through the waterwall. Jim Kay was there and taught me how to fix a zip-cut scarf in a wall tube by opening the cut, and stuffing rice paper inside it through the excavation. We buttered the edges to build them up, hand-dressed the opening, rerooted it, and made the repair. This was crazy, Wild West welding. When replacement parts and materials were not available they figured out ways to make it work. The methods were not conventional, and not always legal, but I learned a lot of tricks in Port Alice.

One of them was how to repair your boots when you're fifty kilometres from a store.

"Now you're a cobbler?" One of the foremen was watching me wrap a roll of duct tape around and around my boot. I shrugged.

"Everyone needs a side hustle."

"Don't quit your day job."

ONE AT A TIME the old waterwalls came down, and the new ones were prepped and rigged into place. I was partnered with Conner, who went on to become an excellent TIG welder, making a lot of money running with the big dogs, but he started out welding with me in lowly Port Alice. Conner was on the inside of the furnace, and I was on the outside. We dropped a couple of grapes, blew the odd hole, but fixed them and moved on. We finished our wall in excellent time, and they told us they had decided to X-ray all of our joints. Some welders were getting stress cracks from the old material. We were nervous, but when we arrived the next day, the QC guy was painting all the joints with green spray paint.

"Don't let it go to your head," he said.

ALL THE ROOMS in town were taken. The crappy hotel was full, and so was the campground. I had lucked out with the B&B, which had a lawn that sloped down toward the inlet. Some distance from the house, there was a little grotto, a clearing, right on the beach. There were a couple of plastic chairs set up, and a fire pit. The unseasonably late snowstorm I had arrived in was followed by a warm and early spring. Occasionally, different pals would stop by after work for a beer in the early morning, and sometimes there was good Scotch, and sometimes snacks. It was an exclusive club, membership was limited and by invitation only, and guests were sworn to secrecy.

But most mornings I had the plastic chairs, and the panoramic view of the inlet, to myself. At five o'clock it was still dark, and the sky would slowly lighten, revealing a band of thick fog hanging over the water. The sea lions were always there and you could hear them before you could see them, letting out long breaths, moving, hunting. Several times a pod of orcas swam into the inlet, trapping fish there, surfacing and diving just offshore. And sometimes a black bear would walk past on the beach, making her way by stepping from log to log, walking their lengths, and never setting a foot down on the gravel.

MAKE WORK

We'd all been waiting for Northwood. 2018 had been slow, and there were a lot of boilermakers who were ready for a cash infusion. It was a power boiler rebuild, and promised four or five weeks of steady work. When I arrived they had the panel sections cut out of three walls and were working on the fourth. The boiler was a hive, with welders and fitters stacked up on top of each other on three levels of staging. My station was at the bottom, sitting on a little wooden box on the floor tubes, tacking in the bottom cut line. I was looking forward to seeing everyone again, as well as a month of paycheques. I had a great fitter, and would be welding wall tubes, which made me very happy.

One of the welders had a Bluetooth speaker set up, blasting loud enough so that you could still hear it over the air tools and electric grinders. The air was filled with smoke and dust, the lighting dim. I was looking for tools to set up my station, had found a halogen light and was looking for my wooden box under the lower scaffold, when a Rolling Stones song came on, "Happy," from *Exile on Main Street.* I gave the welder a thumbs up and he smiled and turned the volume up. I turned back and my heel slipped off the edge of the plywood staging. I heard an audible pop in my right knee and went down.

The emergency room doctor was an anaesthetist putting in some extra hours in the ER.

"It's a sprain," he said. "Take a few days off."

"It's not a sprain," I said. My knee was swelling up like a balloon and I couldn't put any weight on it. He shrugged and handed me a prescription. I called my friend Dave, a retired emergency room doctor who I trusted completely.

"Please don't tell me he said it was a sprain," Dave said.

"He said it was a sprain," I answered.

"There is no such thing as a sprained knee," he said. "The knee is a complex joint with multiple inter-related moving components, any one of which could be damaged. You won't have a definitive diagnosis until you get an MRI." The first aid attendant from work pushed some paperwork at me and asked me to make a statement. Under "Description of Injury," I wrote down *undiagnosed joint injury requiring MRI.* Next to my statement the first aid attendant wrote *Sprain.*

For four days I sat on the bed in the hotel room, my knee packed with ice and propped up on a couple of pillows, watching customers come and go from the crack dealer's room next door. I was waiting for the company to decide what to do with me, whether I was going back to the site to work in the tool crib, or going home, but it was a weekend and the contractor offices in the city were closed. There was no one to make a decision. I didn't hear anything from the site office, not that I expected a bouquet of flowers, but a phone call would have been nice. On the fifth day I decided to break camp, and paid the handyman at the Carmel twenty dollars to load my gear into the car. I stopped at the liquor store for a six-pack. They had a very nice organic pinot grigio from California on sale.

"I'll take a case of that too," I said. I was on crutches. "If someone can carry it to my car."

IT WAS A nine-hour drive to Horseshoe Bay, and I stopped overnight at a hotel in Cache Creek. The drive was fraught with worry, but two ferries later I was home. The sofa became my command centre, a nest of pillows and ice packs with my computer, phone, printer, and charging devices within easy reach. Friends stopped by to make sure there was enough firewood, and occasionally someone from the Workers Compensation Board or the contractor's office would call, trying to negotiate a plan of action. I completed some safety courses from home, but eventually the options narrowed and I was given a choice: I could relocate to a hotel in a suburb of Vancouver, work in the warehouse on light duty, and continue to get paid for forty hours a week. Or, stay home, unable to work, and not get paid. Option one was half the money as working in the field because there was no overtime, and I'd be away from my home, friends, and everything I liked. Option two meant a very broke and unpleasant winter, on crutches. It was known that if you got injured and went to the warehouse it was going to be a made-up job. The guys said you'd be cutting pieces of string all winter, or counting hammers.

"The contract says the employer has to provide meaningful work," I told my WCB case worker. "Can you specify exactly what I will be doing in the warehouse that will be meaningful?" I resisted as long as I could, then reluctantly packed a couple suitcases and my crutches and headed into town.

THE WAREHOUSE WAS a vast 6,000-square-foot storage space with racks that reached the ceiling. This was where the tools and consumables for all the jobs came from. The workers received lists, the stuff was collected from the shelves, strapped onto pallets and loaded into semi-trailers that were shipped to the job sites. There was an entire aisle of safety equipment, another for lighting and ventilation, one for small hand tools, and another for power tools. Socket sets, saws, clamps, tube cutters, pipe stands, air lines, hammers, mill hogs, welding machines, gougers, buckets, wrenches, compressors, any of the tools I had ever used on a job were here. In the back was the rigging equipment. Rows of come-alongs hung from racks and chain falls of all sizes, coiled into galvanized buckets. There were also huge tote-baskets of lifting slings, made of either wire or synthetic webbing.

The people who worked there were nice enough. They said there was always one or two guys doing what I was doing, helping out in the warehouse while they came off an injury — someone was always hurt. They set me up at a table sorting small tools, then later in the rigging area inspecting slings. For eight hours a day I would untangle individual synthetic webbing slings from a massive, tangled pile, inspect them for tears and burns, sort them by length and put them away.

The Workers Compensation Board sent me to a consultant, who said that I had a sprain, so I arranged to see my own surgeon, a handsome sports medicine specialist who had operated on my other knee seven years earlier. He sent me for an MRI. The follow-up meeting was brief: I had severed my right ACL and could undergo replacement surgery. Or I could undertake an intense regimen of physiotherapy, which studies had been proving to be equally effective as surgery in some cases. That's what he recommended.

"I have the same injury," he said. "I just wear a knee brace when I play squash."

"You're a surgeon," I pointed out. "And you decided against the surgery?" He shrugged.

"Because I don't trust anyone but me to do the operation."

"If it becomes a problem," I said, "I'll be calling you."

FOR A MONTH I lived a monotonous loop, seeing a physiotherapist two or three times a week, hydrotherapy at the swimming pool, riding the stationary bike in the hotel gym, and inspecting slings at the warehouse. The company hoped I'd quit, but I kept hobbling in to claim my place in the lunchroom with a bunch of twenty-something warehouse workers, who were obsessed with junk food and video games. There was a day when one of them elbowed his buddy and whispered something, nodding at me.

"What?" I asked. I was cutting up a tomato with a pocketknife.

"It's just..." he said softly, "that's the kind of knife a cowboy would have." I stared at him.

"Have you ever seen a cowboy?" I asked. He had not, not a real cowboy, there were no real cowboys, he said. But they were all deeply involved with an interactive video game where you *are* a cowboy. The game was called Red Dead Redemption, and was wholly realistic, he explained, enthusiastically. You got to make your own choices, and travel through an immersive cowboy world, robbing trains, hunting down outlaws, and having gun fights.

Synthesized, enhanced, with multiple camera angles and surround sound, it was a violent, action-packed interactive experience that came with the same warnings as a restricted movie. While they had never experienced actual cowboyness, this fabricated, cowboy reality was zealously embraced.

"I have a horse," my young friend explained. "He's black, and he's got these awesome powers. He's the fastest horse of all of them, he can beat any other horse."

"Have you ever ridden a horse?" I asked.

"A horse? A real horse?" he shuddered. "No. Not a real horse." Then he asked, "have you?" I nodded.

"I used to have horses," I said, "a long time ago." He just stared.

THE ONLY BRIGHT spot in this dark winter was that I had a new sweetheart, my bicyclist. He came every weekend with his big brown dog and we explored the city like tourists. I switched from crutches to a cane, the hours of physio paying off. Then I swapped the stationary bike for a real one and we started riding the trails and greenways, short distances at first, stopping to eat snacks and watch the river. The Christmas break came and went, and I went back to sorting slings.

I lobbied hard for the company to start breaking me into the Quality Control department, putting my welding inspector's certification to use, but they sidestepped those conversations. At the end of February, I was moved from inspecting slings to sorting office supplies. The warehouse manager apologized.

"I just don't have much else for you," he said. "It's the time of year." I assured him I was fine with it, as long as I was getting the rate.

"I have a high boredom threshold," I said. "I'm a welder."

In fact, office equipment was preferable because I have a stationary fetish. I love pens and notebooks, highlighters, sticky notes, glue sticks, erasers, and HB pencils. There were piles of this stuff returning to the warehouse from site offices and it all needed to be organized and put away. There were wastebaskets, in and out boxes, staplers and electronics. I started setting up a fake office.

ONE MONDAY MORNING I hobbled in with my cane and found a roll of paper towels and a bottle of Windex on my worktable. The warehouse manager explained that I was going to be cleaning welding helmets. He knew how I felt about "meaningful" work.

"Actually, I'm in charge of document control and archiving," I said. If you have anything, I'll be in my office." His brow furrowed. "Just shoot me a text," I said. Back at the folding table I set up a label maker and paper shredder. There was a nice wire wastebasket, an electric cord with a power bar, a three-hole punch, stapler, tape dispenser, and Post-it notes. By the end of the day it looked like an office, and the next day I added an In-box, and a wire Out-basket.

I swapped the metal folding chair out for a threadbare swivel chair that leaned to the left, installed a desk lamp, and assembled a selection of rubber stamps, paper clips, pens, and file tabs. Every day it became a little more real, like the cowboy video game, and soon I was reporting daily to the office where nothing happened. No decisions were made, no policy developed, no budgets hammered out, no correspondence returned. It was an existential space. The trick was going to be to tap into the consensual reality, to get the rest of them to believe. Then I could give my horse any powers I wanted.

"It's a game," I told the guys in the lunchroom. "It's called Warehouse Redemption."

I brought in my own laptop and started working on a few personal projects, since I had no actual office work, and quickly discovered what real office workers have known all along: there is plenty to do in an office where nothing happens. I opened my laptop, logged in, and ordered flowers for a friend who had broken an ankle. Different people walked by. Supervisors came down and talked to the warehouse manager and glanced my way.

After a few days, Bonaparte came down from the real office, upstairs. He'd been on a job in Trail, and on returning was told that one of the welders had bunkered down in a fake office in the warehouse and was refusing to count hammers.

"What the fuck is going on here?" he asked.

"Nothing," I told him, truthfully. He stood on the perimeter, just outside the line of duct tape I'd made on the floor. "You can come in if you want." I gestured expansively to the ten-foot by ten-foot square of floor space I was inhabiting in the middle of the warehouse, like a little diorama set in an airplane hangar. He stepped carefully over the line of tape. I pulled out a folding chair and opened it for him. "Water? Pop?" I opened the tiny fridge plugged in under my "desk." I leaned back in the ragged office chair and propped my bad leg up on a file box. Bonaparte leaned back in the metal folding chair like he was sitting at the head of the boardroom table and stretched out. He cracked a Pepsi. I explained that it was the existential office where nothing happens. "Here. Watch this," I said. I stapled two pieces of blank paper together and punched them with the three-hole punch. Then removed the staple with a staple remover and ran the papers through the shredder. "See?" He nodded.

"This is really something," he said, finally.

"I am aspiring to nothing." I admitted. He nodded again and toasted me with his Pepsi.

"That's a step in the right direction," he said.

"I think so too," I said. "I'm going to requisition a new chair."

THE NEXT DAY I was in my office, researching different kinds of harnesses for the brown dog, so we could take her on bicycle rides, when a forklift came around the corner, carrying a pallet of banker's boxes. It dropped the pallet in front of my desk, disappeared, and returned with another one. The boxes were full of documents. By noon I was buried in paper. As a willing and under-utilized office worker, I was put in charge of hundreds of boxes of documents, from project drawings to quality control manuals. I unpacked everything, sorted it, and created a Quality Control archive dating back ten years. Did they need it? Yes. Did they even notice? It's hard to say.

For most of March I worked in a fake office on a project that didn't need doing, cataloguing documents that would never be read. I'd go home to the motel room that impersonated an apartment and limp down to the fitness centre to ride the fake bike. I'd heat up a burger patty made from vegetables and make a cup of rooibos that was sort of like tea, with almond milk, and maybe a little dish of non-dairy ice cream. Things were beginning to feel . . . inauthentic.

At the end of March I visited my physio for the last time and told her I was going back to work. I bought two boxes of donuts and delivered them to the warehouse for the boys, because nothing says thank you and farewell like 7000 empty calories. I was at the top of the dispatch list at the union hall because I hadn't had a job in five months, and when the call came to go to Cranbrook, I took it.

PULLING THE PIN

I usually stayed in Cranbrook for the Skookumchuck mill. It was a long commute, fifty-five kilometres. This time I rented an off-season ski chalet in Kimberley, which was a little closer. I drove there with my bicyclist, who spent a couple days helping me get settled, took me for pizza, then gamely got on his bike and pedalled the thousand or so kilometres back home. He made a little holiday of it. My outlook was grimmer.

When I opened the door of the ski chalet, there was a coat closet on the left, and straight ahead a long, steep flight of stairs. No bannisters. Anyone who has had a knee injury will understand what this means. Once I managed to get up the stairs, the apartment was terrific. It would have been a great vacation getaway if I didn't have to go to work. I started wondering why I had to go to work, anyhow. The strange hours, toxic environment, noise, and now the knowledge that with bilateral knee injuries it was only a matter of time before I got hurt again. But I didn't know how to make a living any other way, and apparently was too old for a career change.

I had taken my certification to become a welding inspector and had been trying for two years to break into that part of the industry. The contractor I worked for the most had at first suggested it, then backed away from the idea, and I didn't know why. I finally approached the newly hired Quality Control manager, and asked him outright if I could expect any work as an inspector in the following year. He surprised me.

"You know," he said, "Quality Control isn't just a retirement plan for worn out old welders."

"Pardon?"

"How old are you?" he asked.

"I'm not sure you're allowed to ask me that," I said.

"You're older," he said. "How many good years do you think you have left? Five? Maybe seven? That's just not enough for us to invest in you."

"Wow," I said. "Thanks for not discriminating against me based on my gender."

MY SUPERVISION WAS aware that I was easing back in after an injury, and didn't want to beat me up too badly on my first job back, so they put me on the forklift. The forklift actually is the retirement plan for worn out old welders, the guys forty years in the trade with bad knees and bad backs. I loved driving the forklift. I wasn't on it all the time, but they switched me out enough that I was able to weld sometimes, and get a break once in a while by moving heavy stuff around. I was grateful for that. One thing everyone understood is what it means to be hurt.

Workers Compensation rates go up in proportion to the number of workers who are injured. In a high-risk trade like ours a lot of people get hurt, and the insurance rates for the company were skyrocketing. The company was compelled to limit workplace injuries because of the rising expense. *Safety first*, we used to say, *so long as it doesn't interfere with production.* The truth was, the number of injuries had fallen, and safety practices were improving since insurance rates had become tied to the number of injuries claimed. Our well-being had become linked directly to their profit margin.

At the same time, the topic of discrimination and harassment was coming up more often. It was now common for the company policy on bullying and harassment to be read aloud during the safety indoctrination. Yet instances of discrimination and all varieties of harassment were still daily occurrences. I'm asked from time to time what I think would end it for good, and the solution seems simple: treat harassment as a workplace injury and tie it to the Workers Compensation insurance rates. If the company was monetarily penalized every time an incident was recorded, the number would drop. The behaviour would not be tolerated if it was costing them money. Until then, we would all go on, together. Status quo.

As the contract was wrapping up, a safety meeting was called one day after lunch. It was announced that two of our guys had been fired by the mill after accusations of sexual harassment from mill employees. There was a swell of outrage among the crew, and we were warned that the mill had a zero-tolerance policy, and we should be careful out there, about what we say. This was followed by a boisterous discussion about the injustice of it, and how the offenders' side of the story should have been heard. Running parallel to this somewhat reasonable sentiment, was the less logical opinion that it was the complainant's fault, as usual. This ranged from *she misunderstood*, to *it was a joke*, to *she should have kept her mouth shut* (because we have families to feed), to *she did it on purpose to get the guy in trouble*, to *if there were no women on the job, there would be no problem*.

I was working on a crossword puzzle. I had heard it before, with some regularity, and felt no need to engage. I actually enjoyed it, in a way, listening to them hash it out, arguing, worrying, getting angry. It was a topic that seldom concerned anyone, or even occurred to them. At least they were having the discussion, and no matter how you slice it, someone loudly trying to defend his right to harass or bully someone else, just sounded stupid. Slowly, slowly, that line of thinking was becoming indefensible. Eventually the hoopla calmed down a little, and one of the members, who was younger than me but old enough to know better, asked that question.

"How do we know?"

"How do you know what?"

"How do we know if it's harassment? Like if I tell a joke, how do I know if someone's going to take it the wrong way? I could get fired..."

Reluctantly, I raised my hand.

"Maybe I can help," I said. At this point, the hair sticking out from under my welding hat had some healthy streaks of grey in it. I'd been sitting on those hard plastic folding chairs in lunch trailers for two decades. I was wearing cheap reading glasses way down on the end of my nose to see the newspaper, and looked at the guy over the top of them. I had a cold pack on my knee and walked with a limp. I was fifty years old and morphing into the crew grandmother.

"Rule of thumb," I told the room, "if you wouldn't say it in front of your twelve-year-old daughter, don't say it. OK?"

"You hear that?" the foreman said. "That's good. If in doubt, use that."

"I can make it even simpler," I said. "Don't talk about your penis at work."

"What?" the foreman asked.

"Don't talk about your dong, your schlong, your ding-dong, your king-kong, Mr. One Eye, Old Friend..."

"...your big hairy balls," my friend Carla chipped in.

"Your big hairy balls," I agreed. "Doesn't matter what you call it at home, just don't talk about it at work."

"OK, OK..." The foreman let me know my turn to speak was over.

"Don't talk about what you did with it last night, or what someone else did with it, or what you want someone else to do with it, or what you want to do to someone else with it...OK? Just don't talk about it ... at all."

"Or at the hotel," Carla added.

"That's right," I said. "When you go back to the hotel that's booked in the company's name, don't talk to the desk clerk about your penis. Or your server in the restaurant, or the cab driver, or the person who looks after the laundromat. Don't talk to your buddy about your penis, or about his penis, and don't talk on the phone about it where someone else could overhear you. Just. Stop. Talking. About. Your Penis. But especially at work. I guarantee, you'll be eighty per cent there. Pretty much as soon as you mention your penis, you are harassing someone."

"We don't talk about that all the time," a guy at the next table said, baffled. "Do we?"

"Yeah," Carla said, "you do."

"When's the last time you told someone to suck it?" I asked him.

"Oh," he said. "That."

"But if we can't talk about that," Van Norman finally asked, in the ensuing silence, "what are we gonna talk about?"

BEFORE LEAVING FOR Cranbrook, I bought two new shirts. They were expensive, made of a thin, quick-drying material, and had buttons and collars. One was navy blue, and the other white, with a dark blue plaid pattern. The blue shirt had short sleeves, the white, long. Uncharacteristically, they were women's shirts, not men's, and fit well, with darts sewn into the right places. I owned one pair of semi-professional black pants, that I kept in the closet in case I ever had to have a meeting with a lawyer or go to a funeral, and one pair of shiny black shoes with a slightly raised heel.

I drove back from Cranbrook as quickly as I could, but it still took two days. I had to stop often to stretch and walk around a little, and spent the night car camping in Manning Park. As soon as I got to the Coast I started looking for a jacket, and trying to get a good haircut. The occasion for all these wardrobe preparations was unexpected: I had a job interview. A friend had forwarded a posting, and I'd applied on impulse. Just before leaving for Skookumchuck, I'd been asked to an interview, and the appointment was scheduled for the day after I returned to Vancouver.

I had almost turned it down, because work was getting busy, but it was becoming clear that I needed a career change. I hadn't had a job interview in twenty-five years, and had no idea of the current protocol. But I had a new shirt, and if I could find a jacket and get a good haircut, it would be a start. I had just enough time to go to the interview and get to the airport in time to make a flight to Prince George. I'd been name-requested for a job in Mackenzie.

Patrick was the only stylist on Main Street who had an opening, because someone had cancelled. Along with an excellent haircut, he gave me good advice.

"Should I colour my hair?" I asked him. Patrick was about to retire, stylishly dressed in black and white, with a natty black shirt, striped pedal pushers, and four-hundred-dollar shoes. On the wall there was a photo of a much younger Patrick in LA, posing with Vidal Sassoon. He studied me in the mirror through heavy framed black glasses.

"No," he said. I had already explained about the job interview. "Leave it your natural colour. Because you want them to see that you are experienced. And you want them to know that you're authentic." I was doubtful about the greying. "This is very important," he said. "You're offering them your experience. That's valuable." I asked him about the jacket. I had settled on a new Levi's jean jacket, with a sharp, classic cut. Patrick nodded.

"But over the arm," he said. "It's too hot today. Just carry it."

THE INTERVIEW WAS in a shiny, modern office building with large open areas, chic furniture, and polished concrete floors. It had glass walls, a high-tech media theatre, breakout areas and an open plan cafe with free espresso. There were smiling people of all ages, coming and going, speaking cheerfully to each other. And there were women, lots of women, working in this place. The job itself was an inspector's position, related to welding and boilers, in the field of public safety.

As I waited in the foyer in my dated black pants and new blue shirt, I suddenly very much wanted to work there, and felt a pre-emptive pang of disappointment, knowing it would not come to pass. For this was surely not the retirement ground for worn out old welders. There would be no etched glass walls and steel accent tables in my future. It seemed much more likely that my destiny would be a dirty old forklift.

The three people at the interview were smart, and kind, and asked thoughtful questions. Already convinced I wasn't a contender, I spent the time trying to act like one, practicing professional social skills that were so rarely used. After an hour, I regretfully excused myself, as I was flying to Mackenzie and had to catch a plane. But I told them I really liked the progressive philosophy of the organization, and appreciated what they were doing.

"And these concrete floors ... they are fabulous." In the cab on the way to the airport I thought it had gone well, might perhaps even warrant a second interview, though I wouldn't get the job. I could wear the other shirt.

I WAS FLYING because it was faster, and because my knee stiffened up too much during those ten-hour drives. By comparison, the plane was in the air for half an hour, then I was quickly packing my suitcase into the little red rental car and heading north. I'd done long jobs in McKenzie before, even rented an apartment there, so the town was familiar. But this time I was staying in camp.

I have stayed in a number of work camps. Kitimat, Woodfibre, Port Mellon, Mackenzie, and several in Alberta. In BC the camps were at least forty years old with tiny rooms, that typically had nicotine-stained ceilings, wood panelling, and nasty little beds. McKenzie is one of the oldest, and like the hotel in Port Alice, had been condemned at different times, only to be reopened when needed. My room was exactly as expected, except instead of linoleum it had brown carpet, so worn and matted with filth that it was like some kind of composite flooring. It was like the ground.

The room included the standard issue 1970s brown curtains, itchy blanket, and little plaid bedspread, reading lamp bolted to the wall, chipped mirror, and lopsided wardrobe. It had the characteristic camp smell that is a blend of diesel fumes, rancid fat, bleach, black liquor, stale marijuana, and the distilled, accumulated body odours from fifty years of flatulent, sweaty workers. Common wash house down the hall.

Work camps are artifacts from a previous time when the absolute minimum was offered to workers in exchange for their labour, and are wildly inadequate accommodations for modern living. I like to think of them as little shrines, ceremonial spaces dedicated to indentured workers. Ironically, the idea of a very small space has finally hit fad. What hipster doesn't dream of living in a tiny house? Shared kitchen? Communal living? To any person contemplating the joys of miniature housing, I suggest spending a month in camp.

I peeled back the sheet to check for bedbugs, unrolled my sleeping bag, lay down on the cot, and contemplated my destiny. There wasn't much to contemplate. The canteen opened at four. I ate a piece of chicken and a mound of mashed potatoes off a thick, institutional plate, put my plastic tray in the rack with the others, and headed for the bus.

The job was OK. There was nothing remarkable about it, but I was edgy and discontent. My foreman was giving me easy jobs, because I had been hurt, and I both appreciated and resented it. Four days in, I still felt like I couldn't get in the game. It was making me cranky. I drove into town to pick up a pocketknife because security had taken mine at the airport again. There was only one clerk at the hardware store, and I paced impatiently in front of the glass case where the knives were locked up. A trio of apprentices were joking around at the cash register. Later that night at work, one of them asked me if I'd found a knife. I nodded.

"Yes, I did."

"Yeah," he said. "We were wondering who you were going to shank."

Apparently, my cranky side was starting to show.

It had happened in Cranbrook, too. I was working with a different apprentice, passing ten-pound castings up onto a scaffold deck, when I'd caught him smirking at me, because I was only lifting one up at a time.

"You think that's funny, don't you," I'd asked, smiling. "That I'm lifting those over my head one at a time, and you're lifting three." He smirked a little more, and shrugged. Without thinking, I had grabbed the front of his coveralls with both hands and pulled him toward me.

"I'm FIFTY," I'd snarled. Then dropped him and walked away.

These were the warning signs.

"You're gonna snap," one of my colleagues said. "You're gonna lose it completely. Try to wait until I'm there, OK? I want to get a video."

I didn't exactly snap. My foreman put me in the furnace, welding corner splits. I'd finished one and was moving to the other side when he came in with another welder, a young guy dragging his machine.

"What, you're done already?" he asked. "I was going to put Kai on that side."

"It's a twenty-minute job," I said. "We don't need another welder in here."

"I just want to make sure it gets done," he answered.

"It'll get done," I said.

"I want to make sure."

"It will get done," I repeated. "And it'll get done faster if you stopped underestimating your crew."

"What?" he said.

"You heard me. You always underestimate your crew because you're afraid of looking bad." I started in on an unnecessary lecture on his leadership style when my phone rang. The argument stopped.

"You get service in here?" he asked.

"Not usually," I said. "That's super weird." There was a rule that we weren't allowed to have our phones with us in the boiler house. It was a fireable offense. I took mine out and looked at it. "I have to take this," I said, turning to go.

"Take your time," he said, holding his own phone up, trying to get a signal.

"And tell your welder he can leave," I called back, from the manway. "I don't need him."

"Yeah, yeah. Whatever."

I MISSED THE call, then couldn't get a signal, and when I found a hot spot, the person answered but couldn't hear me. I finally went out on to the third-floor roof and dialled the number again. It was the human resources department of the company I'd interviewed for, in the big shiny building. The person who answered was saying something, but reception was sketchy.

"What?" I said, "Could you please repeat that? It's noisy here and I can't hear you very well..." I took one of my earplugs out and pressed the phone to my ear. The person on the other end was shouting.

"I SAID ... WE'D LIKE TO OFFER YOU THE POSITION..."

A WEEK LATER I was laid off and my foreman came over to shake my hand.

"Thanks for coming out," he said. "I guess I'll see you on the next one."

"Actually, you will not," I said. "I've had another offer and I'm pulling the pin."

"What?" he said. "What offer? Where are you going?"

"Greener pastures," I said. "But maybe we'll cross paths again ... actually no, probably we won't." I shook his hand, dropped my gloves, welding helmet, and knee pads into the garbage barrel, and headed toward the gate.

I DROVE FROM Mackenzie to Prince George in a daze. I already knew I would take the position, but the logistics were overwhelming. The job was in Vancouver. I had a five-acre property on an island with a house, a garden, a blacksmith shop, and a studio. I owned a lawnmower, a chainsaw, and a kayak. I had hundreds of books, and five anvils. I was going to have to disassemble and move it all, rent out the house, find an apartment.

I drove past the place on the highway where I had dropped off the wolf, and the McLeod Lake store (slash post office, slash liquor outlet). Sometimes life changes suddenly, and all at once. In the moments just before that happens, we never know exactly how it is all going to come together. I only knew that in six months, or a year, everything would be different. I was going to have to think about clothing, and commuting, and working in an office. I would buy a steamer. One of those things people use instead of an iron, that you just kind of wave at your clothes, and they suddenly become sharply pressed and professional. I wasn't even sure what my duties were, only that I would be in that shiny glass office sometimes, and sometimes in the field conducting inspections, which is where I thought I wanted to be.

ON THE PLANE from Prince George to Vancouver I started thinking about the people I knew who still lived in the city, who I hadn't seen in a long time. There would be concerts, and book launches, and restaurants, and gelato. I would have to get used to driving where there are traffic lights, and parking in underground parkades, and taking elevators. I would no longer walk across the road to swim in the ocean. I would no longer stop the car on my way home to pick up the mail.

Paycheques would arrive regularly, and I would be expected to go to work on most of the weekdays, but only for eight hours, and would have all the weekends off. I would work in every season, and no longer be away for the entire spring. I would see tulips bloom, and birds fledge. Everything was going to be different. Maybe I would buy a new bicycle, and ride it to work.

EPILOGUE

It was a cool, rainy day in October when I rolled into the parking lot at the college. There was a horse trailer outside of one of the buildings, a chestnut head just visible through the window. She was that day's demo horse at the farrier school, patiently waiting to be reshod by one of the instructors, while the students watched. I drove past the farrier school, through the big chain link gate, and parked in front of a row of argon and oxygen bottles. This was the welding department. I hauled my toolbox out of the car, and went inside.

Two years previously I'd walked out the gate in Mackenzie on my last boilermaking job. I didn't miss it. Not the travel, the driving, the hotels, the bus rides. I didn't miss the cold, the noise, the cramped spaces, or the thick smell of black liquor and decaying wood pulp. I sometimes missed the people, the women and men with whom I had worked and travelled for so long. I missed the banter, and the particular intimacy of working closely with someone in extreme conditions. I stayed in touch via social media, duly noting retirement parties of some of the old guard, and noticing new names and photos. Young up-and-comers I had never met, and a number of women in the mix. Young, confident, stepping up, owning it. Which was amazing. Then I saw a posting on the work board that a friend had died. And then another. And another.

There was a lot of death in my trade. Overdoses. Suicides. Lingering illnesses. Sudden accidents that leave you breathless, alone with the knowing that someone important has just vanished from this world, someone who has been your partner, or a part of your team. Someone with whom you have built things, shared tables and meals, made jokes. Death used to be announced on the dispatch tape when you phoned the job line, and now it is posted on the website, but it never comes with a warning. Every loss is a shock and is felt deeply, because one of the few people who understands the language, the conventions, the way that we do things, is gone. We grieve their loss, and mourn that there is one less of us.

Some of the death is preventable, and we know this. Mental illness and addiction thrive in the dark, and the dark is where we keep it. It's ironic that the most stressful, the most dangerous jobs, the ones with the longest hours and most extreme conditions, where people are separated from their families and support systems, are the same jobs that teach us not to show how we feel. Vulnerability is not valued, so people hide their suffering. We suck it up. We don't bleed in the shark pool. And when suffering is hidden, we don't see it. We miss the signals because our skin is too thick. If I could change one thing in construction culture, that would be it: the introduction of a little more tenderness. A little more understanding that we all have our limits, our soft spots, the places where the knife can go too deep. We have all needlessly lost too many friends.

PART OF MY new job was to invigilate weld tests at the college. The shop was similar to where I had trained, with cutting areas, a grinding room, and rows of welding booths, each with its own machines and gas bottles. Each booth had a little steel table, and an adjustable stand for the student to tack up their coupon. One row of booths near the back was set aside for testing, and outside was a large steel table with an industrial stool. I hefted my toolbox onto the table and set up a laptop. This was my tiny domain for the day, my little place.

On this particular rainy day in October, I had four candidates attempting the exam, one woman and three guys. It was a high-stakes exam, expensive, and for some, employment depended on passing. I flashed back on all the tests I'd failed, the ones where I'd squeaked by but should have failed, and the ones I'd passed. I thought about dropping the slug of stainless in my cap in Montana, and failing the tube test in Michigan, and the excellent coupon I produced in Nova Scotia. My four candidates assembled around the table.

I gave the little introductory talk, confirming that they had read the syllabus, and were clear on the procedure, positions, and sequencing. One of my candidates was shifting nervously from foot to foot, another kept glancing at the door, and one looked like he was going to throw up. The young woman stared straight at me, as though pure grit would get her through.

"Are there any other questions?" I asked, wrapping it up. "No? OK then. I just want to say ... um ... that weld tests suck. They really do. Nobody likes them. But you will have every opportunity to pass this test today. If you have questions at any time, stop welding. Clarify before you proceed. You're smarter than the materials, and you will all go on to have long and illustrious careers. And this? This ... is only a test."

REFERENCES:

Hanson, David T., *Colstrip, Montana* (Taverner Press, 2010)

THANKS

My sincerest gratitude goes to Kate Braid and Kathleen Weiss for their wise counsel through this project, and to Judy Kujundzic, reader, subject matter expert and cover model. Also, to Ian Crawford for his photograph, which was the base image for the cover collage, and S. Grand Black for designing the cover and creating the collage, *Judy Hews A Watering Hole*.

I would like to thank Denby Nelson, Garnet Rogers, Stephan Hederich, the Browning-Millers, Carla Jean, my mom, and all the other folks who appear as themselves in this book, as well as the many people I encountered in my travels who appear under names that are not their own.

This project was assisted by the BC Arts Council, and I am grateful for the support. A big thanks to Mark Mushet, and to the people in the background who kept me on the right path: Ingrid Weiss, Simmah Peterson, Holly "here's-the-thing" Bright, Ian Ferrier, Kaile Shilling, Brian Kaufman, Karen Green and the team at Anvil Press, Jim Oaten, and especially Bruce Gordon, for his sweet and constant encouragement.

Finally, I'd like to express my appreciation and respect for my road family, the sisters and brothers in the Boilermakers' Union: in BC Locals 359 and 191, Montana Local 11, Pennsylvania Local 13, Michigan Local 169, Washington Local 502, Alberta Local 146, Ontario Local 128, and Nova Scotia & New Brunswick Local 73.

ABOUT THE AUTHOR

Hilary Peach is a writer, recording artist, and producer of unusual art projects. She was a founder and the director of the Poetry Gabriola Festival, an infamous interdisciplinary performance event that presented many Canadian and international artists on Gabriola Island. For twenty years Peach also travelled across Canada and the United States, working as a welder in pulp mills, chemical plants, refineries, and generating stations. Anvil Press published her collection of poetry, BOLT, in 2019,and she has released three audio-poetry projects: *Poems Only Dogs Can Hear, Suitcase Local*, and *Dictionary of Snakes*. Hilary Peach is now a welding inspector and Boiler Safety Officer for the provincial safety authority, and is writing fiction.

Kate Braid (Foreword) is a red seal journey carpenter, and has written two memoirs, *Journeywoman: Swinging a Hammer in a Man's World* and *Hammer & Nail: Notes of a Journeywoman* (Caitlin Press) as well as three books of poetry about her experiences in construction.